PATENT READY®

Introductory Book for Executives, Managers, Engineers & Others

PATENT INTRODUCTIONS, INC.
Gregory T. Kavounas

www.patent-introductions.com
www.patent-ready.com

**YOUR PATENT DEPARTMENT
CONTACT INFORMATION:**

**YOUR PATENT ATTORNEY
CONTACT INFORMATION:**

STATUS OF THIS BOOK

This book does not contain legal advice. Obtaining a copy of this book does not form an attorney-client relationship with anyone. For dealing with your specific facts and circumstances, and for how the law is at the time in the country you are interested in, obtain the advice of your Patent Department or a patent attorney. You can also ask them if the patent laws have changed since this version of this book.

PATENT READY®

Introductory Book for Executives, Managers, Engineers & Others

PATENT INTRODUCTIONS, INC.
www.patent-introductions.com
www.patent-ready.com

PATENT READY® v1.4(English)

Also by Patent Introductions, Inc.:

PATENT READY® Engineering Notebook: With Patent Analysis Forms
PATENT READY® Inventor's Journal: With Patent Analysis Forms

TRADEMARK NOTICES:

PATENT READY® and the Scroll Logo: ® are trademarks of Patent Introductions, Inc., registered only in the USA.

COPYRIGHT NOTICES:

Copyright © 2014 and © 2016 by Patent Introductions, Inc.
Authored by Gregory T. Kavounas
ALL RIGHTS RESERVED. This book contains material protected under International and Federal Copyright Laws and Treaties, which were first registered before its first publication. Any unauthorized reprint or use of this material or part of it is prohibited. The drawings are the heart of this work, as they are its most creative elements. No part of this book may be translated or reproduced or transmitted in any form or by any means, electronic or mechanical, including photocopying, recording, or by any information storage and retrieval system without express written permission from Patent Introductions, Inc. Violations of Copyrights Laws can result in severe financial penalties and imprisonment.

ISBN: 1499342101
ISBN-13: 9781499342109
Library of Congress Control Number: 2014908411
CreateSpace Independent Publishing Platform
North Charleston, South Carolina

BRIEF CONTENTS

List of Illustrations xvii

Introduction xxi

The Full Lincoln Patent Quote 1

I. Patents and Business
    1. Introduction to Patent Systems 5
    2. Your Company's Business Can Be Impacted by Patents............ 19
    3. Basic Patent Strategies for New Product Planning 33

II. You, Working for Your Company
    4. Your Relationship with Your Company...................................55
    5. Contending with Patents in Your Work 67

III. Patent Basics
    6. Patents in Time 81
    7. Patent Anatomy 101
    8. Finding Past Documents ("Prior Art Searching")....................119

IV. You, Patenting for Your Company
    9. Reporting Your Inventions for Patenting...............................143
    10. A Patent Application Will Be Prepared from Your IRF 161
    11. The Next Two Decades... 173

About Patent Introductions, Inc. 191
About the Author 193
Acknowledgments 195
Dedication 197
Glossary..199

Appendix A: Image of Patent Document of Sample
　　　　　　US Patent No. 4,369,439.. 215
Appendix B: Invention Reporting Form (IRF) (Starting).................... 221
Appendix C: Personal Patent Organizer (Started) 227

Index.. 231

CONTENTS

List of Illustrations xvii

Introduction xxi

The Full Lincoln Patent Quote 1

PART ONE: PATENTS AND BUSINESS 3

Chapter 1
Introduction to Patent Systems 5

1.1 Theory of Patent Systems 5
1.2 Components of a Country's Patent System 6
1.3 Overview of Patenting in the United States 7
1.4 Overview of Patenting in Another Country 8
1.5 Patenting the Same Invention in Multiple Countries 9
1.6 International Agreements to Facilitate Patenting in Multiple Countries 11
1.7 Differences in Accessing Patent Protection 13
1.8 Defining Patent Rights 14
1.9 Resolving Patent Disputes 15
1.10 Navigating within a Patent System 16
Chapter Summary 17

Chapter 2
Your Company's Business Can Be Impacted by Patents 19

2.1 Your Company's Finances 19
2.2 Your Company's Commercial Battles in the Marketplace 20
2.3 The Patent Plane 21
2.4 Patent Battles in the Patent Plane 22
2.5 Patent Business Risks and Opportunities Due to Patent Systems 24
2.6 PBR-1: The Patent Business Risk of Infringing a Patent 25

2.7	PBR-2: The Patent Business Risk of a Product Being Followed	27
2.8	PBO-1: The Patent Business Opportunity to Reserve Future Exclusive Patent Rights	28
2.9	PBR-3: The Patent Business Risk of Generating Inadequate Eventual Returns from Acquired Patent Rights	29
2.10	Patent Business Risks and Opportunities in the Context of Different Industries	30
	Chapter Summary	31

Chapter 3
Basic Patent Strategies for New Product Planning 33

3.1	Planning a New Product: Risk/Reward Calculations	33
3.2	Business Analysis Review with Patent Business Risks	34
3.3	Basic Company Strategies about Some of the Patent Business Risks and Opportunities	36
3.4	Will Your Company Patent Its New Product?	39
3.5	Patent Marking of Products	39
3.6	Does Your Company Permit Searching Others' Patents?	41
3.7	Planning Your Product According to the Patent Business Risk of Infringing (PBR-1)	41
3.8	IP Alignment	43
3.9	Patent Applications That Are Not Findable by Patent Clearance Searches	45
3.10	Mitigating Now the Future Risk of Infringing by Filing a Patent Application	47
3.11	The Progress of Filed Patent Applications Further Helps in Understanding the Risk	49
	Chapter Summary	50

PART TWO: YOU, WORKING FOR YOUR COMPANY 53

Chapter 4
Your Relationship with Your Company 55

4.1	Your Résumé and Job Interview	55
4.2	Your Employment Agreement	55
4.3	Your Company's Rules	57
4.4	You Must Keep Your Company's Trade Secrets Confidential	57
4.5	Company Revelations	58
4.6	Non-Disclosure Agreements with Other Parties	60

4.7	Preventing Internal Records from Being Unduly Damaging during Litigation	60
4.8	The Trap of Work Groups for Setting Technical Standards	62
4.9	Following Business Processes and Your Personal Patent Organizer	63
	Chapter Summary	64

Chapter 5
Contending with Patents in Your Work 67

5.1	Your Company Operates within the Patent System	67
5.2	Your Company's Patent Operations	67
5.3	You May Impact Your Company's Eventual Patent Position	68
5.4	Your Tasks Include Inventive Problem-Solving	69
5.5	Implementing Your Invention into Your Future Product	70
5.6	Concern: "Would My Implemented Invention Avoid Infringing All Patents of Others?"	71
5.7	Hope: "Is My Invention Patentable?"	72
5.8	The Requirements for Patentability of an Invention	73
5.9	Limits to the Patentability of Your Invention: Past Events	74
5.10	Limits to the Future Patentability of Your Invention: Your Present Actions	75
5.11	The Emerging Time Domains of Your Patent Tasks	76
	Chapter Summary	77

PART THREE: PATENT BASICS 79

Chapter 6
Patents in Time 81

6.1	Time Line of Events for a Sample Patent	81
6.2	Time Line of Events for Some US Patents	84
6.3	Observation: Only Some Inventions Become Patented	86
6.4	A Typical Result: The Patent Application Filed the Earliest Generally Wins the Patent Race	87
6.5	Defensive Publications	89
6.6	Observation: When You File a Patent Application, You Can Never Be Certain That You Will Win the Patent Race	91
6.7	Planning When Your Patent Application Will Be Filed	92
6.8	The Challenge of Imminent Public Disclosures	92
6.9	Provisional Patent Applications for Tentative Protection	93

6.10   Misconceptions about Provisional Patent Applications.............96
6.11   Provisional Patent Applications for Start-Up Companies...........98
Chapter Summary...98

Chapter 7
Patent Anatomy 101

7.1   Patents Can Be of Different Types.. 101
7.2   Patents Are Multidisciplinary 102
7.3   A Single Patent Can Have Different Appearances 102
7.4   Published Patent Applications 104
7.5   Reading Your First Patent 106
7.6   People Look at Patents for Different Purposes............................106
7.7   Before Looking at Another Patent, Decide on
Your Purpose 107
7.8   Parsing a Patent Document into Its Basic Parts 107
7.9   The Formalities (F)... 110
7.10   The Claims (C).. 111
7.11   The Specification (S).. 113
7.12   Patent Families... 114
7.13   Information That Is Not Included in a Patent............................. 115
Chapter Summary... 117

Chapter 8
Finding Past Documents ("Prior Art Searching")........................ 119

8.1   About "Prior Art" Searching.. 119
8.2   Reasons for Searching the Prior Art 120
8.3   Confirm That Your Company Permits You to Search 121
8.4   About "Patent Searching" 121
8.5   Update Your Personal Patent Organizer 122
8.6   Your First Few Patent Searches 123
8.7   Your Other Patent Searches 124
8.8   Searching Patents by Field 125
8.9   Expected Effectiveness of Patent Searching............................... 127
8.10   Engaging Patent Searchers...129
8.11   Patent Watch Programs 131
8.12   Patent Searching to Clear a Prospective Product 131
8.13   Dealing with Potentially Threatening Patents without
Disputing Them.. 133
8.14   Dealing with Potentially Threatening Patents by Disputing
Them 134

8.15	Challenging Potentially Threatening Patent Applications	135
8.16	Searching Patent Specifications for Novelty—Patentability	136

Chapter Summary... 138

PART FOUR: YOU, PATENTING FOR YOUR COMPANY 141

Chapter 9
Reporting Your Inventions for Patenting 143

9.1	The Prospect of Your Patenting	143
9.2	Start Managing Your Ideas	144
9.3	Streamline Your Process for Reporting Inventions	145
9.4	Two Types of Inventions to Report for Patenting	145
9.5	Improve Your Invention's Chances of Being Patented	146
9.6	You Are Responsible for the Invention Reporting Form (IRF)	147
9.7	An IRF Is a Separate and Different Deliverable	149
9.8	Writing the IRF	151
9.9	Generating Words	152
9.10	Generating Drawings	153
9.11	Reporting Prior Art	154
9.12	Coordinating with Coinventors	154
9.13	Submitting Your IRF for Patenting	155
9.14	Your Company Will Decide Whether to Patent Your IRF or Not	155

Chapter Summary... 158

Chapter 10
A Patent Application Will Be Prepared from Your IRF 161

10.1	Preparing to Patent	161
10.2	Initial Inventor Interview	162
10.3	Receiving a Drafted Patent Application for Review	162
10.4	Preparing a Document for Your Feedback	164
10.5	Perspectives for Reviewing the Drafted Patent Application	164
10.6	Criteria for Reviewing the Drafted Patent Application	165
10.7	The Updated Drafted Patent Application	165
10.8	Who Will Be Named as the Inventor(s)?	166
10.9	The Inventor Legal Forms for Signing	166
10.10	The Patent Application Will Be Filed	167
10.11	Update Your Personal Patent Organizer	168

10.12 Update Your Calendar for the Expected Publication Date 168
10.13 Update Your Calendar for the 19-Month Clearance
       Milestone 169
10.14 Update Any Relevant Internal Presentations 169
10.15 Maybe You Will Receive a Small Patent-Filing Bonus 171
Chapter Summary 171

Chapter 11
The Next Two Decades 173

11.1   Your Patent Application Is Filed and Pending 173
11.2   Your Patent Application Becomes Published
       While Pending 174
11.3   The 19-Month Clearance Milestone for Managing the
       Risk of Infringing 175
11.4   Third-Party Prior Art May Be Submitted against
       Your Patent Application 178
11.5   Reporting Follow-Up Inventions 178
11.6   The Patent Office Examines Your Pending Application 178
11.7   Helping with Responding to the Office Action 180
11.8   The Examination Clearance Milestone for
       Managing the Risk of Infringing 181
11.9   Your Patent Application Becomes Issued as a Patent 182
11.10 A Patent Protects the Product Better 183
11.11 Revision of Granted Patents 185
11.12 Is Your Patent Infringed? 185
11.13 Patent Litigation 187
11.14 Your Patent Expires 188
Chapter Summary 189

About Patent Introductions, Inc. 191

About the Author 193

Acknowledgments 195

Dedication 197

Glossary 199

**Appendix A: Image of Patent Document of Sample
US Patent No. 4,369,439** 215

Appendix B: Invention Reporting Form (IRF) (Starting) 221

Appendix C: Personal Patent Organizer (Started) 227

Index 231

LIST OF ILLUSTRATIONS

PART ONE: PATENTS AND BUSINESS

Chapter 1. Introduction to Patent Systems

FIG. 1A. Patenting in the USA 7
FIG. 1B. Patenting in Sample Country A 9
FIG. 1C. Sample Patenting of Single Invention in
         Multiple Countries (Non-Priority) 10
FIG. 1D. Sample Patenting of Single Invention in
         Multiple Countries (Using Priority) 11
FIG. 1E. International (PCT) Patent Application for
         Single Invention 12

Chapter 2. Your Company's Business Can Be Impacted by Patents

FIG. 2A. Your Company's Commercial Activity 19
FIG. 2B. Your Company's Product Competes Against
         Products of Rival Companies 20
FIG. 2C. Company Competition in Market Plane and in
         Patent Plane 21
FIG. 2D. Patent Business Risks and Patent Business
         Opportunities 24
FIG. 2E. Proposed Product's Prospect of Infringing
         Another's Patent 26

Chapter 3. Basic Patent Strategies for New Product Planning

FIG. 3A. Project's Business Analysis Review
         (Searched, but No Patenting) 34
FIG. 3B. Some Patent Business Risks, and Basic Strategies to
         Mitigate Them 37
FIG. 3C. Product with Patent Marking 40

FIG. 3D. Planning the Product According to Differing
        Risks of Infringing a Patent..42
FIG. 3E. IP Alignment.. 44
FIG. 3F. Some Patent Risk Is Invisible, and Continues to
        Be Renewed 46
FIG. 3G. Filing a Patent Application Prevents Others from
        Eventually Succeeding in Patenting................................47
FIG. 3H. Cut-Off Effect: Patenting Prevents Renewal of
        Patent Business Risk PBR-1 49

PART TWO: YOU, WORKING FOR YOUR COMPANY

Chapter 4. Your Relationship with Your Company

FIG. 4. Confidentiality of Your Organization's Information.................59

Chapter 5. Contending with Patents in Your Work

FIG. 5A. Typical US Organization's Arrangement for
        Patenting Operations..68
FIG. 5B. Could Your Invention Become Added to Your
        Company's Future Product?...70
FIG. 5C. Concern about Past Patenting Precluding the
        Considered Product 71
FIG. 5D. Hope That Your Invention Can Also Become a Patent..........72
FIG. 5E. Other Concern That Past Activities Preclude
        Your Invention from Becoming Patented 74
FIG. 5F. Time Domains of Your Patent-Related Tasks 76

PART THREE: PATENT BASICS

Chapter 6. Patents in Time

FIG. 6A. Typical Event Time Line for Patent (Non-US Plus
        Most US: Publish while Pending)..................................82
FIG. 6B. Typical Event Time Line for Patent (Some US:
        Publish Only if Issue, When Issue).................................85
FIG. 6C. Not All Inventions Become Patented.......................................86
FIG. 6D. Typical Patent Race between Rival Companies
        for the Same Invention..88
FIG. 6E. Defensive Publication Cuts Off Future Patenting
        for the Same Invention.. 90

FIG. 6F. Even with a Prior Art Search, When Filing a Patent
Application You Can't Know Whether You Are
the Earliest..91
FIG. 6G. Imminent Public Disclosure Risks Forfeiture of
Patent Rights 93
FIG. 6H. An IRF Should Be Submitted At Least 1 Week before the
Disclosure..94
FIG. 6I. An IRF Submitted Timely Enables Filing a Provisional.........95
FIG. 6J. A Provisional Enables Filing a Long-Term Regular
Non-Provisional...96

Chapter 7. Patent Anatomy

FIG. 7A. Sample US Patent Document ("Not Parsed").....................104
FIG. 7B. Partial Image of Cover Page of Sample US Published
Patent Application (Before Issuance as a Patent).................105
FIG. 7C. Separating ("Parsing") the Basic Parts of a Patent...............108
FIG. 7D. Sample US Patent Document with its Basic Parts
Separated by the Patent Reading Prism 109
FIG. 7E. Some Formalities from Cover Page of
Sample US Patent Document... 110
FIG. 7F. Version of How Patent Text Is Presented in the
US Patent Office Website..112
FIG. 7G. Sample Browser Appearance of the Beginning of a
US Patent in Website of USPTO..113
FIG. 7H. Child Patent Application May Be Filed 115

Chapter 8. Finding Past Documents ("Prior Art Searching")

FIG. 8A. The Prospect of a General "Prior Art" Search......................119
FIG. 8B. The Prospect of a Usual "Patent Search" 122
FIG. 8C. Searching Patents by Field 125
FIG. 8D. Some of the Fields That Can be Searched
among the Formalities..126
FIG. 8E. The Level of Confidence in the Reliability of a
Patent Search When Seeking Clearance Improves
with Resources & Effort.. 128
FIG. 8F. Clearance Search to Mitigate Risk That Past
Patenting Precludes the Newly Considered Product............ 132
FIG. 8G. Novelty Search for Higher Confidence That Your
Invention Can Also Become a Patent That Will Protect
the Exclusivity of the Possible Future Product 137

PART FOUR: YOU, PATENTING FOR YOUR COMPANY

Chapter 9. Reporting Your Inventions for Patenting

FIG. 9A. Patenting 143
FIG. 9B. Patenting Starts by You 148
FIG. 9C. Differences between Inventions for
    Patenting and Science Papers for Publication 150
FIG. 9D. Sample Decisions of Patent Committee 156

Chapter 10. A Patent Application Will Be Prepared from Your IRF

FIG. 10A. A Patent Application Will Be Drafted from Your IRF 161
FIG. 10B. Reviewing the Drafted Patent Application 163
FIG. 10C. Your Drafted & Approved Patent Application
    Becomes Filed with the Patent Office 167
FIG. 10D. Project's Business Analysis Review (Filing Clearance
    Milestone: Searched, Then Filed Patent Application) 170

Chapter 11. The Next Two Decades

FIG. 11A. Your Patent Application Has Just Become Filed 173
FIG. 11B. Your Filed Patent Application Becomes
    Published while Pending 174
FIG. 11C. Project's Business Analysis Review (19-Month
    Clearance Milestone: After Filing, then Searched &
    Cleared Again) 177
FIG. 11D. Your Filed & Pending Patent Application Is
    Examined by Patent Office 179
FIG. 11E. Patent Office Examines Claims of Your Pending
    Patent Application against Prior Art 180
FIG. 11F. Your Filed Patent Application Becomes Issued
    as a Patent 182
FIG. 11G. Project's Business Analysis Review
    (Patent Issuance Milestone) 184
FIG. 11H. Your Issued Patent Becomes Revised 185
FIG. 11I. Patent Litigation 187
FIG. 11J. Your Patent Expires 188

INTRODUCTION

This book is for **you, a person working in an organization** in a country that has a Patent System. Many patent concepts are the same across different countries.

Your Organization can be a company providing a product to the market, a start-up company, a design firm, a university, a research institution, and so on. For simplicity, in this book we will mostly say "your company" to mean any such organization.

Your company operates within a Patent System. This book explains **basic patent concepts** that apply in almost all Patent Systems.

It is increasingly understood that *patents are multidisciplinary*. Beyond technology, they involve law and business strategy. They do not fit neatly under any traditional categorization or company department. People from different functions within a company need to cooperate to do things right for their company, in view of the applicable Patent System.

Accordingly, this patent book is intended for people with different functions within a company. It uses common terms throughout, to facilitate dialogue across the vertical and horizontal lines of the organizational chart. It starts from a high-level overview of Patent Systems, presents the main **patent business risks and opportunities** that Patent Systems create for companies, proceeds with the main **patent strategies** that companies use to mitigate these risks and execute on these opportunities and, in increasing detail, shows an engineer's patent tasks for helping his or her company execute these patent strategies.

So, if you are in **Senior Management**, understanding patents can help you appreciate the related patent business risks and opportunities that apply to your company, the basic patent strategies that you should consider, and what the people from different functions must do to pursue them. You can further ensure that everyone knows and will play their part, and has the resources to do so. If you are **a manager**, you can define and execute **business processes** for your company's development of new products in order to execute these basic patent strategies. If you are **an executive** from, say, the Marketing Department, you might be interested in having your company act to legally reserve a new feature for a future version of your product by patenting it before building it. Or, if you are in Business Development, you might see how patents can play a role in a deal you are contemplating.

If you are **an engineer** or **a scientist**, you likely also work with patents, yet doing so is different from anything else you do. You will need to be able to find others' patents, learn from them, and understand what it is that your designs are expected to avoid. Plus, you will recognize that some of your ideas are new, and you can help your company patent them. When a patent application is filed for your work, you will be named as an inventor and remain so even if you leave the company. Once a patent is issued, the patent information will remain publicly available forever. You can list your patents in your résumé to help you with the next steps in your career. You may receive a commemorative patent plaque that your friends and family can see, and from which they will learn something more about you.

Importantly, *regardless of your position or title in your company, you are permitted to invent* to further your company's success. Your invention can be a useful new product or an extension of a product that your company can offer. If your company likes your invention, it might build it into a product. This book also shows you what to look for so that you can get your invention patented. It further shows how, when you start the patenting process, you initiate a chain of events that reduce your company's future patent-related business risks in building your invention into a product.

Students in engineering, science, business, and law will undoubtedly benefit from reading this book, before starting their professional lives. After starting, one is often expected to magically know how to work with patents.

Reading this book once will give you a rather complete picture of the basics. Spaces have been provided at the ends of the chapters to help you take notes.

As you read, you will notice that the book examines patents from different perspectives. Necessarily, some key points are repeated, as they are seen from these different perspectives. You may find some chapters less applicable to you, as they may be addressed more to people in other departments. Still, *such chapters may help you understand the points of view of others in your company, when they ask you to do things or to support what they do*. Plus, if the beginning of a few chapters feels too basic for you, stay with them anyway. The basic beginnings are done for defining common terms, plugging gaps, and giving student readers a chance to come up to speed; the material advances later in the chapter.

After you read this book, you can keep it as a reference. When you encounter a patent situation, hopefully you will be able to identify some place in this book that guides you about it.

To maintain its general applicability, this introductory book purposefully avoids going into depth. Indeed, beyond the basic principles in this book, patent strategies, tactics, techniques, analyses, and scholarship can diverge quickly in the field of patents, especially in the context of different industries.

Beyond the basic principles, this book does not teach patent law and often cautions that additional patent-related facts and details might make an outcome different than what is written. It is important to emphasize that this book is not legal advice. Although it enables you to ask smart questions of your patent attorney, it does not enable you to answer them by yourself. After all, your company would not want you to be making legal judgments without the background of legal training. Moreover, this book does not teach you how to write by yourself a patent application that will succeed in becoming a useful patent, nor does it train you to become a Patent Engineer or an expert witness or a specialist negotiator. It will not help you determine with finality what is in the realm of legal opinions, such as whether a threatening patent should be treated as valid or not, whether a product infringes a patent or not, or what exactly penalties your company can face for infringing a patent in a specific country. Patents are legal documents, and patent attorneys know the complex legal rules and can apply them to your situation. Still, this book orients you as to what legal determinations your patent attorney will seek to make in order to help you in your situation; and it guides you as to what factual circumstances you can create so you can help your patent attorney help you better and faster.

Good luck!

THE FULL LINCOLN PATENT QUOTE

Before then [the adoption of the US Constitution], any man might instantly use what another had invented; so that the inventor had no special advantage from his own invention. **The patent system** *changed this; secured to the inventor, for a limited time, the exclusive use of his invention; and thereby* **added the fuel of interest to the fire of genius, in the discovery and production of new and useful things**.

Abraham Lincoln, 1859, eventual US President[1]

(emphasis added only to the usually quoted portion)

---

[1] Quote from second lecture on discoveries and inventions, February 11, 1859; quote accessed on 2013-11-18 from http://en.wikiquote.org/wiki/Patent. At the time, Lincoln was already a patentee.

PART ONE

PATENTS AND BUSINESS

CHAPTER 1. INTRODUCTION TO PATENT SYSTEMS

CHAPTER 2. YOUR COMPANY'S BUSINESS CAN BE IMPACTED BY PATENTS

CHAPTER 3. BASIC PATENT STRATEGIES FOR NEW PRODUCT PLANNING

INTRODUCTION TO PATENT SYSTEMS

1.1 Theory of Patent Systems

Every country has an **Innovation Landscape**. An Innovation Landscape of a country includes a web of people, culture, economic circumstances, institutions, and laws that relate to innovation.

Within an Innovation Landscape, a country typically has a **Patent System**. A Patent System is a system of laws and institutions intended to reward inventors indirectly, by changing the risk/reward calculations of decision makers in companies and of those contemplating starting new companies.

A Patent System (a) offers aspiring inventors the opportunity to write descriptions of their inventions and (b) publicizes these descriptions so that they can be read by their commercial rivals, plus would-be commercial rivals. The descriptions are publicized in writings called patents. Patents are considered to be a type of **Intellectual Property**, or **IP**.[2] In exchange for the effort and the expense of writing these descriptions and submitting them for publication, the inventors may receive a patent, which is a bundle of temporary legal rights for the new parts of their inventions. After the patent rights expire, the patent documents remain, their writing benefiting all the participants in the Innovation Landscape. In the future, it will be cheaper for everyone to learn a field by reading these voluntarily contributed writings than by having to invest time, effort, and money to recreate this information every time.

---

[2] Other types of IP include **trade secrets**, trademarks, and copyrights.

By these patent rights, then, *the Patent System alters the risk/reward calculations* of companies and would-be companies. While those who would commercialize a new invention face a risk that is increased because their product is new, the Patent System provides them with the possibility of more reward by granting a temporary monopoly for their invention. While those who would merely follow a leader face less risk, the Patent System adds more risk to them in the form of potential legal liability for patent infringement. Accordingly, the Patent System can systemically influence the decisions of companies as to whether to pursue more inventions or more following.

Each country decides on its Patent System and therefore also on its Innovation Landscape. For example, China instituted a Patent System in the mid-1980s for the first time.

The Patent Systems of various countries share many general attributes. They also have differences, whose results affect their Innovation Landscapes.

Many notions have been given summary in this section. We develop them in more detail in the rest of this book.

1.2   Components of a Country's Patent System

A country's Patent System generally has three main components, which we introduce in this section.[3] We will develop each of them in the remainder of this chapter.

First, a country provides **an avenue for inventors to access patent protection.** As the avenue, the country typically establishes a Patent Office that gives to inventors patents in exchange for reporting their inventions. More particularly, inventors can send to the Patent Office patent applications that describe their inventions. If a patent application and the invention it describes meet certain criteria, then the Patent Office grants the owner a **patent** based on the application. This activity of obtaining a patent is also called **patenting**. The granted or issued patent is publicly available for everyone to read. As we will see, a country shapes its Innovation Landscape by how much access it permits to patent protection.

Second, a country defines **what the patent rights are**—that is, what are the legal rights of someone due to owning a patent. As we will see, a country can shape its Innovation Landscape by adjusting what the patent rights are.

Third, a country provides **an avenue for parties to resolve disputes about patents**. If two parties cannot resolve their dispute with each other, one or both of them can go to court. A

---

[3]   There are additional components to a Patent System—for example, a country can have applicable provisions in its accounting rules about whether a company's developed patents are permitted to be treated as capital, employment laws, and so on.

country can shape its Innovation Landscape by controlling how parties can resolve their disputes in court according to the patent laws. As we will see, a country can improve its Innovation Landscape by striking the right balance for how fairly, quickly, and economically parties can resolve their disputes.

The Patent Systems of countries sometimes have different mixes of these three main components. For each country, the functioning sum of these three components shapes its Patent System to be strong, weak, or something in between.

Now we examine individually the main components of Patent Systems.

1.3 Overview of Patenting in the United States

The US Patent System is shown in Figure 1A. The right-hand column shows that the US Constitution mandates that patent protection should be given to inventors. The US Congress passes patent laws for implementing patent protection. The US courts enforce the patent laws when a party has a dispute with another. The US Patent and Trademark Office (USPTO) must operate within the patent laws, and has its own procedures.

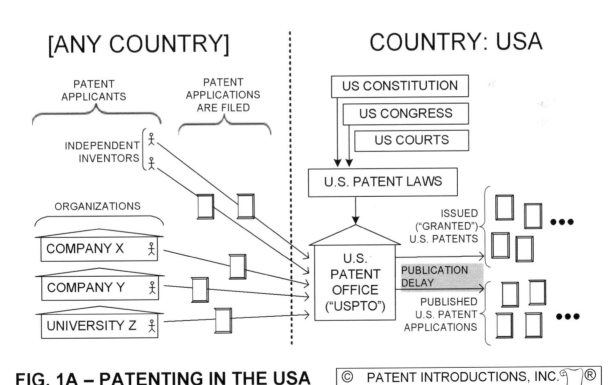

FIG. 1A – PATENTING IN THE USA

© PATENT INTRODUCTIONS, INC.
2014 www.patent-introductions.com

The left-hand column in Figure 1A shows that possible **patent applicants** include independent inventors and organizations. The applicants create specialized writings, which are called **patent applications**. A patent application describes the invention that the applicant seeks to protect by a patent. Even when the applicant is an organization, a human inventor is always involved.

The applicants then file the patent applications with the USPTO, as shown by the arrows. Upon filing, the applicants also pay fees to the USPTO, and the filed patent application is then pending.

An entity does not need to be a US citizen or a resident of the United States to apply for a US patent. If an applicant is not a resident, that person may act through a representative. Typically, such representatives are **patent attorneys** or **patent agents**. The USPTO regulates who can become a patent attorney or a patent agent.

Sometime after a patent application is filed, it is examined by the USPTO. Not all filed patent applications are approved. If the patent application is approved, then it is issued as a **patent**. Accordingly, a patent is a formal document created by the USPTO. A patent has formalities generated by the USPTO, while the remainder of the document reproduces the writing of the patent application.

In addition, the USPTO *publishes many of the patent applications while they are pending* before they are issued, and often before they are examined. Publishing occurs after a delay that is often necessary for institutional and practical reasons. This delay we call the **publication delay**. For most new patent applications the publication delay is 18 months, but sometimes applicants in the United States can effectuate substantially different durations.

Accordingly, the USPTO generates two types of public documents—namely, patents and pending applications. We will study them in more detail in the remainder of this book.

In some cases, the US patent application is not published at all; the only document that is published is a US patent, and only if it is approved. In fact, the entire US Patent System used to be this way. The policy reasons are explained in chapter 6.

1.4 Overview of Patenting in Another Country

Many countries in the world have Patent Systems similar to the US Patent System. Figure 1B shows an overview of patenting in a sample Country A.

The civil authority of Country A creates patent laws and institutes a Patent Office. The same people and organizations that can apply for a US patent can also apply for a patent in Country A.

An entity typically does not need to be a citizen or a resident of Country A to apply for a patent in it. A non-resident may use a representative in Country A, such as a local patent attorney or a local patent agent.

Though similar in basic structure, the Patent System of Country A can differ in a number of ways from the US Patent System. For a first example, of course, the patent documents of Country A are printed in the language of Country A. Some elements may be printed in additional languages.

For a second example, different countries have different patent laws and patent rules. For instance, most countries other than the United States require that *all* pending patent applications be published 18 months after being filed with the Patent Office, regardless of whether or not they will succeed in becoming issued as patents.

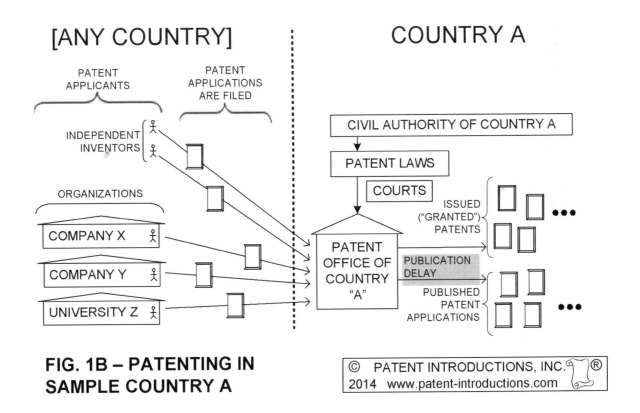

FIG. 1B – PATENTING IN SAMPLE COUNTRY A

© PATENT INTRODUCTIONS, INC.
2014   www.patent-introductions.com

1.5   Patenting the Same Invention in Multiple Countries

A patent in one country will protect the invention in that country only. Companies that sell their innovative products in many countries typically want patent protection in each of those countries.

Figure 1C shows a strategy that companies can implement to protect one of their inventions in other Countries A, B, etc. Company X can be in any country as we saw above. Company X creates a single patent application, creates copies translated in foreign languages, files the translated copies as different patent applications in Countries A and B, and pays fees in each country.

Then the different patent applications for the same invention will be published and maybe issued as patents by the different countries. These different documents form an international **patent family**.

In the patenting of Figure 1C, the first patent application in each country is filed independently of the other patent applications. Accordingly, in this kind of patenting, none of these patent applications claims any **priority** from another, as we will understand better from the next section.

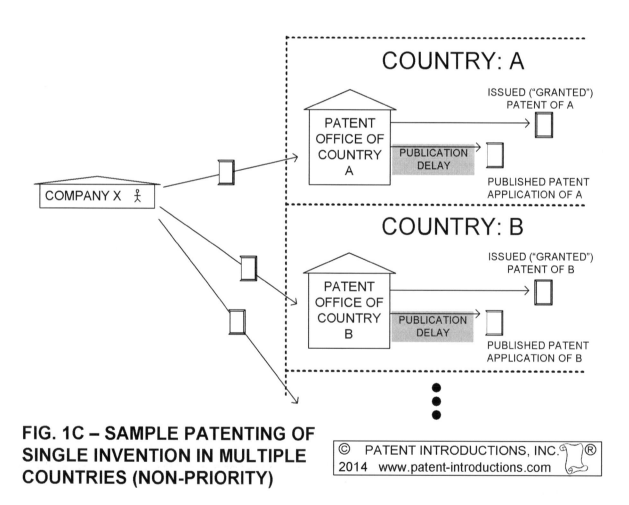

FIG. 1C – SAMPLE PATENTING OF SINGLE INVENTION IN MULTIPLE COUNTRIES (NON-PRIORITY)

The non-priority approach of Figure 1C, however, has inefficiencies. As we will see later in this book, there are strict legal deadlines for filing patent applications, and it is cumbersome to create multiple patent applications, often under tight deadlines. In addition, companies want to file their patent applications as early as possible, so as to win **patent races**, in the event their rivals are patenting the same invention. These challenges have been addressed as we see below.

1.6 International Agreements to Facilitate Patenting in Multiple Countries

Countries have been trying to make it easier for companies to receive patents for a single invention. For this reason, countries have reached **international patent agreements**.

One type of such agreements permits a patent application to claim **priority** from another patent application that was filed previously. As we see, for example, in Figure 1D, the countries are shown more simplified than before. Company X creates a regular patent application and files it in Country A.

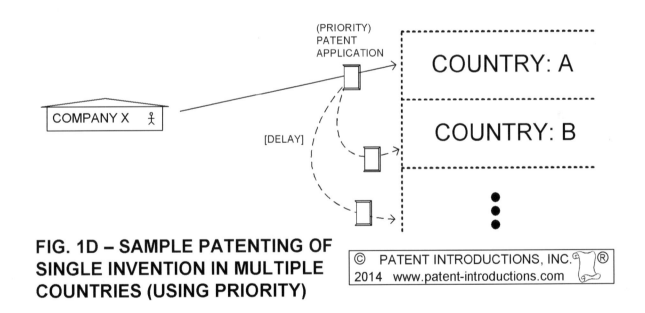

FIG. 1D – SAMPLE PATENTING OF SINGLE INVENTION IN MULTIPLE COUNTRIES (USING PRIORITY)

© PATENT INTRODUCTIONS, INC.®
2014 www.patent-introductions.com

Then, Company X has the option to file the same application in additional countries. The originally filed patent application is then used as a **priority patent application**. Company X can create translated copies of the priority patent application, and can delay up to one year before filing them in the other countries, as long as it does that by **claiming priority** from the priority patent application. The other countries then may treat the delayed patent applications as if they had been filed on the same day as the priority patent application, since the delayed patent applications are for the same invention.

The delay of up to one year in Figure 1D benefits Company X because it has additional time to prepare the applications for the other countries. Beyond creating translated copies, this time can be spent also in customizing each translated copy for particular aspects of patenting in its intended country.

While the priority patenting of Figure 1D helps, patent filing in multiple countries is still cumbersome. For example, an error discovered in the priority patent application by the Patent Office of Country A must be fixed with each patent application in each of the other Patent Offices. Moreover, if the priority patent application is to be rejected over prior art found by the Patent Office of Country A, then it will also be rejected by the other Patent Offices, and the applicant will have wasted the money in applying in all the other countries. This problem has been addressed as described below.

Figure 1E shows the result of a further international patent agreement called the **Patent Cooperation Treaty** (PCT). According to it, the **World Intellectual Property Organization** (WIPO) operates an International Patent Office ("International Bureau") in cooperation with the Patent Offices of some countries.

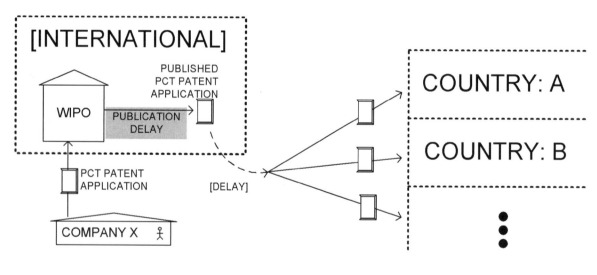

FIG. 1E – INTERNATIONAL (PCT) PATENT APPLICATION FOR SINGLE INVENTION

Company X can then file a **PCT application** with the International Bureau, which sometimes works in cooperation with a national Patent Office. The PCT application will be published after a publication delay of 18 months, which will produce a useful international record. Additionally, the application can be examined while pending at the WIPO, at the preliminary level or also at a deeper level.

The PCT application should not be thought of as a "foreign" application, but as an "international" application. Indeed, the PCT application has no country; it is only an application. It will never become issued as a patent in any country *by the WIPO*, because the WIPO does not speak for any country in particular.

Then, after some delay, Company X can file copies of the PCT application as national patent applications in multiple countries. These national patent applications claim priority from the PCT application, which means that these countries treat their national patent applications as if they had been filed on the same day as the PCT application. Moreover, some countries choose to adopt the deeper examination of a PCT application, and grant their national patents accordingly.

The delay permitted by the PCT is usefully longer than the one-year delay of Figure 1D. The detour via the WIPO will have cost more money to Company X, but will have bought extra time. The preliminary examination of the PCT application gives Company X feedback and opportunity to adjust the PCT application in a single proceeding and make a more updated decision about patentability. This saves much larger costs later, if the examination turns out unfavorable.

Additional international agreements about patents include the formation of regional organizations to simplify their processes. For example, many European countries subscribe to the **European Patent Convention** (EPC). As such, you may see patents granted by the **European Patent Office**, which have been patented ("validated") in some European countries but not others. There are other organizations, such as the **Eurasian Patent Organization**, the **African Regional Intellectual Property Organization** (ARIPO), the **Organisation Africaine de la Propriété Intellectuelle** (OAPI), the **Gulf Cooperation Council**, the **Nordic Patent Institute**, etc.

The international cooperation efforts are continuing. In some instances, examination in one country can expedite examination in another. Moreover, to save costs for applicants, there is an effort to have a single European patent, and a single European Patent Court.

1.7 Differences in Accessing Patent Protection

As mentioned before, each country shapes its Innovation Landscape by how much access it permits to patenting, and what conditions it places on the patenting. You can compare the amount of access by how certain questions are answered about Patent Systems.

For one example, you can ask: "Are there any special accommodations for inventors on the lower rungs of the economic ladder?" Most independent inventors do not find patenting cheap.

For another example, you can ask what kinds of inventions may *not* receive a patent in that country. More particularly, countries seem to agree that "technological-type" inventions are patentable, but various countries have various exceptions about new and useful inventions related to certain types of software, medical diagnostic methods, pharmaceuticals, business methods, tax planning strategies, etc.

Of course, you can ask more questions.

1.8 Defining Patent Rights

The intent behind having patent rights in the first place is best understood in terms of the prospect that an inventor who innovates by bringing their invention to market is likely to be followed and even copied. Such an inventor may be called a leader, although not all leaders innovate on their own inventions. **Following** means the business strategy of competing against a leader with a product that is similar or even identical to that of the leader. Following *is a legitimate business strategy* as long as laws are not being broken. Following is being taught in business schools and in the business literature, and is treated in this book accordingly.

The business strategy of following is compelling to adopt, because it has a more advantageous risk/reward calculus than that of being a leader. A **follower** could generate comparable returns as the leader, while not bearing much of the leader's initial expense or risk. Indeed, *a leader who is both an inventor and an innovator is creating a new paradigm that others will be tempted to follow, exactly or with changes.* Such a leader bears the expense of developing a new technology and the risk that it will not work; the expense of developing a new product; the expense of attempting to break entry barriers and the prospective risk that some cannot be broken; and the expense of educating the market with the prospective risk that the market will not accept the product. Even when a follower's product is not identical to the leader's product, that follower's product has nevertheless been planned and designed with insights and information learned from the publicly known efforts and experiences of the leader.

Given the great economic advantages of being follower as opposed to being a leader, *innovators should expect that others will want to follow them if they succeed.* Additionally, innovators who anticipate success should further plan ahead what to do about being followed in the future.

The point of a Patent System is to create for inventors the opportunity to acquire patent rights that would demotivate or slow down those who would follow them. Conversely, if inventors do acquire such patent rights, those who would follow them would face legal risks related to patents, which we call **patent business risks**.

While patent rights are created for the benefit of inventors as opposed to followers, securing patent rights presents additional expense and even risk to inventors. Indeed, patenting enables their would-be followers even better, because it can be more economical for a would-be follower to read a patent for an explanation than to invest in analyzing a leader's new product. This additional risk is sometimes so high that inventors sometimes forgo patenting and maintain their invention as a **trade secret**.

First we will describe analytically how patent rights operate, and then we present questions regarding how far they should reach. Analytically speaking, *patent rights are legal property rights that operate somewhat similarly to property rights in real estate*. After all, patents are often referred to as Intellectual Property (IP). Property law for real estate defines property rights in a so-called "negative" manner, at least in the United States. The negative manner is in terms of excluding others. For example, when you own your house, legally you have the right to exclude all others from being in it. Therefore, no one else can live in it, and that is how you can live there exclusively. Plus, you can transfer all or some of your rights; for example, you can rent your house to someone else, who will then be permitted to live in your house instead of you. Moreover, you can sell these property rights in the same way that you bought them, when you bought your house from someone else, perhaps even the builder.

Additionally, you *can buy patent rights* from others who own them, such as the original inventor. You *can sell or license patent rights*, which is like selling or renting. The similarities with real property law do not stop there: for example, patent rights can also be pledged as collateral for a loan. Plus, patent rights can be legally enforced in courts against those who infringe them.

Similarly, with the "negative" definitions of real property rights, a patent in itself does not *directly* permit you to build or do what it covers legally. Rather, it only permits you to nominally exclude all others from making, using, selling, offering for sale, etc. what the patent covers, and only in the country that issued the patent. To actually build or do, you still must avoid what is claimed by all other valid patents that you do not have access to.

A country can shape its Innovation Landscape by deciding what patent rights are and what they are not. One question—and there can be more—for probing the extent of patent rights in a country is whether all the patent rights expire when a patent does, or whether some of them expire only within several months of granting the patent.

1.9 Resolving Patent Disputes

A **patent dispute** is a disagreement between two or more parties. The disagreement typically concerns whether or not the patent rights of one party are infringed without permission by the products, services, operations, or other activities of another party.

Patent disputes are resolved in courts because patents are legal documents and patent rights are legal rights. At that time, the courts will apply the patent laws to the pertinent **patent-related facts**, arrive at legal determinations such as whether there is infringement, and then decide any penalties according to the laws. People like you plus those in rival companies *will have created these patent-related facts* based on the history and timing of public disclosures, introduction of products to the market, creation of patent rights, etc.

Sometimes, patent disputes are resolved by negotiation between the interested parties. If the negotiation fails and no mediation or arbitration occurs, one of the parties may resort to the court system against the other.

Negotiations, mediation, and arbitration are often based on how both sides expect that the court system would rule on the dispute. As such, patent negotiations are resolved by specialists who know the patent laws, some of which are obscure. Patent rights are such that, if you don't know the patent laws and say something wrong, your side's legal position can be made worse than it was, if the dispute is eventually resolved in court.

A country further shapes its Innovation Landscape by how effectively its courts actually enforce patent rights. Some initial questions—and there can be more—for reaching answers include the following:

(a) Do courts take a long time to reach judgment? (Often reaching answers that are fully fair takes some time.)
(b) Do the court proceedings cost a lot of money until judgment is reached? In particular, does the structure for legal costs:
  (i) inhibit too much those with legitimate patent claims from trying to enforce them?
  (ii) not inhibit enough those with illegitimate patent claims from trying to enforce them?
(c) What are the penalties for infringement? And, prospectively, are these penalties severe enough to actually deter infringing in the first place?

1.10 Navigating within a Patent System

In subsequent chapters we will see how, by its Patent System, a country influences the economic behavior of its participants. More specifically, we will see:

(a) that the Patent System creates certain foreseeable **patent business risks and opportunities** for its existing businesses and would-be businesses;
(b) a framework for how the patent business risks and opportunities impact the risk/reward calculations for a proposed new project, and more particularly the impact in how the Net Present Value of a proposed new project is computed from a Business Analysis Review; and
(c) basic **patent strategies** that companies use to mitigate these patent business risks and for executing according to the patent business opportunities so that they capture more value.

So, for basic answers about how to navigate and work within a Patent System, continue reading this book. In doing so, you will start asking many of the right questions, and you will understand how your actions can become patent-related facts that put your company at an advantage or avoid a disadvantage.

For reaching final answers, however, *ask your patent attorney*. He or she will point out the particular patent business risks your organization faces in each case.

> **Chapter Summary**
>
> In this chapter, we saw an introduction to Patent Systems. The three main components of a country's Patent System are (a) an avenue for inventors to receive patent rights in exchange for reporting their inventions, (b) a definition of what are the legal rights of a patent owner, which behave much like real property rights, and (c) an avenue for parties to resolve their disputes about patents. We saw overviews for patenting in the United States, in typical other countries, in groups of countries, and international agreements to facilitate patenting of a single invention in multiple countries. Moreover, we examined how different aspects of the main components can shape a Patent System to be strong, weak, or something in between.

Notes:

2

YOUR COMPANY'S BUSINESS CAN BE IMPACTED BY PATENTS

2.1 Your Company's Finances

Your company's strength today generally arises from its commercial activity, which we discuss using Figure 2A. Your company offers a product to the Market. The product, which can be a service, is also called an offering. In exchange, your company receives revenue as payment. Revenue improves your company's finances. This example outlines the basic structure, although other business models are less direct.

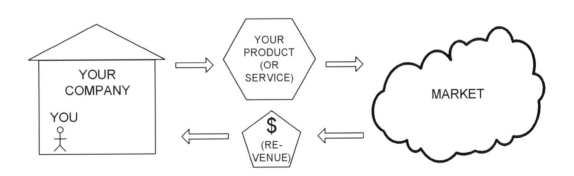

FIG. 2A – YOUR COMPANY'S COMMERCIAL ACTIVITY

Your company's revenue has an impact on you; it helps pay your salary, provides for the expectation that your employment will be continued, and so on. In turn, you contribute by doing your part so that the revenue will continue in the future.

2.2   Your Company's Commercial Battles in the Marketplace

Other companies will want the revenue that your company receives, and so they will try to create rival products for the market. In Figure 2B these rival products are shown as shaded.

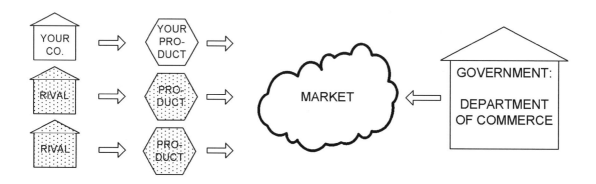

FIG. 2B – YOUR COMPANY'S PRODUCT COMPETES AGAINST PRODUCTS OF RIVAL COMPANIES

© PATENT INTRODUCTIONS, INC. ®
2014   www.patent-introductions.com

The products from rivals compete with your company's product, and accordingly dilute the revenue that your company is receiving. The success of each product relative to the others is measured by its **market share**.

In Figure 2B, the three competing products are shown by identical icons, but that does not necessarily mean they are identical. They may have differences. **Differentiation** in any aspect of a product that a consumer cares about may be important to gain or preserve market share. Plus, differentiation in how a product is made can help protect an advantageous cost structure and profitability relative to rivals. As we will see, *patents can protect the differentiation*. When products lack such differentiation and are sold by numerous sellers, they can become **commoditized**. Such products compete mostly on the basis of price, squeezing revenues, profits, and the occasional employee bonuses.

There are additional influences in the market, one of which (i.e., the government) is also shown in Figure 2B. For competition to work legitimately, laws about commerce must be obeyed by all participants. Plus, the governments of many countries have ministries or departments whose purpose is to help the wheels of commerce work for the benefit of a country's domestic businesses. For example, in the US Government, the **Department of Commerce** has the stated mission to "help make American businesses more innovative at home and more competitive abroad."[4]

2.3 The Patent Plane

Think of the operations of Figure 2B as occurring in a single plane, which is the plane of the drawing. Let's call that the **market plane**, where there are products and payments.

In addition to the market plane, companies also compete in a different plane, which we can call the **patent plane**. Figure 2C shows the patent plane together with the market plane, visualized in three dimensions.

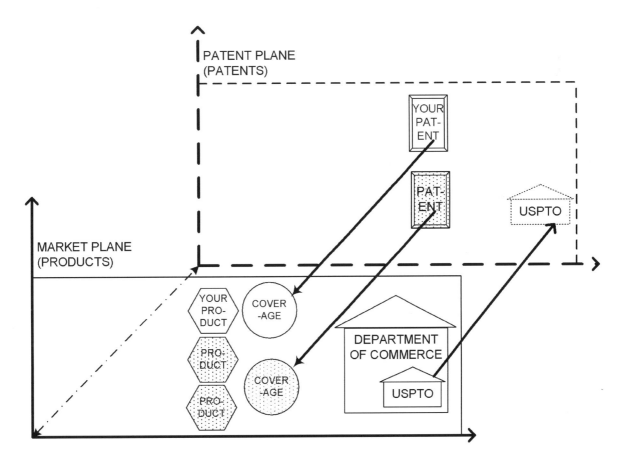

FIG. 2C – COMPANY COMPETITION IN MARKET PLANE AND IN PATENT PLANE

© PATENT INTRODUCTIONS, INC.®
2014 www.patent-introductions.com

---

[4] Quote from website of US Department of Commerce at http://www.commerce.gov/, accessed on 2013-09-21.

In Figure 2C, the market plane seems lower, but is intended to be thought of as being at the "front". The market plane in Figure 2C repeats some elements of Figure 2B.

The patent plane is shown as higher than the market plane, but is intended to be parallel to and "deeper" than the market plane, with its contours in dashed lines. The patent plane in Figure 2C repeats some elements of Figure 1A.

The patent plane is where patents reside. Only one of your company's patents is shown, and only one rival's patent. In practice, of course, there could be more.

In Figure 2C, we see that the US Department of Commerce exerts its authority in the market plane. In addition, the **US Patent and Trademark Office** (USPTO) exerts its authority in the patent plane. The USPTO is part of the Department of Commerce because patents and trademarks are empowered to impact commerce in the market plane.[5]

Patents legally cover market spaces. Figure 2C shows the patents projecting their coverage on spaces of the market plane even though they themselves are in the patent plane. In each case, the space with the patent coverage is shown—arbitrarily—by a circle. Your company's patent and its legal coverage are shown as clear because your product can often enter that space without infringing any patents of others. (There is an important caveat here, which we explore in chapter 3.) Your rival's patent and its legal coverage are shown as shaded because, if your product goes into that space, it would infringe that patent. In the example of Figure 2C, all products avoid the coverage of all patents and there is no infringement.

2.4   Patent Battles in the Patent Plane

Since patents affect the market plane, companies also compete in the patent plane in **patent battles**. Patent battles have at least one element in the patent plane. We will see more of them in detail later in this book.

You can think of a patent battle that is confined to the patent plane as part of a patent "cold war". In such patent battles, companies *create patent rights for themselves* and *prevent, spoil, and outright destroy patent rights of others*. Here are some examples:

Companies create patent rights for themselves by filing patent applications. A company that is first to invent can receive a patent to protect the differentiation of its product or its contemplated product. From the perspective of business strategy, such an innovator uses a patent as a **barrier to entry**. Even if a patent does not completely deter followers, it operates as a barrier by potentially increasing the followers' entry costs and uncertainty. The costs include

---

[5]   A misconception is that patents are really only technical papers, and that the USPTO is a "technology" department of the US Government.

the costs of (a) patent searching, and (b) designing a product so as to further avoid the legal coverage of the patents found by the searching. The uncertainty increases because the would-be follower would need to invest in these operations without knowing whether they will achieve a favorable outcome—namely, that their prospective competing product will eventually survive the adverse consequences of a **patent infringement** legal challenge.

Companies also prevent others' *potential* patent rights by creating **defensive publications** for spaces in the market plane that they predict could become important. A defensive publication may prevent or limit others from patenting in those spaces in the future. Of course, a company that creates the defensive publication also forgoes any rights that the company could patent what is published, even if that company's employee thought of it first.

Companies further spoil and outright destroy their rivals' actual patent rights. As will be mentioned in chapter 3 and developed in chapter 8, armed with appropriate documents that you can help find, patent attorneys are sometimes able to create and file specific legal papers that challenge their rivals' pending patent applications and prevent them from becoming issued as patents. In other instances the challenges are made against issued patents, which can become forcibly revised or even invalidated this way. Patent Systems recognize that this destructive activity usefully complements the efforts of Patent Offices to prevent patents from having broader legal coverage than the laws would allow them to, and even permit some of these challenges to be made without disclosing who made them.

It is often difficult for your company to know how much its patents affect its rivals—in other words, to know how much the rivals worry about their patents. After all, your rivals will usually not easily admit openly that they are *not* competing against your company because of its patent, even if that is the case. One can, however, get a partial indication of that by asking their patent attorney which of their company's patents and patent applications are being challenged by rivals.

Patent litigation is fought in courts, and usually involves products from the market plane and patents from the patent plane. You can think of patent litigation as an example of a patent "hot war". This happens if two sides have a patent-related dispute that they cannot resolve by negotiation, mediation, or arbitration. For example, in Figure 2C there could be additional patents legally covering one or more of the shown products, additional products that are covered by the shown patents, or both.

Patent litigation often starts with a patent owner asserting that its patent is infringed by one or more products of the rival.[6] The accused rival then may offer defenses, as we will see in chapter 11. Since a product is involved, more money is at stake, and typically far more money is spent in a patent "hot war" than a patent "cold war".

---

[6] In some instances, patent litigation can be started by a party concerned that a patentee will sue it. Your patent attorney can tell you when that is permitted.

2.5 Patent Business Risks and Opportunities Due to Patent Systems

The prospect of the patent battles of the previous section creates certain foreseeable **patent business risks and opportunities** for existing businesses and contemplated would-be businesses. These risks and opportunities may influence what companies decide to invest in.

The table of Figure 2D summarizes some of these patent business risks and opportunities, and we elaborate on some of them in the remainder of this book. For easier reference, we identify the patent business risks as PBR-(number) and the patent business opportunities as PBO-(number).[7]

PATENT BUSINESS RISKS ("PBR-#")	PATENT BUSINESS OPPORTUNITIES ("PBO-#")
PBR-1) Product will infringe another's patent	PBO-1) Try to reserve future exclusive patent rights
PBR-2) New Product will be followed, and its market share & pricing power will be eroded	PBO-2) ...
PBR-3) Investment to acquire patent rights will generate inadequate or no returns	
PBR-4) ...	

FIG. 2D – PATENT BUSINESS RISKS AND PATENT BUSINESS OPPORTUNITIES

© PATENT INTRODUCTIONS, INC. ®
2014 www.patent-introductions.com

Figure 2D shows that a company that provides products faces the **patent business risk of infringing (PBR-1)** another's patent without the patent owner's permission. A company found to infringe risks being legally forced to pay money damages for past infringement, being stopped

---

[7] There are additional patent business risks and opportunities, as patent consultants will tell you. We invite the literature on patents to further identify them and number them sequentially PBR-(next number) and PBO-(next number).

from continuing the activity that infringes and, even if not, paying money for a license to be allowed to continue using the patent.

Additionally, a company faces the **patent business risk that its new product will be followed or copied (PBR-2)**. The reasons for this are the economic advantages of following as opposed to leading, as we saw in chapter 1. In fact, the pervasiveness of risk PBR-2 is the very reason that the US Patent System was created in the first place, as Abraham Lincoln observed.[8] We can define risk PBR-2 as patent-related in this context, since patenting is a potential mitigation to the risk. If there is no mitigation and the company is then actually followed by rivals, it risks losing the differentiation provided by its innovative product or feature, missing out on some of its market share and having its future pricing power eroded.

A first patent business opportunity due to the Patent System is to prospectively **try to reserve future exclusive patent rights (PBO-1)** in a new invention, before offering it as a product or service. Reserving can be by patenting it, or by buying an unused patent. Briefly, opportunity PBO-1 is risk PBR-1 from the other side's point of view, and in a possibly different time frame. Indeed, being the one to acquire the patent on an invention enables the company to offer the innovation, now or in the future, free from the business risk of infringing *another's* patent for *that* invention. Moreover, opportunity PBO-1 is the main mitigation of risk PBR-2.

One more business risk due to the Patent System is that **inadequate or no returns will be generated (PBR-3)** for the investment made in acquiring patent rights. This may occur when one executes on patent business opportunity PBO-1.

In this book, we will stay only with the patent business risks and opportunities of Figure 2D because that is where you can help as an employee. Now we discuss each of them in more detail.

2.6 PBR-1: The Patent Business Risk of Infringing a Patent

As mentioned above, a company providing a product to the market has a first **patent business risk that the product infringes another's patent (PBR-1)** without the patent owner's permission. Figure 2E shows the prospect of risk PBR-1 for the situation in which your company contemplates providing a product to the market.

Figure 2E addresses two relevant questions by the question marks. The first question mark is in the patent plane, and considers whether there is a patent that has legal coverage at the

---

[8] From the Lincoln Patent Quote at the beginning of this book, see the first sentence.

location of the market plane where you are contemplating placing your product. Briefly, this is the kind of question that can be answered with patent strategies that we will see in the next chapter.

The second question mark is in the market plane and indicates that, even when you do know about all possible patents, you often do not know *with certainty* whether a particular design will infringe. The potential of infringement is shown by your prospective product overlapping the circle only partially. There are reasons for the uncertainty.[9] Later, we will see that a patent attorney can answer some of these questions and where you can help.

If the owner of the patent suspects that your company's product does infringe, then he or she may sue your company for **patent infringement**. If successful, the owner may legally force your company to stop providing the product, or pay a **license fee** to continue providing it. The patent owner may also force your company to pay them **money damages** for past infringement.

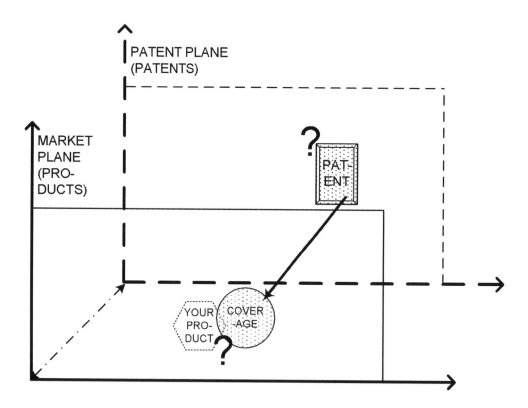

FIG. 2E – PROPOSED PRODUCT'S PROSPECT OF INFRINGING ANOTHER'S PATENT

© PATENT INTRODUCTIONS, INC.®
2014 www.patent-introductions.com

---

[9] The reasons are legal, driven by desire for fairness to all involved. Think of an issued patent as a tip of an iceberg in terms of how it will be legally interpreted by a court. At least in the United States, a patent will be interpreted not only from what it says, but also from other factors, such as dictionaries, legal "equivalents", the prior art that was known when the patent application was filed, and so on.

In the US, the money damages can include **compensatory damages**, plus **punitive damages** if your infringement is proved to be willful because, after all, patent rights are a type of legal property rights.[10]

Patent business risk PBR-1 is foreseeable, because it is known that sellers face the risk of liability of infringing another's patent. The seller's ignorance of the patent is not an excuse for the infringement.

Risk PBR-1 arises in a number of ways, even indirectly. For example, your company's product is not excused if it incorporates an infringing component or a design purchased from a separate firm.

Risk PBR-1 is greater if your company is executing a follower strategy against an original innovator. Follower strategies are common and have advantages, as we mentioned in chapter 1. Percentage-wise, the risk of infringing is even higher if the innovator you are following tends to patent its innovations. The downside risk is even worse if the innovator you are following tends to enforce its patents. If the product you want to follow is very recent and you cannot find yet any of their patents or applications, changing your product to differ somewhat from their product may decrease, increase, or leave unchanged your risk PBR-1.

Patent business risk PBR-1 can be mitigated with some diligence. In the next chapter, we will list basic patent strategies for such mitigation. In addition, through the rest of this book we will see increasing detail of business processes and actions to implement these strategies.

2.7 PBR-2: The Patent Business Risk of a Product Being Followed

As mentioned above, a company providing a product to the market has a second **patent business risk that its product will be followed (PBR-2)**. More specifically, a rival can execute the business strategy of following, which is copying substantially or even exactly. If a rival eventually does follow, the company offering the innovation risks losing the advantage of its differentiation and its eventual market share and pricing power. If many rivals follow, the followed product risks becoming commoditized.

Patent business risk PBR-2 is foreseeable because follower strategies are common. A rival might adopt a follower strategy because it provides economic advantages, as we saw in chapter 1. The risk of being followed may not matter immediately after the product is released. But it will likely matter significantly more over many fiscal quarters and fiscal years after the fact, which is why those who fund you often insist on advance mitigation.

---

[10] You can ask your patent attorney what exactly "willful" means in the US.

Patent business risk PBR-2 can be mitigated with some diligence. In the next chapter, we will list basic patent strategies to this effect. Of those, patenting is the most economical portion of the investment in a new product.[11] Patenting may deter a would-be follower. Even if following has started, timely patenting may compensate for the following afterward, and may even stop it. In fact, *a patent essentially provides a form of legal monopoly and its attendant pricing power* for the product or feature it covers. Through the rest of this book we will see business processes and actions to implement the patenting.

2.8 PBO-1: The Patent Business Opportunity to Reserve Future Exclusive Patent Rights

As mentioned above, an entity such as a company has a **patent business opportunity of reserving future exclusive patent rights in an invention (PBO-1)**, so as to have an option to offer it in the future. Opportunity PBO-1 is the main mitigation of risk PBR-2 of being followed.

You can execute on opportunity PBO-1 by buying a patent, or by applying to patent in advance your own invention. Of course, you cannot apply to patent just the *what*; you also need to disclose the *how* you would implement it, as we will see in chapter 9.

Prospective patenting is permitted because there is no requirement that an entity such as a company or individual be "working" the invention, for purposes of being able to patent it. Accordingly, entities can patent their inventions even if they do not "practice" them. More specifically, entities such as companies that sell products, start-up companies, universities, research firms, and individuals pursue patent business opportunity PBO-1 by prospective patenting. These entities invest in developing and patenting inventions while keeping their options open as to whether they will eventually:
(a) practice the inventions, or
(b) sell or license the patents they generate from the inventions.

As time passes, these entities can observe the progress of their patenting. They can also take into account their own circumstances. If patenting does not succeed, then these entities may choose to not develop a product under certain circumstances. If patenting does succeed, then these companies, universities, research firms, and individuals in some instances launch products and even companies, based on these patents that they have prepared in advance. Or, according to their situation at the time, instead of launching, these entities can transfer the developed patent rights to other companies, which is an activity called "monetizing". For a company that sells products, classic candidates for patents to monetize are their unused ("non-core") patents—that is, patents on inventions that they initially invested in and developed enough to be able to patent, but eventually chose not to make the much larger investment of launching products or subsidiaries.

---

[11] The amount invested in a new product also properly includes the time that a company's employees and founders spend on developing it, multiplied by their salary rate, plus materials costs in some cases.

Sometimes patents are among the most prized assets of a business. Plus, when a business fails, its assets including its patent portfolio are typically sold to reduce the creditors' losses.

Some transfers of patent rights are private transactions, whereas others are public, such as in patent auctions. The companies that receive the patent rights also include companies that specialize in patents, such as brokers. All the companies that receive patents in turn have the same options as those who generated the patents. In fact, valuation of patents is sometimes derived by considering patents under options theories.

Advance patenting generates more certainty as to patent rights in the area. The increased certainty will be regarding as to who has which patent rights, which patent rights are not (yet) reserved, and which patent rights cannot be reserved by anyone anymore. Indeed, as patent applications are filed and examined, documents are created and referenced, all producing findable writings. The activity of patenting generally enables one to resolve rights to inventions from the writings with far more certainty.

The increased certainty can increase the confidence in New Product Development. As patent rights become settled, development can proceed with lesser risk of infringing (PBR-1) and possibly also with lesser risk of one being followed (PBR-2). Businesspeople looking for wholly new areas to enter tend to ask those who hold patents whether they have any patents they want to sell. In fact, those who specialize in monetizing patent portfolios sometimes show on a website the areas in which they have patent portfolios available for sale or license.

You, too, can help your company as an employee. If you want your company to eventually pursue an idea, you can propose developing and patenting your idea in advance. Your patenting will generate certainty and possibly reduce the future patent business risks for your implemented idea, which in turn will remove obstacles when you later try to convince your company to develop your idea into a product.

In the case of a proposed start-up company, **Venture Capitalists (VCs)** appreciate the patenting because of its durability and cost-effectiveness. They sometimes use the word "traction" for early patent filings of a start-up company. The more sophisticated VCs also ask *what* has been patented, and thus mentally project what is *not* patented and can therefore be followed easily in the long term by rivals. They know that patenting will make the differentiation more durable.

2.9 PBR-3: The Patent Business Risk of Generating Inadequate Eventual Returns from Acquired Patent Rights

There is a risk with acquiring patent rights before one needs them. **The risk (PBR-3) is that inadequate or no returns will be generated** from the investment in the acquired patent rights. At risk are the invested resources, such as the time and money spent to evaluate the ideas and patents, and the funds and other capital used to acquire the patent rights. The risk applies to entities that patent their own inventions or buy patents from others.

Risk PBR-3 can be manifested in many ways. For example, patenting might not succeed for a multitude of reasons. The most frequent such reason is that someone else has patented or described the same invention earlier. Or the patenting could succeed, but no one wants to practice the invention. Or another company will want to practice the invention, and that company will find legitimate ways to avoid the legal coverage of the patent.

Risk PBR-3 is faced by all the companies, universities, research firms and individuals that acquire patent rights. Companies and universities that develop and patent inventions mitigate this risk by having an internal Patent Committee evaluate their patenting prospects, as we will see in chapter 9.

2.10 Patent Business Risks and Opportunities in the Context of Different Industries

While all of the above is generally true for those operating within a Patent System, the patent business risks and opportunities apply markedly differently in the context of different industries, according to their market realities. Here are some examples.

First, patent laws define time periods, the most important of which is the duration of patent validity (about 20 years for a new utility patent). These patent time periods interact with each industry's typical durations, an important one of which is the duration of the product life cycle. For example, exclusivity for products with a hoped-for life cycle duration of much longer than the two decades of a patent may be able to be maintained better with trade secrets, such as is the case with the chemical formula of the Coca-Cola® soft drink.

Second, patent laws define the penalties for a product infringing a patent. Before developing a product in a risky market position relative to the legal coverage of a rival's known patent, a prudent company will evaluate the risks. If the cost of ameliorating infringement is prohibitive and the product life cycle duration is long, then it may be safer to just develop products that use patents that are owned or expired. This situation is more pronounced where the market appreciates innovation less than it appreciates low cost to purchase, low total cost of ownership, etc.[12]

Third, patent laws define that the legal coverage of a patent is implemented by a part of a patent that is called **claims**. Sometimes the nature of the industry and the science behind it play a large role in conjunction with what can be claimed. For example, if one tries to avoid a patent

---

[12] The reader can determine whether this applies to his or her industry.

for a pharmaceutical compound claiming a chemical formula by making minor modifications, the result will be a different compound that can have different pharmaceutical properties and often does not function the same way. Thus, simple modifications of a chemical formula can fail to design around a patented pharmaceutical compound, and therefore are not worth making by a would-be rival. The science of chemistry simply works this way. So, a single chemical patent can effectively protect a chemical product having pharmaceutical activity. However, the result could be different for products in other industries, such as technology type industries (electronics, computers, software, optics, medical devices, aircraft, maybe some materials, etc.)

Fourth, different industries seem to have different amounts of **competitive convergence**— i.e. competition in products and patenting by different entities. For example, in some areas of the life sciences there seems to be less patenting competition, with patent applications rarely overlapping. This is not true, however, in many areas of the technology type industries for commercially important products. Accordingly, the risk of infringing a patent and the need to patent before others so as to win **patent races** are more pronounced in the latter fields.

There are additional reasons for which patent business risks and opportunities apply differently in the context of different industries. This book applies to all industries, and more for the technology type industries.

Chapter Summary

In this chapter, we saw how patents can impact your company's business. Your company may have revenue in the marketplace where its products compete against the products of rivals. Beyond that competition, companies also compete in a patent plane, which may affect the eventual commercial outcome. The competition in the patent plane occurs because the Patent System creates patent business risks and opportunities. Risk PBR-1 is the foreseeable patent business risk of infringing a patent. Risk PBR-2 is the foreseeable patent business risk of being followed, or copied, if your new product is successful—as you are planning it to be. Opportunity PBO-1 is the known patent business opportunity to reserve future exclusive patent rights, either by buying a patent or by patenting one's own invention. Risk PBR-3 is the foreseeable patent business risk of generating inadequate or no eventual returns from acquiring patent rights. The patent business risks and opportunities apply differently in the context of different industries, according to the realities of the latter. The remainder of this book is focused more on the technology type industries.

Notes:

3

BASIC PATENT STRATEGIES FOR NEW PRODUCT PLANNING

3.1 Planning a New Product: Risk/Reward Calculations

In many cases, companies contemplate developing additional products. As we saw previously, the contemplated products could be new or following other products, or a combination of both.

When contemplating investing in the development of a new product, your company will usually make risk/reward calculations as to whether it expects to make a profit. In addition your company may consider other strategic factors.

The risk/reward calculations will sometimes be performed in terms of a **Business Analysis Review** that computes a **Net Present Value** (NPV) for the project. The NPV will be computed from the expected revenues of the new product, less the costs invested to create it and continuing to produce and sell it. The computed number for the NPV will guide the decision of whether or not to develop the product.

The Patent System affects the NPV, and therefore the risk/reward calculations. As we said in chapter 2, the Patent System creates patent business risks and opportunities that can impact your company's expected revenues and the expected investment. However, *NPV computations often do not account for patents*. The rest of this chapter tries to help you appreciate which components of the NPV patents can impact.

3.2 Business Analysis Review with Patent Business Risks

Figure 3A is an example of how a Business Analysis Review could be structured if we also account for patent business risks PBR-1 and PBR-2 of Figure 2D. The top few lines are intended to provide numbers for calculating the NPV, as is known. These are numbers about future performance, and understandably include guesses.

BUSINESS ANALYSIS REVIEW – COMPUTATION OF NPV
NEW PROJECT: [NAME]

DEVELOPMENT COST	$...	
RAMP-UP COST	$...	
MARKETING & SUPPORT COST	$... / year	
UNIT PRODUCTION COST	$... / unit	
PRODUCTION VOLUME	... units / year	
SALES VOLUME	... units / year	*N1, *N2
UNIT PRICE	$... / unit	*N2
SALES REVENUE	$...	*N1, *N2
PROJECT NPV	**$...**	*N1, *N2

*N1 PBR-1) PATENT BUSINESS RISK
   OF INFRINGING A PATENT: * VISIBLE TYPE: There is some; we have spent some resources in patent searches, and we have cleared what we found today, but the searches will be stale next week.

   * INVISIBLE TYPE: There is some, and it will continue being renewed (for as long as we don't patent or introduce commercially). Patent searches & clearance need to continue.

*N2 PBR-2) PATENT BUSINESS RISK
   OF BEING FOLLOWED: Risk will be higher if project succeeds; rivals will be unfettered if we don't patent.

FIG. 3A – PROJECT'S BUSINESS ANALYSIS REVIEW (SEARCHED, BUT NO PATENTING)

© PATENT INTRODUCTIONS, INC. ®
2014 www.patent-introductions.com

The patent aspects in the NPV calculation can be implemented by considering notes N1 and N2. These notes indicate key components of the NPV that are affected by patent business risks—namely, that the new project, if implemented, would infringe another's patent without permission (PBR-1) and would be followed (PBR-2) by a rival.

According to Note N1, patent business risk PBR-1 can impact the Sales Volume. This is because the risk of patent infringement includes the chances that (a) a patent infringement lawsuit will be filed against the company by the owner of the patent, and (b) if the lawsuit succeeds, sales will be forced to be interrupted or stopped completely, and your company may be required to pay money to the patent owner. Accordingly, the Sales Revenue and the NPV can also be impacted.

In this example we also observe a more advanced feature, which we will explain later in this chapter. Risk PBR-1 has two categories—namely, the **visible type** and the **invisible type**. The categories are separated because basic patent strategies address these categories differently, as we will see in more detail later in this book.

If risk PBR-1 is considered high, then the computation of the NPV should be further burdened with the costs of litigation, in case the company is sued for patent infringement due to the new product. Perhaps various scenarios can be considered. The costs to defend against a lawsuit would burden the company as a whole, above and beyond the usual volume of its legal expenses. (At least in the US, patent litigation is very expensive, and these legal defense costs should not be ignored due to the fact that they will be faced by a different department within the company.) Worse, if your company loses in the litigation, it will also have to bear any assessed money damages for past infringement. Moreover, even if a license per-item is available and ultimately obtained after a lawsuit, it will add to the unit cost.

In Figure 3A, according to Note N2, for a brand-new product or feature, patent business risk PBR-2 of being followed can impact the Unit Price, or the Sales Volume, or both. This is because being followed can reduce the differentiation, and therefore the eventual market share, or the pricing power, or both. Accordingly, the Sales Revenue and the NPV can also be impacted. If patent business risk PBR-2 is mitigated by patenting, then the cost of patenting for this project could be fairly ascribed to the development cost.[13]

The impact of notes N1 and N2 in these numbers will depend on how much, and for how long, your company will have followed patent strategies such as we present later in this chapter. In the example of Figure 3A, it is assumed that patents have been searched and cleared, but no patent applications have been filed. Updated versions of this Business Analysis Review will be seen in the last two chapters, as milestones in the progress of a patent application become respective milestones in patent clearance and patent protection.

There are challenges in determining how notes N1 and N2 would impact these components of the NPV. First, these notes really represent different scenarios, each with a different probability.

---

[13] As a practical matter, it is administratively more difficult for a company with multiple products to continue allocating its patent expenses to different products under development.

More work, such as preliminary patent searches and research of rivals, can give a sense for what the chances are for each scenario.

The second challenge arises when the NPV computations are not extended beyond five years, because doing so can miss potentially high future values for truly new products that are also patented. Any objections to extending the computations beyond five years can be questioned explicitly. For example, although many types of such computations already favor those candidates for New Product Development that are shorter-term and less-risky,[14] there is no prohibition from computing the NPV for the longer term of beyond five years.

Other objections to the longer term computations can also be questioned, when possible patent protection is involved. For example, the fact that the initially guessed numbers of an NPV computation become even less certain beyond five years is not a reason to not study them at all. Different scenarios can be presented for different possibilities. It should not be automatically and pessimistically assumed that, after five years, the product will have been followed, and its pricing power and market share will have deteriorated—this might just not happen in the scenario where the product succeeds and strong patent protection has been procured. The patent protection will further present the real option of licensing perhaps without losing much pricing power, and real options are not even accounted for by the NPV model.

Moreover, planning for only up to five years does not benefit from the timing characteristics of a patent's power to exclude rivals. Although this power starts from zero at the time the patent application is filed, within four years this power has typically become established. Indeed, as we will see in chapter 6, when a patent is applied for it is still a secret. Even when your company's patent application is published, it has no immediate power of enforcement in a court. The Patent Office will examine it and fairly try to prevent it from issuing more broadly than is legally permitted. Even after the patent becomes issued, there can be a short time when the ability of your company's rivals to have it forcibly revised is temporarily stronger. Usually, however, four years after filing, much of the uncertainty will have receded, the proverbial dust will have settled, the power of the patent will have been more established, and in some scenarios that power will be large.

It is true that some product tastes shift in the technology-type industries within four years. Often these tastes are on the surface, however, while this does not happen as much to good underlying value propositions.

3.3 Basic Company Strategies about Some of the Patent Business Risks and Opportunities

Companies also execute **patent strategies**, which are decided in the context of the company's industry, as we saw at the end of chapter 2. These patent strategies are intended to

---

[14] Christensen, C. M., van Bever, Derek (2014). The Capitalist's Dilemma. Harvard Business Review, 92(6), 60-68, HBR Reprint R1406C.

have a better chance of winning the patent battles in the patent plane, to ultimately improve financial results.

Patent Business Risks:	PBR-1) Proposed Product will infringe another's patent	PBR-2) Proposed new Product will be followed, and its differentiation and pricing power will be eroded.
Solo Patent Strategies to mitigate:	PSD1) Check rival products for patent markings PSD2) Search to discover existing prior patents & pending patent applications PSD3) Identify potentially threatening prior patents & pending patent applications from what was discovered PSD4) File patent applications for new aspects of Product to cut off others from applying. PSD5) Design-around the claims of existing threatening patents PSD6) Search to discover reasons why a threatening patent should not be deemed valid; maybe force revision, or even invalidation PSD7) Challenge threatening pending patent applications	PSI1) File patent applications for new aspects of Product PSI2) Perform patent marking for the Product
Interactive Patent Strategies to mitigate:	PSD8) Acquire at least non-exclusive rights to threatening patents & pending patent applications	PSI3) Acquire exclusive license to threatening patent or pending patent application with rights to enforce PSI4) Acquire outright a threatening patent or pending patent application
(no patent strategy to mitigate) Create & sell Product ignoring patents	Consequence about business risk: no mitigation; might avoid patents by chance, or incur litigation costs and/or be forced to stop selling and/or be forced to pay money damages	Consequence about business risk: no mitigation; Product can be copied freely

FIG. 3B – SOME PATENT BUSINESS RISKS, AND BASIC STRATEGIES TO MITIGATE THEM

© PATENT INTRODUCTIONS, INC.
2014 www.patent-introductions.com

There are many possible patent strategies. Since this book is about companies that develop products, we focus on the most applicable patent business risks PBR-1 and PBR-2, and patent strategies to mitigate them. These are also the risks that you can most help mitigate.

Figure 3B is a table about patent business risks PBR-1 and PBR-2 of Figure 2D, and basic patent strategies to mitigate them. These patent strategies are used for patent battles in the "cold wars" that we saw in chapter 2. The top row lists the titles of the columns. The next two rows show two categories of patent strategies to mitigate them. The bottom row also shows what happens when one has no patent strategy—i.e., ignores patents.

The two main categories of patent strategies are **Solo** and **Interactive**. Solo patent strategies are those that a company pursues alone, and Interactive patent strategies are those that a company pursues while partnering with others in the patent ecosystem, assuming these others are amenable to it. In this book we develop the shown Solo patent strategies.

In Figure 3B, the middle column shows patent strategies PSD1 through PSD8, which can be used to mitigate risk PBR-1. Strategies PSD1 through PSD8 aim to accomplish **Freedom To Operate** (**FTO**), and are called **defensive patent strategies**. The last column shows strategies PSI1 through PSI4, which can be used to mitigate risk PBR-2. Strategies PSI1 through PSI4 aim to accomplish **exclusivity,** and are called **innovator patent strategies**.

The strategies of Figure 3B are shown as separate, according to their effect of mitigating risks. Sometimes, however, executing a strategy for one objective may also promote another objective. For example, the single act of filing patent applications is both an innovator strategy (PSI1) and a defensive strategy (PSD4). Indeed, as an innovator strategy (PSI1), filing patent applications can accomplish exclusivity. In addition, as we will see later in this chapter, filing patent applications can work also as a defensive strategy (PSD4), by cutting off the possibility of rivals filing patent applications before your new product goes to market, perhaps while it is being developed for a long time.

Often some of these strategies are not available. None of these strategies is guaranteed to always succeed. For example, it may not be possible to design around a threatening patent (PSD5), dispute its validity (PSD6), or challenge a patent application (PSD7). Plus, you should not expect that those who own threatening patents will want to license (PSD8, maybe PSI3), or sell them to your company (PSI4). It could be that those who own patents that you find threatening may have had their own plans about these patents when they applied for them.

Given that not every strategy is guaranteed to be available, focused companies implement at least the easy and predictable strategies. Implementation is typically performed by instituting business practices and internal controls. For example, a New Product Development Process can define milestones, and each milestone can have patent-related deliverables. Such deliverables could include checking rival products for patent markings (PSD1), searching for patents and pending applications (PSD2), identifying the threatening ones (PSD3) and dealing with them (PSD5, PSD6, PSD7), reporting new aspects of a proposed product as inventions for patenting, filing at least provisional patent applications for them (PSD4 and PSI1), etc.

Now we will examine more closely how to mitigate these risks.

3.4 Will Your Company Patent Its New Product?

No law requires companies to patent the new inventions in their products. In fact, a few companies ignore risk PBR-2.

According to strategy PSI1, a company will also patent the new features of the product it is developing. Since patenting deals with a patent business risk, the decision of whether or not to patent a new upcoming product belongs to the company's Senior Management. Inexperienced companies may release new products to market without having patented them and eventually lose the right to patent them, a phenomenon that is called **loss of IP**—i.e., loss of legal rights in Intellectual Property. Loss of IP can be caused by a number of reasons, such as Senior Management not implementing the right business processes, not establishing controls for these processes to be followed, and so on. Examples of such processes are mentioned in this book.

When processes are followed, patent aspects can be integrated more tightly within the company operations. For example, some patent attorneys recommend that, as part of releasing the new product, an internal **Product Patent Report** be generated that lists which patents and patent applications cover the product. The same patent attorneys will also give very good reasons as to why this report should remain attorney confidential.

3.5 Patent Marking of Products

When a company's product is indeed legally covered by one of its patents, then the company can implement **patent marking** (strategy PSI2). As shown Figure 3C, patent marking is the act of indicating on the product the numbers of patents that cover it, or that it is covered by one or more pending patent applications.

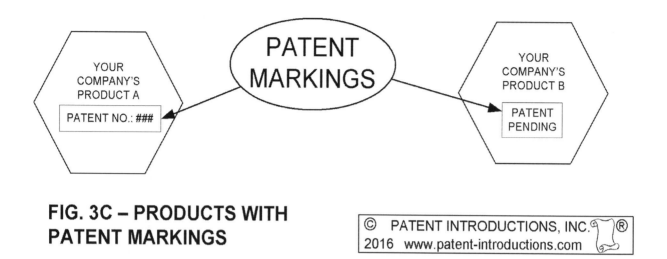

FIG. 3C – PRODUCTS WITH PATENT MARKINGS

© PATENT INTRODUCTIONS, INC. ®
2016 www.patent-introductions.com

Companies choose to implement patent marking because then the rivals' penalties for infringement can be higher. At least in the United States, patent marking of a product can be the same as giving legal notice about the product being protected by the indicated patent. It is *as if*, when your company plans a product for the US market, the US Patent System *expects* that your company will have (1) searched *the US market* for all rival products, (2) found all of them, (3) examined each of them for any patent marking, and (4) cleared at least the patents that are marked from the prospect of infringement. Similar considerations apply also with the Patent Systems of other countries. It should be recognized, however, that reading all the marked patents on a product may not constitute an adequate patent clearance search. For example, some companies may mark their product with some but not all their eligible patents, for advanced strategic reasons.

When a company desires to implement patent marking for a new product, a list of candidate patents should be generated. Good starting points for the list are:
(a) the previously mentioned internal **Product Patent Report** for this product, and
(b) what was covered by previous versions of the new product, as determined from their patent markings or their Product Patent Reports.

Then, for each candidate patent in the list, a determination needs to be made as to whether it legally covers the product. This determination should be made by a patent attorney because it amounts to a legal opinion, and there can be penalties for **false marking**, or **false patent marking**. Plus, there are other ways of false marking. False marking is illegal, and there are ways that rivals can discover it. False marking is punishable, by money in the US, by jail time in other countries, etc.

Moreover, the exact way that the product is marked should be confirmed with a patent attorney. There are legal rules as to where the writing should be, what exact words should be used, how large the writing should be, and so on.

3.6 Does Your Company Permit Searching Others' Patents?

A frequent defensive strategy is to search patents in the prior art (PSD2). Accordingly, some companies search for patents as carefully as they can, and plan their products accordingly.

Other companies, however, have the policy of not allowing their technical employees to learn about others' patents. Or, they permit only some employees to search, and artificially isolate their work from everyone else's—a practice that is sometimes called "working behind a firewall."

Unless you are told not to search for rivals' patents, *the default is that your company expects you to be searching for patents, and clearing your proposed designs from the patents that you find.* If that is not the case, it is up to your company to tell you very clearly. Learn what your company policy is and follow it.

3.7 Planning Your Product According to the Patent Business Risk of Infringing (PBR-I)

As mentioned above, companies first search patents (strategy PSD2) to achieve Freedom To Operate. You will read about patent searching in chapter 8. In your company, *you can plan your product according to the results of your patent searching, so as to avoid or minimize risk of infringing (PBR-1).* In particular, you will need to create a proposed design for the product, and check it with the results of patent searching. In some cases, the results themselves will guide the design, for example as shown in Figure 3D.

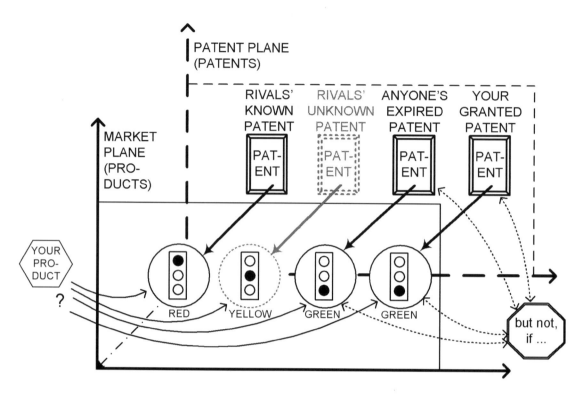

FIG. 3D – PLANNING THE PRODUCT ACCORDING TO DIFFERING RISKS OF INFRINGING A PATENT

© PATENT INTRODUCTIONS, INC. ®
2014 www.patent-introductions.com

Figure 3D is an example of a **patent landscape**. It shows a patent plane with four sample results of such patent searching. Each result is shown as a single patent in the patent plane. Each of these four patents projects its legal coverage on the market plane. Each time the coverage is annotated with a "traffic light" to indicate where your product can be positioned to avoid or to minimize the risk of infringing (PBR-1).

First, your rivals' known patents are a clear, known risk that should be avoided, which is why they are indicated as a "red traffic light." If your design needs to come close, there is a chance that you will be able to avoid these patents, as we will see later in this book about patent clearance.

Second, you should assume that at least your known rivals have unknown patents or patent applications. These do not appear explicitly in the patent landscape of Figure 3D, which is why they are shown as faded. You will not have found any, but you should always suspect them. There are multiple possible reasons for which you did not find them. You possibly did not find a patent document that you could have found, perhaps because not enough resources were used in the patent search. Another possibility is that what needs to be found is not yet findable, as we will discuss later in this chapter. For these reasons, this area is indicated with a "yellow traffic light."

Third, anyone's expired patent may become a safe space to operate in *for the feature it covers*. Then you will have a "green traffic light" for that feature, except for a caveat indicated by an octagon: if someone later obtains a subsequent patent, for example on an improvement of the feature, you must also clear that subsequent patent. The challenge of expired patents is that they describe the state of the art a long time ago, such as 20 or more years ago, and in many industries using 20-year old technology is not good enough.

Fourth, your own company's granted patent often defines a safe space for your own product for the feature it covers. Then you will have a "green traffic light" for that feature, except for the same caveat indicated by the octagon: if someone has a later patent, for example on an improvement, the feature must also clear that later patent.

When planning your product, therefore, you can group the patent search results according to the colored traffic lights. There will be no results today for the group with the yellow traffic light, but we show the yellow traffic light because such patents may appear later. The grouping will instruct about risk PBR-1, so you can make product planning decisions.

3.8   IP Alignment

In Figure 3D, the location of the second green light is a noteworthy special case. If you indeed position your product where your own patent already protects it, then the situation becomes as shown in Figure 3E.

The positioning of Figure 3E is a special case called **IP Alignment**. More fully, it is called "Alignment of one's product with one's patent coverage."

In terms of uncertainty for risk PBR-1, IP Alignment is optimum for the aspect of the product that the patent legally covers, because there is high confidence that the product does not infringe anyone else's patents. (Of course, as before, IP Alignment applies only to what your own patent covers. So there is no IP Alignment if your patent covers only an improvement over an invention of a rival's unexpired patent.)

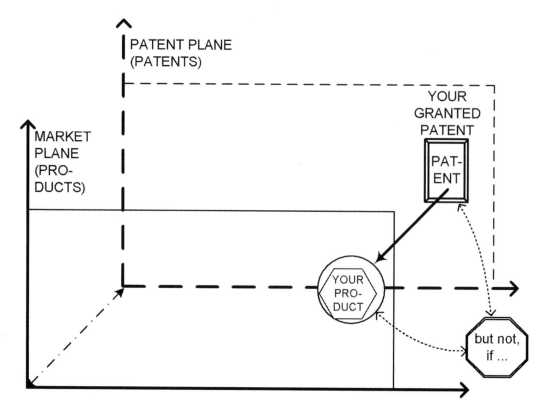

FIG. 3E – IP ALIGNMENT

Given the relatively higher confidence that IP Alignment gives against the uncertainty for the risk of PBR-1, it is good to strive for IP Alignment. Some patent attorneys have distilled the effort to strive for IP Alignment into a mantra, which you can mentally repeat when choosing from options that otherwise seem similar. Here it is:

> The IP Alignment Mantra:
> *Patent what you make;*
> *make what you patent.*

Achieving IP Alignment in a technology context is not easy for many reasons. First, issued patents can be narrower than initially hoped for. Second, IP Alignment for a product is understood only "per feature." For example, in a technology context, a product may have many features; while IP Alignment may exist for one of the features, it may not exist for the rest.

A technology company developing a new product can achieve a large degree of IP Alignment if: (a) it understands the value proposition and the new product is optimized accordingly, and (b) all foreseeable implementations of the value proposition are truly new, patentable, and patented well, while no rival appears or patents anything for enough time.

3.9 Patent Applications That Are Not Findable by Patent Clearance Searches

In the Business Analysis Review of Figure 3A we pointed out that the patent business risk of infringing (PBR-1) has two categories—namely, **visible type PBR-1 risk** and **invisible type PBR-1 risk**. Now we explain in more detail.

Reviewing again Figure 3D, certain earlier patent documents are shown faded and indicated as not found, and their risk was indicated by the "yellow traffic light." We clarified that a possible reason is that they are not yet findable, and we elaborate in this section.

As we first saw in Figures 1A and 1B, when a patent application is filed, the Patent Office does not publish it immediately. Rather, the patent application is published after a publication delay, which in most instances lasts about 18 months. Before the patent application is published, no patent search can find it. While such patent applications are not findable, they can be called **invisible**. Correspondingly, patent applications that are findable can be called **visible**. For this kind of categorization, all issued patents and published patent applications are considered visible.

Figure 3F shows the problem of clearing a contemplated product from patent business risk PBR-1 of infringing another's patent. You could make a decision at time NOW on the time axis to invest in developing your product so you can release it in the future.

Patent business risk PBR-1 includes **visible type PBR-1 risk**, which is from patent applications that you can find with a patent search. These patent applications are the documents that have been published within time range TR1 in Figure 3F, and are visible and findable. An example in Figure 3F is filed patent application titled "VISIBLE & FINDABLE."

Risk PBR-1 also includes **invisible type PBR-1 risk** from invisible patent applications filed during time range TR2. These documents may have been filed 17 months ago, yesterday, or could be filed next week. The invisible type risk is from patent applications cloaked by the confidentiality of the Patent Office before their publication. Of course, a pending patent application that is not yet visible today is not a threat *today*. However, as shown Figure 3F, such a patent application can still be on its way to becoming a patent that your product could infringe in the future.

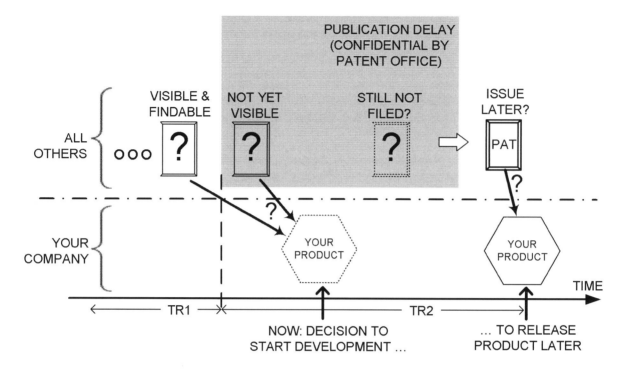

FIG. 3F – SOME PATENT RISK IS INVISIBLE, AND CONTINUES TO BE RENEWED

© PATENT INTRODUCTIONS, INC.®
2014 www.patent-introductions.com

You should especially think about the invisible type risk if you have been asked to create a product that competes with a rival's recent new product. Will the rival have applied for patents? Some rivals apply for patents only rarely or not at all. Others apply, file **child patent applications**, and even revise existing issued patents to broaden them. These patents and patent applications were indicated as a "yellow traffic light" in Figure 3D. Of those, the patent applications will eventually be resolved into a "red traffic light" or a "green traffic light" for your proposed design, but not soon enough for the decision that your company faces today (the NOW moment).

Now we examine in more detail the invisible type PBR-1 risk of time range TR2 in Figure 3F. It has two categories—namely, the first category from patent applications that have been filed before NOW and the second category from patent applications that may yet be filed after NOW. Figure 3F shows an example of the first category—a possibly filed patent application titled "NOT YET VISIBLE." If your company's rivals have indeed filed this patent application, you cannot cancel it; that application would be already on its way to becoming a patent. As time passes, it will become findable.

The second category of invisible type PBR-1 risk arises from patent applications that rivals may file after NOW but before your company's product is released to the market. An example shown in Figure 3F is a possible filed patent application titled "STILL NOT FILED?" Every day that passes, rivals could be filing such a patent application that would be on its way to becoming a patent that will eventually threaten your company's future contemplated product. In other words, *the invisible type risk to your company's future intended product is being renewed every day, even after your company's decision to develop the product.* Your company's patent business risk of infringing (PBR-1) will be more acute if it will take you a long time to develop the product, whether due to the development taking a long time or due to your experiencing delays or both. Your risk PBR-1 can be even more acute if your company has leaks. Fortunately, you can do something about that, as we will see in the next section.

3.10 Mitigating Now the Future Risk of Infringing by Filing a Patent Application

Some of the second kind of invisible type of patent risk of infringing can be mitigated by filing a patent application (strategy PSD4). Figure 3G explains why this is, by repeating aspects of Figure 3F. Invisible patent applications are in time range TR2. When your patent application is filed at time NOW, it will define a **Cut-Off Time**. The Cut-Off Time divides time range TR2 of Figure 3F into time ranges TRA and TRB.

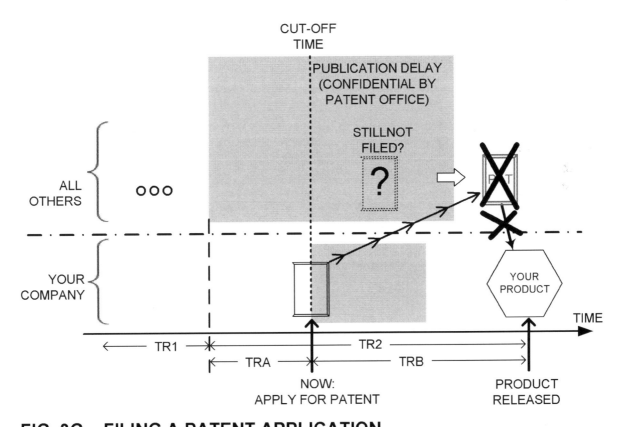

FIG. 3G – FILING A PATENT APPLICATION PREVENTS OTHERS FROM EVENTUALLY SUCCEEDING IN PATENTING

© PATENT INTRODUCTIONS, INC.
2014   www.patent-introductions.com

As noted previously, you cannot cancel or undo a rival's patent application that may have been filed during time range TRA for the same invention. However, such a patent application that could be filed by a rival during time range TRB, i.e. after the Cut-Off Time, will likely fail to become issued as a patent because your company's filing will have been earlier. The filing of your patent application will thus have a **Cut-Off Effect**, which averts such threats to your company's future product.[15] In chapter 6, we explain in more detail how the Cut-Off Effect takes place in the context of a patent race.

Note: *Figure 3F should not be confused with Figure 3G*. Figure 3F does not include a Cut-Off Time because the Cut-Off Effect does not take place when you *decide to develop* your product, or by the fact that you are developing it. Rather, as in Figure 3G, the Cut-Off Effect takes place when you file a patent application for your idea.

Figure 3F describes the renewable risk, and Figure 3G describes the remedy of filing a patent application. As you contemplate the cost/benefit of the remedy, it can be instructive to consider the *evolution* of risk PBR-1 as time passes *without* filing a patent application. In other words, what is the chance that the "STILL NOT FILED" patent application will be filed by rivals? Figure 3H attempts an answer.

We suggest that the diagram of Figure 3H depicts the typical time evolution of patent business risk PBR-1 for a contemplated product. Without your intervention, risk PBR-1 increases monotonically, meaning it can only stay constant or increase. It will increase faster the more rivals and would-be rivals your company has, the more inventive they are, and so on. Even though it may not increase much from one day to the next, risk PBR-1 can become appreciably larger if it takes your company a long time to introduce your product. In addition, the risk will increase more if your company makes early announcements, etc.

Figure 3H also depicts the Cut-Off Effect. At time NOW your company has the option to file a patent application, and therefore define the Cut-Off Time for a feature. If a rival's patent application is filed after the Cut-Off Time, then it will be subject to the Cut-Off Effect, so risk PBR-1 will stop being renewed and remain at a constant value.

---

[15] Although the concept applies generally, there are variations in the result if you were to involve the complexity of provisional patent applications. Your company's patent application for Figure 3G cannot be only a provisional. Provisional patent applications are preliminary and tentative patent applications, which we will discuss in chapter 6. Plus, the rival patent applications could have their own provisionals, and so on. The complexities multiply, as each country has their own rules for resolving who wins the **patent race** in every contested scenario, how complete are the provisional patent applications, and so on. Your patent attorney will tell you the particulars about your specific scenario.

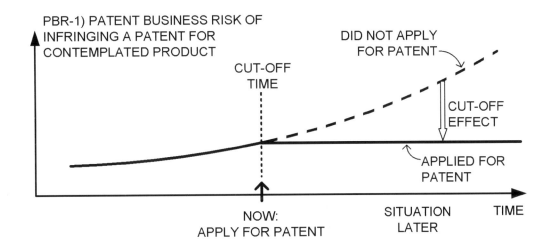

FIG. 3H – CUT-OFF EFFECT: PATENTING PREVENTS RENEWAL OF PATENT BUSINESS RISK PBR-1

You can even obtain experience with possible actual shapes of the graph of Figure 3H, after you learn how to do patent searches. Try performing a patent search in a competitive area for a few key terms, to get some results. Then plot along a time axis how many results you got per year *according to their filing date*. Then look at different instances of your time axis, recognizing that the earlier the search would have been performed, the fewer the results would have been. Additionally, think of why the number of the results is not increasing as fast beyond some point. Also be cautious about the fact that sometimes it takes a while for terminology to become settled.

Therefore, the general strategy should be clear: *The Cut-Off Time you create to protect your company's product should be started as early as possible.* In addition, patenting should be started before new product announcements and the like, lest competitors become alerted prematurely and start filing patent applications that could interfere with the plans your company announced. Fortunately, creating the Cut-Off Effect against rivals by patenting is something your company can do much faster and much more economically than the product development itself, by simply patenting.[16]

3.11 The Progress of Filed Patent Applications Further Helps in Understanding the Risk

In addition to the Cut-Off Effect, filing a patent application on a new feature of your company's product has further consequences for mitigating risk PBR-1. More specifically, your

---

[16] In addition, your company's product introduction itself will create a Cut-Off Time against rivals, in theory. If later others apply to patent what is in the earlier product and if the Patent Office knows about the earlier product, then the later patent application should not be allowed to issue.

company's filing initiates a process of revealing more views of the relevant **patent landscape**, which commensurately adds certainty. As the patent filing progresses, you will understand your risk PBR-1 better than if you had not filed. Even if your company's patent application fails to become issued as a patent, at least you will know some of the prior patents better than if your company had not filed, and you may be able to design your company's product legally around them.

If your company's filed patent application succeeds in becoming a patent, and there are no other documents published before it, your company could be on the road to attaining IP Alignment. The patent application that started as an effort to mitigate the risk of infringing (PBR-1) is the same as the one filed to mitigate the risk of being followed (PBR-2) and as the one to execute according to the opportunity to reserve future exclusive patent rights (PBO-1).

> **Chapter Summary**
>
> In this chapter, we saw basic patent strategies for planning new products. When planning a new product, the expected risk/rewards are calculated by using a Business Analysis Review to compute a Net Present Value. We saw which components of the NPV are impacted by the patent business risks of infringing (PBR-1) and of a product being followed (PBR-2). We listed basic patent strategies for addressing these two patent business risks. These strategies include patenting new products, patent marking, patent searches, and attempting to place the planned new product in a safe space. We further saw how patent business risk PBR-1 really has two categories—visible and invisible—and how patenting can further mitigate a component of the invisible, by cutting off any possible future patent applications by rivals for the same invention.

Notes:

PART TWO

YOU, WORKING FOR YOUR COMPANY

CHAPTER 4. YOUR RELATIONSHIP WITH YOUR COMPANY

CHAPTER 5. CONTENDING WITH PATENTS IN YOUR WORK

4

YOUR RELATIONSHIP WITH YOUR COMPANY

4.1 Your Résumé and Job Interview

An employer might appreciate you more if you have previous experience with patenting. Your résumé (curriculum vitae or bio) may list your patents and your published patent applications that have not yet been patented. The listing can include the document number and the title. You may not reveal your patent applications that have not yet been published—those are likely still a **trade secret** of your previous company.

In case a company invites you to an interview, you can prepare additionally by researching patents of that company. However, you should not search for patents of their rivals, in case this company has a policy forbidding employees to search for rival patents.

As we will see in chapter 10, sometimes companies pay small additional bonuses to employees for their inventions that result in patents. During an interview, do not ask if they pay such bonuses. If they do, they may volunteer this information. In addition, do not judge a company negatively if they don't pay such bonuses—sometimes they have good reasons not to.

4.2 Your Employment Agreement

Your employment by your company will often be governed by an **Employment Agreement**. Both you and a representative of your company will have signed it before you are allowed to start working there.

The Employment Agreement will apply for at least as long as you are employed by the company; some clauses may apply even longer. You are legally bound by this Agreement, as is your company. You can be penalized if you violate it. Worse, if you do violate it, it may become harder for you to find another job.

A typical Employment Agreement has clauses that include what you will be paid, what your starting job title will be, and that you will report to a supervisor who will assign you your tasks. One more common provision is that you will do nothing that is beyond what your position authorizes you to do.

A typical clause is that the **work product** you develop while working for your company will belong to your company. Sometimes this clause will be written expressly, while other times it will be in a company policy that the Employment Agreement refers to. Generally your work product includes those of the ideas and designs you develop that can be used for furthering the prospects of your company.

Therefore, at least in the United States, your work product also includes the inventions you develop and their patent rights. This is why, for example, you may be required to give (**assign**) your patented inventions to your company. Your company will then have the right to patent the inventions you made while working for it. This right does not end after you leave. In fact, your company may seek your cooperation even after you leave to patent the inventions you made while working for the company. And, if your company is contracting to work for another company, these patent rights may be transferred to that other company.

In some instances, companies will permit you to keep for yourself, and also to patent, those of your inventions that are not within your company's actual or foreseeable line of business. For such patenting you would hire your own patent attorney, bear the entire expense, and you would be in effect an independent inventor.

At least in the United States, a covenant is often implied that you owe your company a **legal duty of loyalty**, even if that is not expressly written in your Employment Agreement. This covenant is an open-ended obligation. Briefly, it includes your duty to act in the interests of your company, and not against them. For example, if you become aware that your company could have a business opportunity for a partnership, collaboration, or a new client, you should not divert that opportunity away from your company, such as to a friend or to yourself separately from your company.

Before becoming employed, you may be asked to disclose all your patents and all your published patent applications. In such cases you will be typically asked not to disclose anything that has not been published yet.

4.3 Your Company's Rules

Your company will typically have rules for basic employee behaviors, for example that you are not permitted to steal, harass your coworkers, etc. In addition, they may have Ethics and Compliance rules. Companies have good reasons for creating and following such rules, even though sometimes it feels inconvenient to follow them. Here are some examples.

In some industries, product recalls are expensive and companies are harmed if their reputations are tarnished. Accordingly, your company may have a rule that you should speak up if you see a problem in a product that you are developing.

Additionally, incorporating certain software code into a company's products or internal tools can have adverse effects to the company's legal rights. Accordingly, your company may have a rule that you may not incorporate certain types of software code without permission.

Moreover, you might not be permitted to search for rivals' patents in the prior art, as we have mentioned earlier in this chapter.

The bottom line is: Learn your company's rules and follow them.

4.4 You Must Keep Your Company's Trade Secrets Confidential

A frequent and important clause in Employment Agreements is a **duty of confidentiality**. Your duty of confidentiality applies to your company's **trade secrets** and other confidential information. Your company is making efforts to keep secret its trade secrets and its other confidential information. Your duty of confidentiality is to support these efforts. This means that, plainly, you may not reveal the trade secrets and other confidential information without permission.

Generally, a trade secret of a company is information that gives the company an advantage by the fact that it is being kept secret. Information can have value for your company as long as it is exclusive. In other words, the company would lose value if the information became known to others, especially its rivals or would-be rivals.

Your company's secrecy efforts take many forms. Examples include your company requiring you (a) to sign, in exchange for being employed, an Employment Agreement that includes also a confidentiality clause, (b) to add the words "[COMPANY NAME] CONFIDENTIAL" on internal documents, (c) to use code names for new projects that are being developed, (d) to use Non-

Disclosure Agreements (NDAs) before certain conversations with parties outside your company, etc. In addition, your company might limit access to certain materials to a defined fraction of its employees—those employees who have a work-related need to know regarding the information in such materials.

There are different types of trade secrets. Examples include: aspects that affect company valuation, business plans, strategies including marketing plans, market shares, pricing information, sales strategies and techniques, client lists, contact lists, records of sales, company policies, your company's intranet, formulas, know-how processes and techniques, computer algorithms, computer code regardless of application, product plans and designs, inventions (even if there is no present plan to patent them or build them), unpublished patent applications, Product Patent Reports, timetables, suppliers' lists, and internal costs. You should treat all of these, and more, as trade secrets.

Trade secrets could include technical know-how, and even **negative know-how**. Negative know-how is an accumulation of information about what techniques do *not* work well, or do not work at all, for building your product. Negative know-how is a **barrier to entry** for your company's rivals and would-be rivals and therefore has competitive value to your company, because to them discovering it is an additional cost and risk.

4.5 Company Revelations

Some revelations actually help your company, especially when made at appropriate times. Figure 4 helps visualize that such revelations are exceptions, while everything else should remain confidential. In addition, such revelations can be made only by the appropriate company officials.

A set of exceptions in Figure 4 include what can be learned by looking at your company's product itself, but only to the extent it can be reverse-engineered. As for the trade secrets of other companies, it is acceptable for you to reverse-engineer their products unless there is an agreement otherwise.

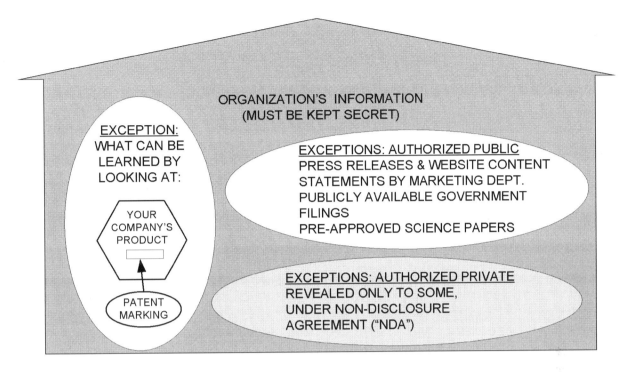

FIG. 4 – CONFIDENTIALITY OF YOUR ORGANIZATION'S INFORMATION

© PATENT INTRODUCTIONS, INC. ®
2014 www.patent-introductions.com

Another set of exceptions is the company's **authorized public exceptions**. These include press releases by an authorized spokesperson, the content of your company's website that is accessible from outside your company, statements by the Marketing Department, publicly available filed government documents, and preapproved science papers.

Sometimes those working in a university or research institution will rush to publicize new information they develop. Do not assume that you have permission to do the same while working for a company that needs revenue to stay in business, and relies on your work to do so. Before publishing a paper, make sure that any requirements are met. For example, you may be required to patent any uses of what your paper discloses, before you submit it for publication.

One more set of exceptions is the company's **authorized private exceptions**. These are usually made under **Non-Disclosure Agreements** (**NDA**s) with other parties.

There are also exceptions that apply to you personally. Unless your company tells you otherwise, you can also tell others your job title, what department you work for, and generally what type of work you do, but without disclosing what specific product or matter you are working on. After all, your business card is typically not a trade secret. Moreover, companies also have policies about what you may or may not share in social media.

4.6 Non-Disclosure Agreements with Other Parties

Sometimes two organizations want to explore the possibility of reaching an agreement. So, they reach an agreement of confidentiality about exchanging information, which is commonly called a **Non-Disclosure Agreement** (NDA), as was mentioned in the previous section. According to an NDA, the parties that sign it disclose some of their relevant trade secrets to each other. The NDA restricts these parties from revealing to others the trade secrets that they learn because of it. You must keep confidential any information that you learn from others under an NDA.

The other party in an NDA can be another entity, such as a consultant or another company, which your company might do business with for the long term. The NDA might be used for an interim phase where your company explores whether it will do business with the other party. Then, if the parties do reach an agreement to work together, the terms of the NDA will also include clauses about maintaining confidentiality.

Your company will likely have a policy about NDAs. The policy will be about who must approve in advance an NDA, what terms should be included, and how the agreement is to be handled after it is reached. NDA policies typically require that that the company's Legal Department receive a copy for archiving and enforcement in case the other party breaches it. In many instances you will also be required to report new ideas for patenting and have a provisional patent application filed before you give or receive any disclosures under the NDA, as we will see in chapter 6. This way, your company will be able to prove that it knew of certain materials on its own before learning it from someone else under the NDA, in case problems develop in the relationship with the other company or person.

When the NDA is in place, follow it. For example, you might reveal some of your company's trade secrets if they fall within the scope of the NDA. Ensure that you mark the header of any such writings with: "CONFIDENTIAL—DISCLOSED UNDER NDA." This way, if the information later becomes revealed improperly, your company has a better chance of proving wrongdoing by the other side. In addition, you should never reveal to the other party any trade secrets that are outside the scope of the NDA.

4.7 Preventing Internal Records from Being Unduly Damaging during Litigation

Your job will typically include generating records of what you do. Records are the documents you create, most of which are electronic and are stored as computer files. Beyond writing and presentations, records now also include voice recordings, etc. Records include not only the content of any computer files, but also metadata about them.

These records are trade secrets of your company. You should recognize that, if litigation happens, at least in the United States a rival company's attorneys will have the opportunity to find and use some of these records.[17] Documents are unduly damaging if they give the other side the opportunity to paint a worse picture of your company than what would be fair.

Accordingly, *you should be careful in how you create records today and keep them*. Here are some good ideas:

(a) When you start a new document, even for just taking notes, write on its header: "[COMPANY NAME] CONFIDENTIAL."

(b) Do consider that, as time passes, you may forget. Ask yourself whether there is something that you will want to remember in the future; if so, ensure at least that it becomes documented. (Being able to remember everything while you are younger is nice, but not a guarantee that you will be able to remember everything when you get older.)

(c) What you write should be what you mean. Before you store it or send it, read it again and ask yourself if it really says what you meant. When an attorney of a rival company reads it back to you in a future litigation, it will be presumed that you wrote what you meant.

(d) In an email chain, do not change the topic because you conveniently have many of the right recipients for your new topic. To start a new topic, start a new email chain with the appropriate topic in the Subject line.

(e) Distinguish facts from opinions. If you must write also an opinion, use a separate sentence starting with "In my opinion..." If you are basing your opinion on any assumptions, write what those assumptions are.

(f) Distinguish opinions that are appropriate for you to have from those that you are not formally qualified to have. If you are not an attorney, it is inappropriate for you to offer legal opinions. Examples of legal opinions about patents include opinions about what inventions are patentable, whether a patent is valid or not in view of prior art, and whether a product infringes a patent. You could say, however, that a proposed new product or feature A *could* be found to infringe a patent X.

For handling records, check your company policies about document retention and emails. Do not try to improvise or be independently helpful or creative in that regard. If you are told not to destroy any documents—don't.

---

[17] The process in which opposing parties in a lawsuit can get access to each other's records is called **discovery**, which we discuss in chapter 11. Some records are exempt from discovery due to some legal privilege.

4.8 The Trap of Work Groups for Setting Technical Standards

In a number of situations, companies collaborate to create a **Technical Standard** for their products. The theory is that a new industry can achieve critical mass and more products will be sold eventually. The business risk of a Technical Standard is that these products can become commoditized quickly and compete only on price, which threatens the continuing viability of some of the companies that collaborate.

A Technical Standard is usually created when a sponsor creates a work group among different companies that could be rivals. Typically, *as a condition for participating in a work group, a company is required to give some kind of a license to its relevant existing and maybe even to its future patents*. This way, products that comply with the standard will not be at risk of infringing a patent, at least from the participants.

An invitation to join such a work group may seem friendly, exciting, and refreshingly different from what you do daily. Beware, however, of the risk of exceeding your authority.

First, whether or not you may participate in such a work group is a business decision for your management—they decide how you are to spend your time. The ones who invited you don't have any authority about your time.

Second, while the invitation may have felt personal, it is possible that it was given in the hope of getting your company to also surrender a license to its patents. Only your Senior Management has the authority to do so. They would rightly hesitate before doing so because, every time they give such a license, your company's product or future product will lose an increment of its future differentiation and pricing power. So, you should not appear in such a group "casually" or "as an observer only" unless the sponsor puts it in writing that the first meeting is informational and attendance does not mean any surrendering of your employer's rights.

When you receive such an invitation, therefore, *you should first request from the sponsor the agreements that will bind the participant companies*. Document the request you made and any reply that you receive. Sophisticated sponsors will be clear about the conditions for participation—they will provide clear forms for officers of participating companies to fill out, and so on. Forward your request and their reply to your Senior Management, as you ask for authorization to participate on behalf of your company.

And, of course, when you do participate, you should be careful not to reveal trade secrets of your company without authorization.

4.9 Following Business Processes and Your Personal Patent Organizer

Companies often have formal business processes for employees to follow. These include filling in forms and so on.

When encountering a new business process, you could ask yourself proactively: "Will I need do this again?" Chances are that you will—some processes happen multiple times, even periodically. In addition to today, you may face the prospect of filling in the same form again in the future.

You can make business processes easier to follow if you proactively create notes for them. More particularly, for each process you can privately create a handy personal reference document, with notes that guide you when a process is not clear to you. If the process requires you every time to enter some standard text, your handy document can have that standard text ready for copying. In addition, you can refine your handy document every time you use it.

For patents you may need to follow business processes that repeat. For example, you may do more than one patent search, or you might report more than one invention for patenting.

Accordingly, we suggest you create a handy document for your patent work. Let's call this document a **Personal Patent Organizer**.

Think of how you want your Personal Patent Organizer to be so that you can consult it quickly. What notes would you want to put there? A started example is in Appendix C of this book. As your experience grows, you can add more notes.

Chapter Summary

In this chapter, we examined your relationship with your company as it may start from your résumé and job interview. Your Employment Agreement will guide the relationship, and you will be required to follow your company's rules. A pervasive rule is that you must keep your company's trade secrets confidential. Your company has its proper ways of making revelations. In some instances, a Non-Disclosure Agreement (NDA) with other parties will permit you to make specific revelations.

You should also avoid traps. One way to avoid traps is by preventing internal records from saying the wrong things that could be used unfairly against your company in a future litigation. Another potential trap is to accept an invitation to participate in a work group intending to create a Technical Standard without first receiving permission, where the intent may be to get your company to surrender a patent license.

Moreover, you will need to follow business processes, which often have repeating procedures. Create notes for following them more easily the next time. In that spirit, you may want to start your own Personal Patent Organizer.

Notes:

5
CONTENDING WITH PATENTS IN YOUR WORK

5.1 Your Company Operates within the Patent System

Your company must follow the patent laws as much as it must follow the tax laws, employment laws, and all other laws. As with all other laws, your company needs your help in following the patent laws so that it will not be at the wrong end of a lawsuit, and so that its new products will remain competitive in the marketplace for a long time.

Accordingly, Senior Management shapes the patent strategies of your company and the business operations that support the patent strategies. Your duties and responsibilities include supporting the business operations. Some of these operations are related to patents.

5.2 Your Company's Patent Operations

Companies are organized so that they can conduct patent operations. Usually companies assign responsibilities regarding patents to a person or a group. If your company gave you this book, look at the first few pages—the relevant contact information might be shown there. Small companies usually have a person responsible for patents. Larger companies may have a **Patent Department**. If your company has a Patent Department, it will typically be staffed with one or more patent attorneys and/or patent agents.

The Patent Department will create your company's policies about its patent operations, taking into account many strategic factors about the company, its products, the competitive landscape, patent laws, etc. For example, your Patent Department will typically decide your company's policies about patent marking, patent searching, foreign filing, and so on.

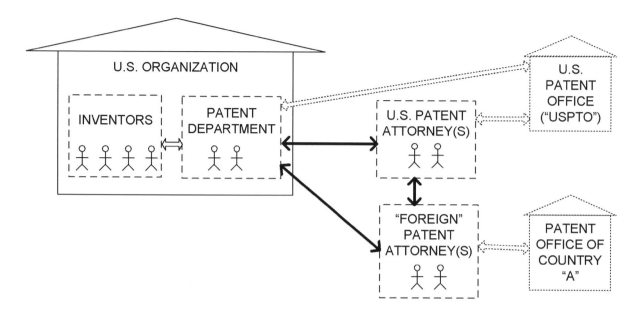

FIG. 5A – TYPICAL US ORGANIZATION'S ARRANGEMENT FOR PATENTING OPERATIONS

© PATENT INTRODUCTIONS, INC. ®
2014 www.patent-introductions.com

Some of your company's patent operations are for patenting. Figure 5A shows how a US organization can be arranged to conduct its patenting operations. For a non-US company, the organizational structure would be analogous. The Patent Department will engage outside patent attorneys who work in law firms. The Patent Department, or the outside patent attorneys, will communicate with the Patent Office.

There are ways for you to be helpful. In this book, you will find information as to where your Patent Department will appreciate learning from you the type of information that you routinely encounter in your work.

5.3 You May Impact Your Company's Eventual Patent Position

You may impact your company's eventual patent position in terms of its products and its patents. While you work, some of your actions can become **patent-related facts** that determine your company's eventual patent position and, therefore, your company's legal risks and rights.

An example is how you may have shaped your company's product. You may have considered different possibilities for a required design, and you may have searched for patents, etc. Your final decisions may have shaped your company's product, and its position in the product plane. These decisions are patent-related facts, if one considers how well they help the product avoid others' patents.

Another example is that you may have reported your invention timely enough for patenting. This reporting is a patent-related fact, if one considers that you will have enabled your company to reserve the patent rights of your idea.

5.4 Your Tasks Include Inventive Problem-Solving

Your company may be considering introducing a new product in the future. As an engineer, there is a chance that you have been asked to help design a part of it.

To proceed, you might first read to expand your knowledge in the field. You might start by reading a textbook, or reviewing a textbook that you read when you were a student. Then you might read on the internet where information has been recently understood enough to be well organized, and is too recent or too specialized to have been written in a textbook. Beyond the internet, the most recent, detailed, or specialized source you can read is frequently a patent.[18]

Second, upon reading patents, you may recognize the problem-solution approach of inventions: **inventing** takes place when you *identify a problem and a solution for it*. Often you are given the problem and arrive at the solution. Other times, you can start with a solution, such as a technology, and look for a problem that you can solve with it. Once you identify that problem and recognize how your solution helps solve it, you will again have an invention that may be patentable.

Third, you can apply the problem-solution approach for recasting prior knowledge as problems that have been identified and solved. You might further start recognizing thought patterns. For example, in a certain industry some general solutions may have been established because of *who* solved them first, and the perspective and priorities they had. Is your perspective different?

Fourth, you might recast what you have been asked to do as a problem to solve. What is really the problem? You may think of new solutions to this problem, or ways for your new product to avoid this problem.

When you solve the problem, *you will have conceived your invention*. You should write it in your Engineering Notebook, if required by your company's business process.

---

[18] For purposes of determining patentability, a hypothetical **person having ordinary skill in an art** is legally postulated, who is deemed to know the contents of the patents in their art, as we will see later in this chapter and also in chapter 7. In addition, the skill level of this person has been legally determined in the US for a number of different fields.

In the above, you had a specific problem to solve. In other instances you might invent in a less directed way, for example when brainstorming on how to improve your product without having in mind a particular technical problem to solve. When you do reach possible inventions, you might ask whether they would enhance the future product's utility to the customers in the existing market segments, whether they would create a new set of customers, and so on.

5.5 Implementing Your Invention into Your Future Product

Your next step can be to visualize your invention becoming added to your company's future product, or becoming a standalone future product. Visualizing can be seen in Figure 5B, in which you are at a moment NOW with your invention. The new or updated product is in the future, and you are considering implementing your invention in it.

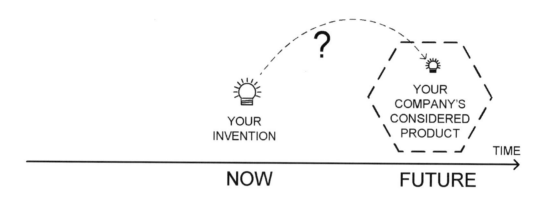

FIG. 5B – COULD YOUR INVENTION BECOME ADDED TO YOUR COMPANY'S FUTURE PRODUCT?

© PATENT INTRODUCTIONS, INC. ®
2014   www.patent-introductions.com

As we will see later in this chapter, for your invention to be implemented in the product you still must complete patent tasks, which include patent searches, reporting of inventions for patenting, and so on. Your patent tasks revolve around two key patent perspectives:
(a) first, the concern that your new invention, if implemented, might infringe any valid patents of others; and
(b) second, the hope that your new idea is patentable.

While addressing these two perspectives, you may find that your patent tasks cause you to think about your invention from multiple points of view, including more abstractly. The more holistically you think, the better your solutions will be.

5.6 Concern: "Would My Implemented Invention Avoid Infringing All Patents of Others?"

First, you should address the concern of whether your invention, if implemented in the future product, would avoid infringing all valid patents of others. We showed this concern as a possibility in Figure 2E; you want to plan now to prevent this from occurring in the future.

Your present situation is shown in Figure 5C, which has been created by starting with Figure 5B. You are thinking along a time axis. You are at the moment NOW with your invention. On the right side, in the future, is the proposition that your future product may incorporate your invention, as in Figure 5B.

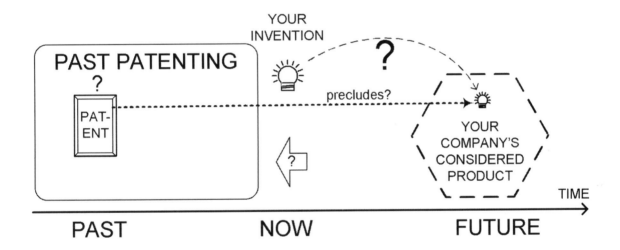

FIG. 5C – CONCERN ABOUT PAST PATENTING PRECLUDING THE CONSIDERED PRODUCT

While at the moment NOW, you are looking toward the left at past patenting. Your concern should be whether any patent by another before NOW precludes you from implementing your invention into your future product. Such a possible patent is shown in Figure 5C as part of past patenting with a question mark because you do not know it in advance. Your concern additionally includes patent applications that can become patented later.

The concern of Figure 5C is about your company's **patent business risk of infringing (PBR-1)** that we discussed in chapter 2. Your company's risk is the highest if you have been asked to design a product that imitates a rival's earlier product. You may be asked this especially when the rival's earlier product is doing well in the marketplace. The risk arises from the possibility that the rival company has patented its earlier product, which now your management considers worth following on the market plane.

The concern of Figure 5C can be mitigated by a **patent clearance search** (patent strategy PSD2 of Figure 3B). Such a search is intended to find as many of these patents as possible. You will read more about these searches, how to start doing them, and their limitations, in chapter 8.

5.7   Hope: "Is My Invention Patentable?"

Second, you should address the hope that your invention is patentable. The hope is shown in Figure 5D, which has been created by starting with Figure 5A. You are thinking along a time axis. You are at the moment NOW with your invention. On the right side is the proposition that your company's considered product in the FUTURE may incorporate your invention. Plus, a patent is shown created between the moments of NOW and the FUTURE.

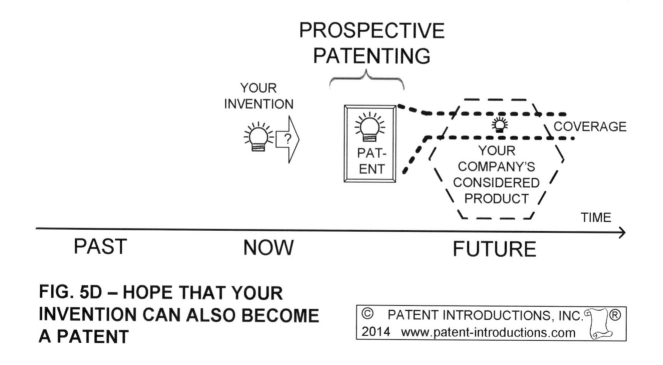

FIG. 5D – HOPE THAT YOUR INVENTION CAN ALSO BECOME A PATENT

© PATENT INTRODUCTIONS, INC.®
2014   www.patent-introductions.com

The patent is later than the moment of NOW, which is why this patenting is called prospective patenting or advance patenting. More particularly, after introducing the product in the FUTURE, your company will face the **patent business risk of being followed (PBR-2)** that we discussed in chapter 2, which means that your rivals may want to copy your invention. If that happens, your future product's eventual market share and pricing power can be eroded. However, your prospective patenting of Figure 5D constitutes strategies PSI1 and PSD4 of Figure 3B for executing on patent business opportunity PBO-1.

There are no guarantees that you will succeed in the advance patenting of Figure 5D. Even if you do succeed, there are no guarantees that the patenting will be broad—that is a matter outside the scope of this book.

5.8 The Requirements for Patentability of an Invention

There are certain requirements for your invention to be patentable. First, it must be invented by you, or coinvented by you in cooperation with other inventors. This means that you cannot claim as your own an idea that you heard from another.

Second, your invention must be useful at something, or be applicable at doing something. In the United States the corresponding legal rule calls for your invention to have **utility**, which is a term one learns in Economics.

Third, your invention must be new—that is, different from all prior applicable knowledge. In the United States the legal rule calls for your invention to have **novelty**, or be "novel". Of course, the determination of whether or not the invention has novelty should be made for the day that its patent application is filed. If this determination is being considered at a later date, then that determination necessarily uses hindsight.

Fourth, your invention must not be suggested from all prior applicable knowledge. In the United States the legal rule calls for the invention to be, among other things, (**not**) "obvious" to the **person having ordinary skill in the art** mentioned earlier. The text of the law does not have the quotation marks of the previous sentence; these quotation marks are given in this book purposely, to prepare you for the notion that *written words in a law can develop meanings different from what you might expect in ordinary writing*. Indeed, for decision outcomes about patentability to be uniform there are specific legal detailed rules about what "obvious" means. These rules are argued by Patent Examiners and patent attorneys, and are decided by the legal process. Moreover, just like with novelty, the determination of whether or not an invention is obvious should be made for the day that its patent application is filed.

Fifth, a patent application must be prepared that legally describes your invention, and which meets some formal and substantive requirements. Your company will do that with your help, after you report your invention for patenting.

Sixth, *the prepared patent application must be filed with the Patent Office before any legal deadlines have passed.* If it is not filed by that time there can be **loss of IP**, i.e., loss of legal rights in intellectual property. Accordingly, you must be aware of how your company's activities create legal deadlines, and report your invention early enough so that the prospective patenting can take place before the deadlines.

5.9 Limits to the Patentability of Your Invention: Past Events

The last four requirements introduce a time dimension, which we explore with Figure 5E. You will notice that Figure 5E has been created by starting with Figure 5B. You are thinking along a time axis. You are at the moment NOW, with the prospect of patenting your invention.

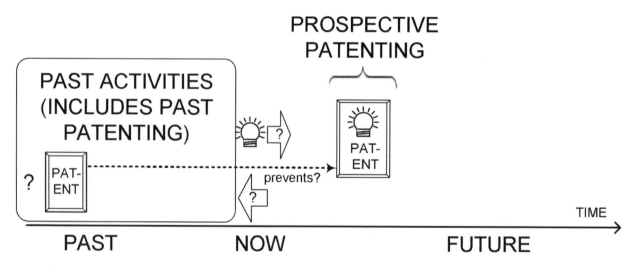

FIG. 5E – OTHER CONCERN THAT PAST ACTIVITIES PRECLUDE YOUR INVENTION FROM BECOMING PATENTED

In Figure 5E, while at the moment NOW, you are looking toward the left at past activities. Two kinds of past activities are of concern to us.

First, applicable past writings may prevent patenting your invention, by causing it to *not* meet the third and fourth requirements of being novel and non-obvious. Your hope of patenting your invention is tempered by the concern that an applicable writing before NOW precludes you from patenting your invention. The past writing includes past patenting, which is a more easily searchable subset of past writings, as we explain in chapter 8.

You can address this concern by performing a **novelty search**, which is also known as a **patentability search**. If a novelty search reveals that someone else has patented or described the same invention before you, then you may no longer patent your invention. You will read more about these searches, how to start doing them, and their limitations, in chapter 8. Ask your attorney as to the effect of prior writings that were done by you, such as from having published a paper.

The second kind of activity can come from your own company, and we discuss it in the next session.

5.10 Limits to the Future Patentability of Your Invention: Your Present Actions

Some activities by your company *at the time it deals with your invention* create legal deadlines, after which it is too late to apply for a patent in the United States and/or other countries where your company will be interested in protecting its product. Accordingly, these activities are patent-related facts. When viewed later, these activities will be considered past activities, but the key is to be aware of these activities as they happen so as to prevent loss of IP.

The activities that can create these legal deadlines can change as the laws change. Your patent attorney can tell you what the activities are, and what deadline each defines for the countries in which your company will be interested to apply for patent protection. Indeed, a frequent trap is to meet the deadlines of one's own country (e.g. the United States), while not considering possibly more restrictive deadlines of other countries in which your company may also seek patent protection.

In general, activities to look for are those that would create a public disclosure of the invention outside your company. Public disclosures include new product introductions, product announcements that announce the invention, market studies, beta testing, and publications. For some countries the deadlines can be the dates of your activities; for other countries the deadlines can be a specified time after these dates.

Companies try to address the concern of missed legal deadlines by having business processes about reporting inventions in enough time to be patented before the deadlines created by such activities. Additionally, if you determine that a public disclosure is scheduled and no invention has been reported, consider warning your Patent Department independently and as soon as possible, so as to avert a foreseeable and preventable crisis.

5.11 The Emerging Time Domains of Your Patent Tasks

Your patent tasks are inexorably connected to the dimension of time. Looking at the previous drawings in this chapter, we can extract some lessons in Figure 5F. Again, think along a time axis. You are at the moment NOW, which defines two time domains.

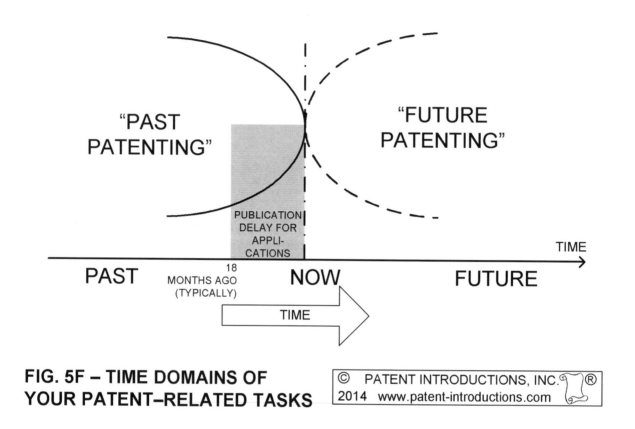

FIG. 5F – TIME DOMAINS OF YOUR PATENT-RELATED TASKS

For the time domain of the past, we can use the term **past patenting**. Past patenting includes patenting that has already been *started* in the past. It includes patent applications that have become patents or have become abandoned. It includes patent applications that have been filed so recently that they are still pending and sometimes are not even published yet, as we will see in the next chapter. Events of past patenting have happened—they are fixed in time. It is harder to affect what has already happened.

For the time domain of the future, we can use the term **future patenting**, which is when inventions may still be patented. These inventions include yours and those of everyone else. When they are patented, they will become past patenting after the NOW moment crosses them in its continual move toward the right. Future patenting has not happened yet, and it is up to anyone.

Chapter Summary

In this chapter, we saw how you may contend with patents in your work. Your company must follow the patent laws, and so it defines business processes that you will be required to follow. What you do may impact your company's eventual patent position. More particularly, your tasks may include inventive problem-solving. Once you invent a new solution, you would have the concern of whether your invention, if implemented in a future product, would avoid infringing all patents of others. You would also have the hope that your invention is patentable. Pondering that concern and that hope will cause you to appreciate the two different time domains, past patenting that cannot be easily affected and future patenting where the possibilities are. You can start addressing that concern—and that hope—with patent searches that you will learn about in chapter 8.

Notes:

PART THREE

PATENT BASICS

CHAPTER 6. PATENTS IN TIME

CHAPTER 7. PATENT ANATOMY

CHAPTER 8. FINDING PAST DOCUMENTS ("PRIOR ART SEARCHING")

6

PATENTS IN TIME

6.1 Time Line of Events for a Sample Patent

A patent can be described in terms of events taking place at different times. In this section, we describe these events briefly, and we will discuss them in more detail in the remainder of this book.

Figure 6A shows a time line of events for many US patents and almost all non-US patents. A time axis has intercepts at times T1, T2, T3, ... T11 for the important events in the life of a patent. The intercepts define intervals between them that are not to scale. In addition, some areas are shaded to convey how confidential a stage is relative to others.

At time T1, an inventor thinks of an invention, by having an idea. This could be you. When this happens, only you know about it. You might even write it in your notes or in your Engineering Notebook. Unless there is a business process where others periodically check your notes or Engineering Notebook, the rest of your company will not know about your idea.

At time T2, an **Invention Reporting Form (IRF)** is written about the invention and submitted. Your company will have its own standard IRF. After submitting the IRF, the invention is still confidential to the company and is known within the channel that can patent it.[19]

At time T3, your company decides whether or not to patent the invention from the submitted IRF. Generally, your company's **Patent Committee** will make that decision, as we will see in chapter 9. The rest of this time line assumes that your IRF is approved for patenting.

---

[19] If the idea is reported to other company channels it will still be confidential to the company and not only to you, but will still not be reported to the channel that can patent it. As we explain in chapter 9, reporting an invention for patenting is a separate deliverable.

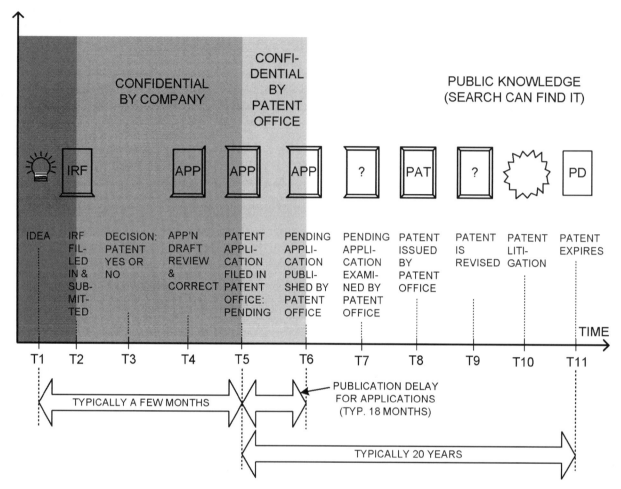

FIG. 6A – TYPICAL EVENT TIME LINE FOR PATENT (NON-US PLUS MOST US: PUBLISH WHILE PENDING)

At time T4, **a patent application** is drafted for your invention. A patent attorney or a patent agent ("drafter") will read the IRF, write ("draft") a proposed patent application, and give it to you for feedback. The patent drafter may make corrections according to your feedback.

At time T5, the patent attorney will *file the finished patent application with the Patent Office*. At this time, **Patent Pending** status is achieved. Now the Patent Office also knows about the invention. It can take a few months from when you had the idea at time T1 until time T5, because some business processes are working in the background.

In addition to the above, it is possible to also file a **provisional patent application**, as we will see later in this chapter.[20] To differentiate, the regular and formal patent application filed at time T5 is sometimes also called a "non-provisional" and/or "regular" patent application. Generally, "patent application" means non-provisional, unless specified otherwise.

At time T6, *the patent application will be published* by the Patent Office as pending. Its text and drawings will be the text and drawings of the application filed at time T5. A well-targeted patent search will now be able to find it.

Time T6 takes place when the publication delay ends for this application. We first saw the publication delay in Figure 1A. The publication delay typically lasts a few days over 18 months after the initial filing, whether the latter was the regular patent application (T5) or a provisional before time T5. The publication delay can be shorter or substantially longer, at least for some US patents.

After time T6, and usually before time T7, the patent application may become **challenged**. More particularly, after watchful rivals find it, they may become concerned that the patent application aims to become a patent with broader legal coverage than they think the laws would allow, and which might interfere with their product plans. Rivals can then challenge the pending patent application by sending the Patent Office reasons why the legal coverage should not be as broad as it is being applied for, if they can find such reasons.

At time T7, *the Patent Office will examine the patent application* to determine whether it meets the criteria for patenting. If the patent application has been challenged, the Patent Office will further consider what has been sent by the challenging rival.[21] Time T7 depends on the Patent Office, which **art**, i.e. field, the patent application is classified in, how many applications have been filed before it, how well-funded the Patent Office is, etc. Upon examining the application, the Patent Office will start a correspondence with your patent attorney.

If the application passes the examination then, at time T8, a *patent will be issued ("granted")*. Time T8 is also when the patent becomes enforceable in court. However, in some instances the rights of a US patent may become retroactive to earlier time T6—ask your patent attorney. The interval between T7 and T8 may seem short in Figure 6A, but it is not always. For example, an appeal alone can take a few years.

---

[20] We do not show provisionals in Figure 6A because they, alone, do not become patents, as we will explain later.

[21] In a perfect world, the Patent Office will not have needed the materials sent by the rival, but in the real world Patent Offices have difficulties finding the best pertinent materials and the rival is not taking any chances. The difficulties include that Patent Offices can be underfunded, the claims of some patent applications are open to different interpretations, and there is prior art in foreign languages that is too expensive for a Patent Office to search for. (Perhaps the latter can be ameliorated with online translation engines that use keywords in possible combination with art classification codes, and an interface where a user can select patent databases of countries so as to at least locate pertinent prior art references.) Due to these real-life difficulties, therefore, patents are sometimes granted that are broader than they should be.

In some cases, at time T9, the issued patent may be **revised**. As we will see in the later chapters, revision may be attempted by the owner of the patent, or forcibly by a rival who finds the patent threatening. Different types of legal revision proceedings may occur, with different names and processes. Not all revision attempts will succeed.

At time T10, the patent might be litigated. As we will see in the last chapter, litigation is a patent dispute that is being handled in court. Litigation may also be combined with a revision proceeding.

At time T11, the patent will expire. When this happens, the patent remains as only a public document that can be found in a patent search. Anyone will be able to make, use, sell, or offer for sale what it describes, as long as no other patent is infringed. Time T11 is shown at "typically 20 years" from time T5, only because that is the **nominal full term** of a US utility patent. In reality, the term of a patent may be adjusted when it is issued. Plus, it may be later extended beyond the nominal full term, or expire before its nominal full term.[22]

6.2 Time Line of Events for Some US Patents

Figure 6B shows a time line for some US patents. Figure 6B differs from Figure 6A in that the patent application does not become published while pending. The publication that takes place at time intercept T6 of Figure 6A simply does not take place in Figure 6B. If the patent is indeed issued at time T8, that is the first time anyone else can see it.

In fact, Figure 6B describes how the US law used to be for *all* US patents until about the end of the 20th century—markedly different from the Patent Systems of the rest of the world. Now someone applying in the United States may use either the system of Figure 6A or 6B—that choice will be made by your Patent Department. As of 2014, a majority of patents issuing in the US have been published while pending.

The rule is that, to be entitled to use the system of Figure 6B, the patent applicant must pledge to not claim **priority** from this patent application when he files a patent application in a different country. In other words, a patent application filed using the system of Figure 6B cannot serve as a priority application in the system of Figure 1D.

In Figure 6B, the examination of time T7 takes place confidentially, with no help from challenging rivals. When the examination is complete and before a patent is issued, the company that applied will know what patent it stands to receive and can decide whether it finds such a patent adequate. If so, then the company will pay the appropriate fees, and the patent will be issued at time T8. If not, then the company that finds the prospective patent protection

---

[22] For example, the owner might not pay the maintenance fees to keep the patent in force, or the patent might have been successfully forcibly revised to have no valid claims sometime after it was issued.

inadequate will not pay the appropriate fees, the inadequate patent will not be issued, and therefore nobody will be able to learn from the USPTO that a patent application had been filed, or what it disclosed. Having failed to receive an adequate patent, at least the company can keep its invention as a **trade secret** this way.

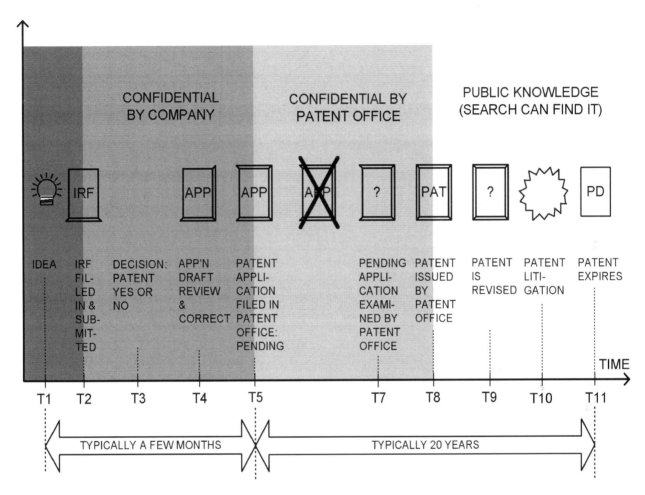

FIG. 6B – TYPICAL EVENT TIME LINE FOR PATENT (SOME US: PUBLISH ONLY IF ISSUE, WHEN ISSUE)

© PATENT INTRODUCTIONS, INC.®
2016   www.patent-introductions.com

The system of Figure 6B further enables a company filing patent applications only in the United States to operate in **stealth mode**. Its patent applications will not be publishing 18 months after they were filed. This way, a rival that would follow the company would have to wait longer. Therefore, stealth mode operation gives the company a longer lead time to develop a product by harnessing a challenging technology, and the chance at achieving a larger degree of **IP Alignment** for what it is developing, as we saw in chapter 3. Accordingly, the US offers an Innovation Landscape where companies may operate in stealth mode, at least with respect to the US market.

A patent issued under the system of Figure 6B cannot be challenged while pending. To compensate, US patent laws have become updated to permit rivals to force more aggressive revision proceedings soon after US patents are issued at time T8.

6.3 Observation: Only Some Inventions Become Patented

Looking back at Figures 6A and 6B, think of time intercepts T2, T3, ... T11 as times of successive filtering. Not every idea conceived at time T1 makes it to T2; not every idea reported at T2 becomes approved for patenting at T3, and so on.

The idea of successive filtering is shown in Figure 6C as a Venn diagram. Some of the sets S1, S2, ... correspond to actions at time intercepts T1, T2, ... of the time lines of Figures 6A and 6B. Not all the subsets are shown, but these are enough to get the picture.

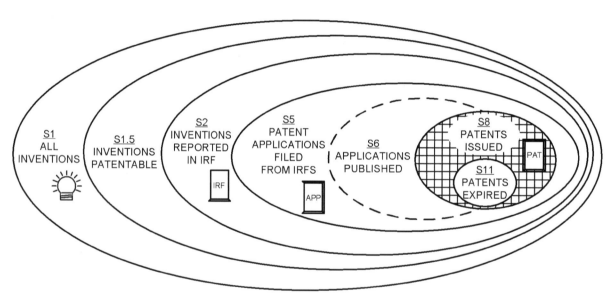

FIG. 6C – NOT ALL INVENTIONS BECOME PATENTED

© PATENT INTRODUCTIONS, INC.®
2014 www.patent-introductions.com

Set S1 is the set of all inventions made. Set S1.5 is a subset of the patentable inventions, so as to reflect the reality that not all inventions are patentable. Some inventions are not patentable because they have been invented previously by someone else, or are the type of inventions for which no patents are granted in a country of interest.

Set S2 is the subset of inventions in set S1.5 that are reported in an IRF. Within set S2, there might be another subset—let's call it set S3 even though it is not shown—of only those inventions approved for patenting. Within set S3, there might be another subset—let's call it set S4 even though it is not shown—of only those inventions in which the process of drafting a patent application is completed successfully. (It does happen that an IRF is approved for patenting, but then funding for patenting is not approved.)

Set S5 is a subset of set S4, of only those drafted patent applications that are actually filed. Set S6 is a subset of set S5, of those filed patent applications that become published.

Within set S5, there might be another subset—let's call it set S7 even though it is not shown—of only those patent applications that survive the examination of time T7.

Set S8 is a subset of set S7 of only those patent applications for which the requirements are met, and the patent applications are issued as patents. Within that, there is a subset of those patents that become invalidated and another subset S11 of patents that are expired. Set S8 is one more reminder that examination by Patent Offices at time T7 is akin to filtering. Filters generally work, but no filter can be expected to work perfectly all the time.

So, not all inventions become patented. When you see something new, sometimes you cannot know with certainty whether it has been patented or not.

6.4 A Typical Result: The Patent Application Filed the Earliest Generally Wins the Patent Race

Another timing aspect of patents is that *patenting is a race*. If two patent applications are filed for the same invention, generally the one filed earlier wins over the other.[23] We give an example of a **patent race** in Figure 6D.

Figure 6D shows a single time axis and a sample patent race between two companies, A and B, to patent the same invention.[24] Each has its own time line for patenting; Company A has Time Line A, and Company B has Time Line B, in which only a few of the salient events are shown. The time intercepts for these events for both applications can also be seen with reference to the single TIME axis.

First, at time TA5, Company A files Patent Application A for an invention, which becomes published at time TA6. At time TB5, Company B files Patent Application B for the same invention, which becomes published at time TB6.

---

[23] This outcome could be changed in some circumstances where there is a provisional.
[24] A and B need not be companies; either one can alternately be a university, research institution, an individual, etc. However, the example of Figure 6D happens mostly between companies that compete in the same space.

Then, at time TA7 Patent Application A is examined to determine whether it is patentable. Among other aspects of the examination, it is determined whether this application was the first to teach its invention *as of the time that it was filed*—i.e., as of time TA5. In this determination, the already filed and published Patent Application B will *not* be considered because it was filed at time TB5—i.e., after time TA5. In this example, the invention in Patent Application A is found to be new and patentable. Therefore, at time TA8, a patent is granted for Patent Application A.

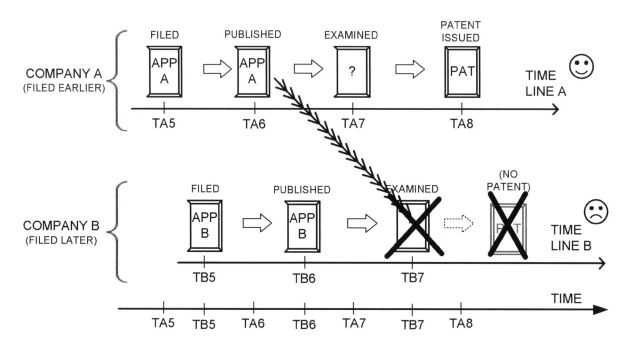

FIG. 6D – TYPICAL PATENT RACE BETWEEN RIVAL COMPANIES FOR THE SAME INVENTION

© PATENT INTRODUCTIONS, INC.®
2014   www.patent-introductions.com

At time TB7, Patent Application B is examined to determine whether it is patentable. Among other aspects of the examination, it is determined whether this application was the first to teach its invention *as of the time that it was filed*, which is TB5. In this determination, the already filed and published Patent Application A *will* be considered because it was filed at time TA5 that is before time TB5. When so considered, the already filed Patent Application A will show that Patent Application B was not the first to teach the invention. So, at time TB7, the Patent Office will reject Patent Application B, which will therefore not be issued a patent.

In the **patent race** of Figure 6D, *Company A won because it filed before Company B*. In other words, Patent Application A of Company A has **cut off** the later Patent Application B of Company B. This is also the more detailed version of what happened in Figure 3G, where your patent application cuts off patent applications filed after it.

Although the patent race of Figure 6D took place in the patent plane of Figure 2C, *the result has an impact on the market plane* in terms of the patent business risks PBR-1 and PBR-2 of Figure 2D for both Companies A and B. Indeed, if both wanted to introduce a product with the invention, their risks have changed as a result of the patent race. After receiving a patent, Company A has less patent business risks of infringing (PBR-1) and of being followed (PBR-2). After losing, Company B has a larger risk of infringing Company A's patent, because Company B applied for patent later than Company A, *even though Company B may have started product development before Company A!* So, real market actions are impacted from battles in the patent plane.

If losing a patent race in a feature you are developing would be painful, a lesson from Figure 6D is *to not delay the part that you control*, which is having the IRF written and submitted, so that time T2 of Figure 6A can start in your favor. Your company cannot file a patent application without it.

The above example of a patent race conveys a basic concept that is generally true. The example works by making some simplifying assumptions, which we examine now:

First, there was exactly a single invention, the same in both instances. In reality, there may be some convergence, but other patent claims might diverge and not be affected.

Second, we assumed that Company A was the first to teach the invention at time TA5. If it were not, neither side will get a patent.

Third, we assumed that there were no disclosures or provisional patent applications before the regular patent applications were filed at times TA5 and TB5. In reality, a provisional patent application may change a few things, but not necessarily the final result or the calculus of the patent business risks.

6.5 Defensive Publications

In some instances, entities may want to cut off all others from patenting an idea, even if they are to receive no patent rights themselves.

A tactic for such entities is to create and publish a document as a **defensive publication**. The document must describe the invention and be published in media that will legally operate as applicable prior art against patent applications that are filed afterward. Such media generally include mainstream scientific journals about the topic of the invention. There can be other media, which your patent attorney can confirm whether they are adequate or not in operating as applicable prior art. Moreover, even though it was not intended as such at the time, a filed and published patent application also operates as a defensive publication, as was seen in Figure 6D. This is true, even if the patent application eventually does not become issued as a patent.

The publications of universities can operate as defensive publications. For example, in Figure 6E, we see how a defensive publication cuts off future patenting by others. Figure 6E is similar to Figure 6D, except a university publishes a document at time T0 of Time Line U. Company B files a patent application for the same invention at a time TB5 that is later than T0, which therefore fails to become a patent. In Figure 6E, however, the university does not receive a patent either, because it did not apply for one.

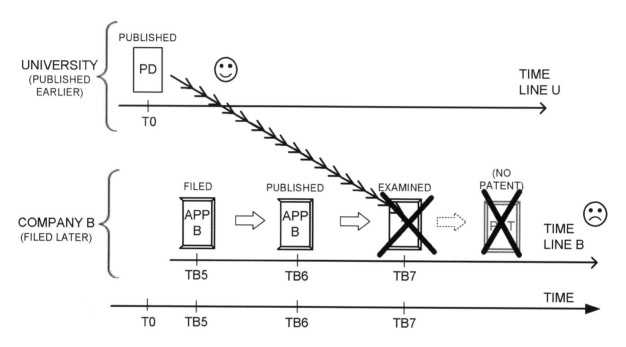

FIG. 6E – DEFENSIVE PUBLICATION CUTS OFF FUTURE PATENTING FOR THE SAME INVENTION

© PATENT INTRODUCTIONS, INC. ®
2014 www.patent-introductions.com

Importantly, publishing a document as *a defensive publication without filing a patent application operates as a waiver of patent rights* on the content of the document. This means that the one who published it will not receive a patent on the content. In this way the disclosed invention can remain unprotected, free for everyone to use. The same may not be true, however, for some later extensions of the content.

Since creating a defensive publication can effectively waive your company's possible future patent rights in some countries, you should first check your company policy for any requirements before publishing a science paper. Often you will be given permission if you first report your invention for patenting before your intended publication, with time lines that we will see later in this chapter.

6.6 Observation: When You File a Patent Application, You Can Never Be Certain That You Will Win the Patent Race

Look again at the patent race of Figure 6D. How early should you apply for a patent, so that you will win for sure? The reality is that *you cannot be certain in advance that you will win*. This is because you cannot tell what patent application has already been filed, which would still be during its publication delay.

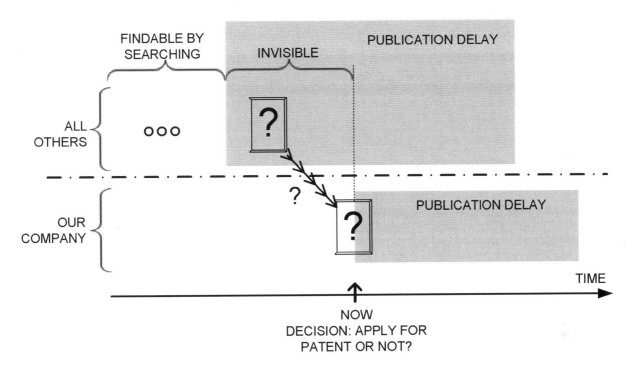

FIG. 6F – EVEN WITH A PRIOR ART SEARCH, WHEN FILING A PATENT APPLICATION YOU CAN'T KNOW WHETHER YOU ARE THE EARLIEST

© PATENT INTRODUCTIONS, INC.®
2014 www.patent-introductions.com

Figure 6F shows this observation. It starts from Figure 3F, at a time when a decision to apply is contemplated. Suppose the time is NOW. You have an idea for which you are considering writing an IRF. You are concerned that another entity has created the kind of publication that will prevent you from patenting, and so you search to find what is findable. Suppose you find nothing—in other words, the search is clear and thus favorable. You know, however, that a patent application may still have been filed before now and is invisible, as described in chapter 3. Its publication delay would be preventing you from finding it today. If there is such an earlier rival patent application, your patent application will eventually lose the patent race, as Company B's application lost in Figure 6D. No matter what you do now, you cannot know for certain that your patent application will win.

Every patent application that is ever filed is thus filed under the uncertainty of Figure 6F. Therefore, this uncertainty would be a misguided reason for *not* patenting!

6.7 Planning When Your Patent Application Will Be Filed

When should the patent application be filed? If you are the inventor or a manager in charge of the inventors, the question reduces to your part: when should you report your invention for patenting, or ask others to do so?

If your invention is not scheduled to be implemented in a product, you have some freedom in timing, and you should find a good time to report your invention for patenting. Your constraint is your other work and the consideration that a rival could patent it before you.

Things are different, however, if your company invests in your invention. Investing could be developing, testing, or concretely planning to implement your invention in an upcoming product. Activities like this create **legal deadlines**, as we saw in chapter 5.

Doing things only by the deadline is not compulsory. For example, sometimes product development may be temporarily paused, with the intent to restart. During the pause you can report inventions for patenting, as typically no budget is required and you may have a respite.

6.8 The Challenge of Imminent Public Disclosures

There will be a number of instances when your company will be making a public disclosure imminently. See, for example, Figure 6G. The time is NOW, and time T1 has already passed because you or a coworker has already had a patentable idea. In fact, since time T1, your company has already invested in developing a product that contains this idea. Now this product and the idea are on course to be disclosed to others outside the company—for example, in ways that we show in Figure 6G. Since this public disclosure is only two weeks from NOW, we call it "imminent."

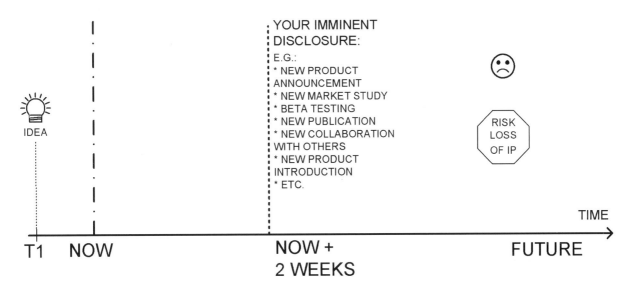

FIG. 6G – IMMINENT PUBLIC DISCLOSURE RISKS FORFEITURE OF PATENT RIGHTS

In Figure 6G, the idea has not been reported for patenting. Because of that, as you can see from the octagon, *your company's disclosure may cause loss of IP—i.e., forfeiting future patenting rights*. In other words, a **legal deadline** is two weeks from today.[25]

Your quandary, then, is how to prevent your company's loss of IP that could happen from your planned disclosure. The quandary can be avoided, as we see in the next section.

6.9 Provisional Patent Applications for Tentative Protection

The Patent Systems of many countries provide a solution to the risk of loss of IP shown in Figure 6G. The solution is with two steps.

For the first step, the Patent Systems of many countries permit the filing of a **provisional patent application**, which is sometimes also called simply a "provisional." Patent Systems do this because they recognize that patenting is a race, and creating and filing a regular patent application takes your company more than just a few hours.

---

[25] These rights might *not* be forfeited if many conditions apply, including all those receiving your disclosure under NDA NOT violating the NDA, not having invented independently, etc.

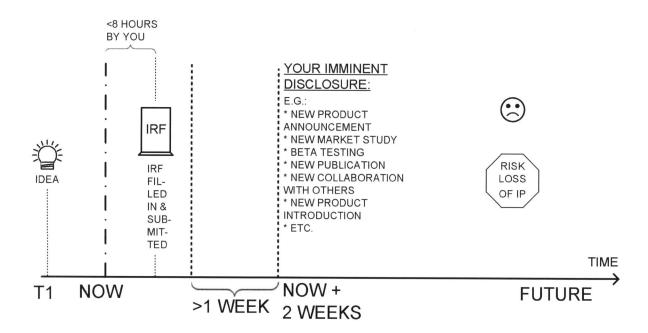

FIG. 6H – AN IRF SHOULD BE SUBMITTED AT LEAST 1 WEEK BEFORE THE DISCLOSURE

As shown by the timing of Figure 6H, to enable a provisional patent application to be created you should, at least one week before the date of the disclosure:
   (a)   find your company's IRF; it could be in the intranet of your Patent Department;
   (b)   fill in the IRF about the invention that will be disclosed (see chapter 9 for more detail);
   (c)   ensure that your IRF is submitted;
   (d)   notify your Patent Department about the special circumstances:
      i.   tell them, or email them, when your imminent disclosure is planned;
      i.   give them a way to identify your IRF from other IRFs; and
      ii. ask them to file a provisional patent application based on your IRF to prevent the loss of IP, and to notify you when they do, so you can stamp "PATENT PENDING" on your disclosed item, if applicable.

Your Patent Department will take care of the rest.

The rest is explained here only for completeness. Since you will not be required to do it, it is shown in faded font in Figure 6I. Your Patent Department will have one week to file a provisional patent application from your IRF before you make the imminent disclosure.[26]

---

[26]   Or it may do another action during that week, since a provisional cannot support priority of certain types of applications such as design patent applications.

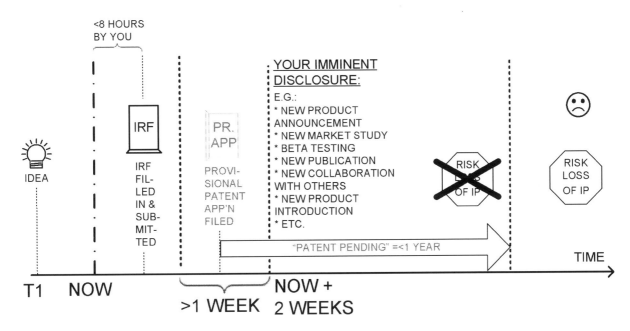

FIG. 6I – AN IRF SUBMITTED TIMELY ENABLES FILING A PROVISIONAL

As we can further see in Figure 6I, the time domain of the future will be divided in two. For times less than one year from when the provisional is filed, the just-filed provisional patent application confers **Patent Pending** status to your disclosure. The risk of Figures 6G and 6H will have been deferred temporarily.

The provisional patent application will expire one year from when it is filed. It cannot be refiled, except in some circumstances that your patent attorney can tell you about. So, for times longer than one year, the risk of Figures 6G and 6H will reappear, predictably.

Notice what will have happened: your Patent Department will typically create and file the provisional patent application from your IRF, without your company having officially decided to patent this invention.

Notice what will *not* have happened: filing the provisional *alone* does not guarantee that your company will make the investment to file the full patent application. Rather, this decision will be made by the Patent Committee, as we will see in chapter 9.

If your imminent disclosure eventually brings promising results, ensure that you update the IRF accordingly, and that the Patent Committee has your last updated version. These results can be from your market studies, beta testing, or experimenting, and will help the Patent Committee make a more informed choice as to whether to patent the invention or not.

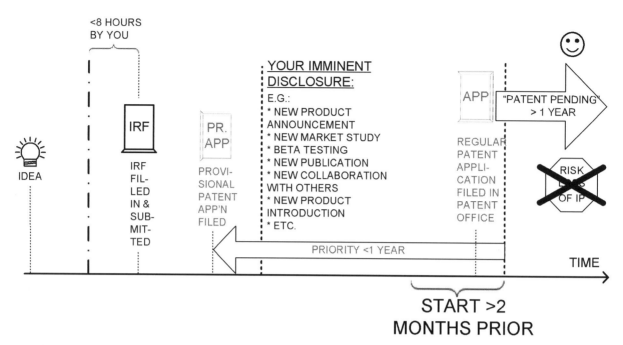

FIG. 6J – A PROVISIONAL ENABLES FILING A LONG-TERM REGULAR NON-PROVISIONAL

For the second step, your company may prepare and file a regular non-provisional patent application from your IRF. The situation will be as shown in Figure 6J.

The latest filing must be completed within one year from the filing date of the provisional, and can claim **priority** from it. Once done, the risk of loss of IP will have been averted.

Your patent attorney preferably should start more than two months before the deadline. Of course, starting earlier may also cause the Cut-Off Time to start earlier in your favor.

6.10 Misconceptions about Provisional Patent Applications

Provisional patent applications are useful in the above scenario, but one should be careful. They have important differences from regular, non-provisional patent applications.

In terms of names, both regular patent applications and provisionals are called "patent applications." The similarity in the names creates misconceptions and dangers from relying on provisionals alone. To prevent confusion, it is useful if one thinks of provisionals as **tentative pseudo-patent applications**. Here are the reasons.

A misconception is that you can apply for a provisional *instead* of a regular, non-provisional patent application. This is true, but only for the moment of NOW in Figures 6G, 6H, and 6I, since provisionals are tentative—they last only a year. Before the year is over, you will need to file a regular, non-provisional patent application *in addition to* the provisional you already filed, so that you can get to the benefit of Figure 6J.

A danger is that one will rely on a provisional without filing a regular, non-provisional patent application. Unlike with a regular patent application, a provisional will not be examined by the Patent Office to determine whether it is new. A provisional will not be published by itself as a patent document. A provisional will never become a patent. Alone, a provisional will not protect your product from the patent business risk of being followed (PBR-2, described in chapter 2). To protect your product, a regular non-provisional patent application should be filed in due time relative to your disclosure, not relative to the provisional.

Another danger occurs because a provisional patent application by itself may not achieve the Cut-Off Effect of Figures 3G and 3H. Accordingly, filing a provisional alone will not help you prevent the renewal of patent business risk PBR-1. In the scenario of filing a provisional before an imminent disclosure, the provisional will tentatively save your company from forfeiting patenting rights due to the action of your disclosure, but not necessarily from any patenting by others. To prevent losing those, a regular patent application may need to be filed.

One more danger with provisional patent applications is that, at least in the US, they cannot help where the eventual patent application will be a design patent application. Accordingly, before resorting to a provisional, one should ensure that eventually they will file a utility patent application, and not a design patent application.

Another misconception about provisional patent applications is that they require *no* effort by you, the inventor. It is true that a provisional requires less effort and expense from your company than a regular non-provisional patent application. Plus, you might not be required to proofread a prepared provisional patent application before it is filed. However, effort is still required from you—you must write and submit the IRF as described above. Indeed, much of what you write in the IRF will often create of the body of the provisional patent application.

A great appeal of a provisional is that it confers Patent Pending status. While marking "Patent Pending" appears identical for having filed a non-provisional application as a provisional application, the right to do so cannot last for longer than one year. If that year has passed and a non-provisional has not been filed, this amounts to **false marking,** with all the risks it entails. Rivals may suspect it when time passes and no patent application has been filed, then try to prove it, etc.

6.11 Provisional Patent Applications for Start-Up Companies

Provisional patent applications can also be used by start-up companies. Some business books advise start-up companies to innovate by lean methodologies, bootstrapping, spending minimum cash, and so on. All these are useful; however, these books often do not mention patent business risks and opportunities or patent strategies.

Moreover, sometimes these books suggest that a company quickly try many different ideas, or versions of an idea ("experiments"), to find the better ones heuristically. Of course, trying includes disclosing to many people without an NDA! As we saw earlier in this chapter, disclosure is a patent-related fact that can result in loss of IP.

In our opinion, cash-constrained start-up companies that are still trying different directions can benefit from a patenting strategy that uses provisionals to balance controlling costs against the risk of loss of IP. Of course, this strategy does not guarantee cutting off others or protection outside the United States, and patent clearance should also be considered.

This provisional-based patenting strategy includes first writing the proposed experiments and filing provisional patent applications about them before trying them, as seen in Figure 6I. If a number of the experiments will be similar, they can be combined into a single provisional. It is especially important to do this every time the start-up company changes direction ("pivots"). Then one can show their ideas to others, while they can fairly claim Patent Pending status.

Second, after trying the ideas, one can identify those of them that appear promising—for example, based on their meaningful metrics. Then, for the reasons discussed in the previous section, one should start applying for non-provisional patents only for the promising ideas within 10 months of each provisional, as seen in Figure 6J.

Chapter Summary

In this chapter, we saw how patents are strongly associated with time lines. A patent application can be created and filed from your Invention Reporting Form (IRF). The patent application must survive examination by the Patent Office against prior art references that existed before the application was filed, so as to become an issued patent. Since patenting is a race, Patent Systems make some provisions for preserving the right to patent when disclosures are imminent, as sometimes happens in real life. Start-up companies can benefit from a patenting strategy based on filing provisionals before experimenting, and then timely filing non-provisionals only for those ideas that experimenting shows as promising.

Notes:

7

PATENT ANATOMY

7.1 Patents Can Be of Different Types

This chapter is intended to help you better understand existing patent documents.

Patents can be of different types. Specifically, the United States has two types of patents: **utility patents** and **design patents**.

A **utility patent** includes text and, most frequently, drawings. Very briefly, a utility patent can protect embodiments of machines, processes, articles of manufacture, compositions of matter, and their improvements, often regardless of their exact appearance or even size. The legal coverage of a utility patent is based primarily on its text. While drawings are provided, they only support the text. The emphasis on text can be challenging if, as is true for many technically minded people, you understand faster from a good drawing than from text.

A **design patent** always includes one or more drawings. Very briefly, a design patent can protect shapes and the appearance of things ("designs"). The legal coverage of a design patent is based primarily on its drawings. A design patent may include some text that explains relevant aspects of its drawings.

US design patents have further differences from utility patents. First, design patent applications cannot claim priority from provisional applications. Second, they are not eligible for being published, and therefore the time line of Figure 6B applies to all of them. Third, the nominal full term (time T11) of a design patent lasts 14 years from issuance (time T8), not 20 years from filing date (time T5).

Other countries also have different types of patents. For example, along with utility patents, some countries have a utility model, which is a form of a patent that corresponds somewhat to a US design patent.

The remainder of this book focuses primarily on US utility patents. However, much of the discussion applies also to other types of patents and patents of other countries.

7.2 Patents Are Multidisciplinary

As we delve into the content of patents, keep in mind that *patents are multidisciplinary*—they have different aspects. Indeed, a patent is (a) a *legal* document (b) that teaches an *invention* and (c) was generated for a *business* reason. Patent writing may seem strange, and that is because it tries to serve all these aspects at the same time.

From the technical discipline, the part that teaches the invention uses a combination of text and drawings. The drawings and especially the text are written to serve also the other mentioned aspects.

Since patent documents are also legal documents, *legal rules will be applied to interpret them* in various contexts. These legal rules will be applied by the Patent Office, by licensing specialists deeply trained in patent rules, by patent attorneys on all sides of a dispute, and by courts. The interpretation will impact the eventual coverage of a patent and your company's risk or benefit. A patent could be held invalid for a number of reasons, including that the writing does not meet the standards set by these legal rules.

7.3 A Single Patent Can Have Different Appearances

A "patent" can have different appearances. We will look now at a few examples.

First, when a patent is granted, the Patent Office mails the owner a **patent certificate**. A US patent certificate is a document in the form of a booklet. The front and back covers are made from thicker cardstock and contain no information distinguishing their particular patent from any other patent. The front cover is adorned with a gold seal and a red ribbon. The patent certificates of many other countries have equally aesthetically pleasing designs.

In your case as an employee, you will likely not see any of the patent certificates that the Patent Office sends to your company. This is true even when the certificate is for a patent for *your* invention. Rather, your Patent Department will store the patent certificate in their files or corporate vault.

Between the front and the back covers is the **patent document**, which is created by the Patent Office at time T8 of Figures 6A and 6B. Copies of the patent document are freely available—anyone can get an image file from the Patent Office or from the internet.

The Patent Office designs the format of the patent document. Formats have improved over the years. The USPTO format presents text very compactly.

A sample patent document of a US utility patent is included in Appendix A of this book. It has only five pages, while most utility patents have more. Figure 7A aggregates these five pages into a single drawing by diminishing their size.

Figure 7A shows pages #1 and #2 arranged side by side in the top row. Page #1 is also called the **cover page**, which is not the same as the front cover of the patent certificate mentioned above. After the cover page come the pages with the drawings—in this example only page #2. After the drawings are the pages with solely the text, which here are pages #3, #4, and #5.

To see pages #3, #4, #5 in more detail, refer to Appendix A. Each text page contains two columns of text, and these columns have sequential **column numbers** at the top. So, page #3 contains columns 1 and 2, page #4 contains columns 3 and 4, and page #5 contains columns 5 and 6. In addition, between the two columns in each page, **line numbers** are indicated down the middle. These column and line numbers make it easy to identify specific portions of the text when discussing and analyzing the patent document.

As we will see below, patents have different parts. We characterize the image of Figure 7A as "not parsed" into its parts, so as to distinguish from what comes later in this chapter.

In addition to the patent document format of Figure 7A, a patent can have other appearances. For example, some services provide patent content with parts arranged in a different order than the format of Figure 7A.

FIG. 7A – SAMPLE US PATENT DOCUMENT ("NOT PARSED")

7.4 Published Patent Applications

A patent is created from a corresponding patent application. Often the patent application is published while pending at time T6 of Figure 6A. Publishing will create a **published patent application document**.

Figure 7B shows a partial image of a cover page of a sample US published patent application document. You can contrast this with the cover page of the sample patent in Appendix A. The main difference is that the words "Application Publication" appear after the word "Patent".

FIG. 7B – PARTIAL IMAGE OF COVER PAGE OF SAMPLE US PUBLISHED PATENT APPLICATION (BEFORE ISSUANCE AS A PATENT)

The document of Figure 7B is not the patent application that resulted in the patent of Appendix A. It is, however, from the patent application that resulted in a patent shown later in this chapter.

A published patent application has a different status than a patent. A published patent application is still pending, and it may be changed by the applicant while it is pending. A patent application is intended to become a patent in the future, but it may not succeed. If it does succeed, then an additional document will be created for the patent. This patent document will have content generated from the content of the patent application.

There is no "certificate" for a published patent application as there is a patent certificate for an issued patent. Otherwise, however, the appearance of a published patent application document is rather similar to that of a patent document. The two types of documents have similar parts. And, while a patent application is not a patent, a patent application that became published is a warning of a patent to come.

7.5 Reading Your First Patent

If you have read an entire utility patent before, you may skip this section. If you haven't, now is a good time for you to read a whole patent document. The exercise will increase your experience with patents, and no one else can do this for you.

First, decide which patent you will read. It can be the patent of Appendix A or another patent you choose. You may appreciate that, for this exercise, the patent of Appendix A is both short and not difficult to follow for many people.

Second, choose a time when you can concentrate without interruptions.

Third, prepare mentally. It will be helpful to first look at the drawings of the patent, and then read the text. Prepare to read all the text, starting from the cover page. If you don't understand something, write a question mark in the margin next to it and continue reading. Where you see titles or headings, try to understand what they stand for; they will be easier to find the next time you read a patent. Notice if the language seems strange to you and if any phrases are repeated. Where the text refers to a drawing, go back and look again at the drawing. Where the text has a **reference numeral**, see if you can find it in the drawings, identify what it points to. Then go through the drawings, pick a reference numeral at random, and try to find it in the text.

Now, stop reading this book, and read the patent you chose. When you finish, continue reading below.

7.6 People Look at Patents for Different Purposes

Patents are reference documents. Since patents are multidisciplinary, different persons will look at them for different reasons, purposes, or answers that they seek. Beyond engineers and scientists, other people may look at a company's patents. For example, they might be trying to understand where a company is technologically when they contemplate buying it, and so on.

Here is the trick: *Most people do not always read all the parts of a patent* because they do not need to. Rather, people only read the parts of patents that contribute to answers they seek to find, and this way they do not waste time.

7.7 Before Looking at Another Patent, Decide on Your Purpose

When previously you read the patent of Appendix A, your purpose was to familiarize yourself with every part of a patent by reading it at least once. Now you no longer have that purpose. From now on, you will only read patents when you are interested in something about them (or when you are very bored).

If you are a technical person, you also have a vulnerability about the patents you read. The vulnerability is that, if the patents are in a field that interests you, you may find them so interesting that you may spend too much time reading every part of them, including the parts that you do not need to for your purpose.

To prevent wasting time, be alert about this vulnerability. *Before reading a patent, decide why you will be reading it.*

So, what is your purpose for looking at a specific patent? For example, you may want to advance your knowledge on a particular topic. Or you could be helping your patent attorney prepare a response to the Patent Office about a patent application that was filed earlier for your invention. You will see sample purposes in chapter 8 when you read about patent searches.

Once you decide on your purpose, then you can *determine which parts of the patent you should be reading*. You will save time by *not* reading the other parts. For this, you need to be able to parse the patent into its basic parts, and understand what each part does.

7.8 Parsing a Patent Document into Its Basic Parts

In this section, we will learn a mental visualization technique for parsing a patent to its basic parts. Always apply this technique when first looking at a patent, because a patent (almost) always has these parts, and applying this technique will orient you.

Figure 7C shows the visualization technique. Imagine a patent passing through a mental **patent reading prism**. The content will be separated into three parts: (a) the **formalities**, (b) the **specification**, and (c) the **claims**. In fact, a patent can be drawn as seen at the right, with three small boxes for F (formalities), S (specification), and C (claims).

These three basic parts of a patent serve different legal purposes, and we will discuss each of them. Because these are different parts of the same document, there may be some phrases that are repeated from one part to another.

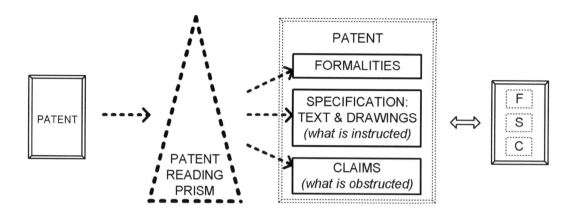

FIG. 7C – SEPARATING ("PARSING") THE BASIC PARTS OF A PATENT

© PATENT INTRODUCTIONS, INC.®
2014   www.patent-introductions.com

For completeness only, we shall mention that there may be additional parts to a patent, which could have been added after the patent was issued. For example, there can be a **Certificate of Correction** issued by the Patent Office that is intended to be appended to the patent document. It is important to recognize that such a certificate might not show up in the easy web searches that we will discuss in chapter 8.

Returning to the three basic parts of a patent, reading the rest of this book will be a lot easier if you memorize their names: Formalities, Specification, and Claims. You can close your eyes, and try to repeat them from memory. (Then open your eyes again, and continue reading!)

Now let's try the parsing of Figure 7C with a real patent document. Figure 7D shows the patent document of Figure 7A, parsed by the patent reading prism of Figure 7C. You can see the three basic parts.

The **formalities** are—very conveniently—aggregated on the cover page. The cover page also includes a section called an Abstract, which is regarded as part of the specification.

The **claims** are numbered clauses in the end.

PATENT READY®

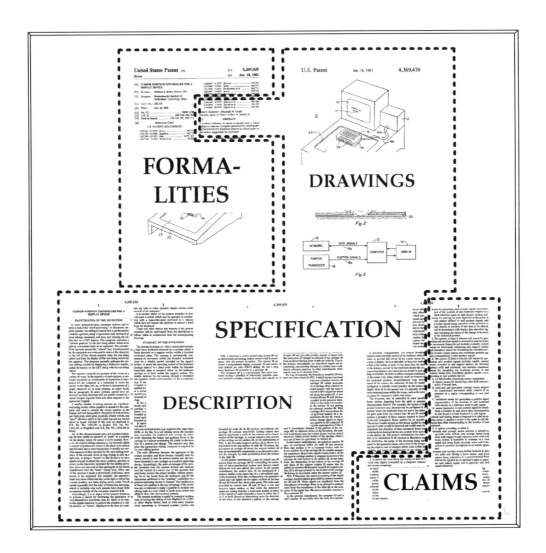

FIG. 7D – SAMPLE US PATENT DOCUMENT WITH ITS BASIC PARTS SEPARATED BY THE PATENT READING PRISM

The **specification** is everything else between the formalities and the claims.[27] It includes the drawings plus the text of the description.

Now we look at each of these basic patent parts in more detail.

---

[27] Sometimes for advanced purposes, the claims are considered to be part of the specification, but that is beyond the scope of this book.

109

7.9 The Formalities (F)

Formalities are administrative data about a patent. This data is on the cover page, if one excludes the Abstract. For a patent document, also look at the page after the cover page; the formalities may extend there, before the description of the invention starts.

Figure 7E highlights formalities in the top portion of the cover page of a US patent. You may recognize that the patent of Figure 7E is the one issued from the patent application of Figure 7B.

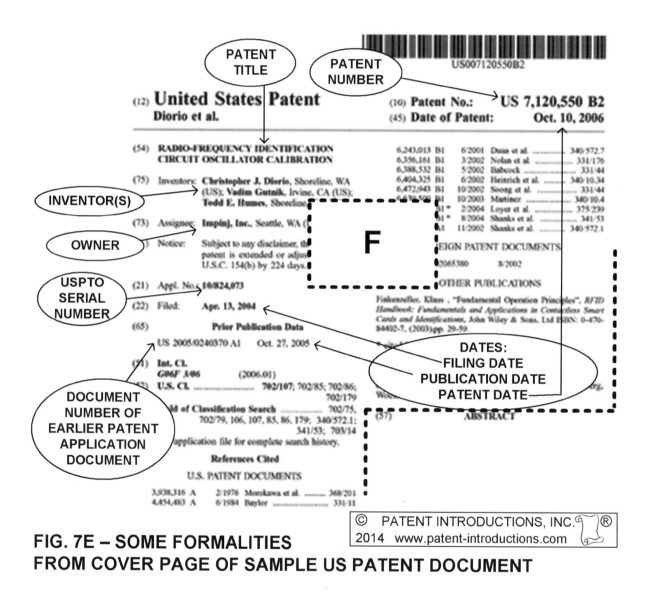

FIG. 7E – SOME FORMALITIES FROM COVER PAGE OF SAMPLE US PATENT DOCUMENT

In Figure 7E, the highlighted formalities include the **patent number**, which is unique to each patent. The **patent date** is the date on which the patent was issued, which is also time T8 in Figure 6A.

You can also see what happened at earlier events for this patent, which relate to the patent application, before it issued as a patent. The patent application was filed on a day that is called the **filing date**, which is also time T5 in Figure 6A. At that time, the USPTO assigned a **serial number** to the application for tracking it. Then, the patent application was published as pending on a day that is called the **publication date**, which is also time T6 in Figure 6A. At that time, the USPTO assigned a **document number** for the published patent application document. Notice how the publication date and the document number in Figure 7E are the same as those in the top right at Figure 7B.

In Figure 7E there is a field for the names of the **inventors**. Look for a field about the name of the owner at the time that the patent was issued (**assignee**). An assignee might not be listed. Even if an assignee is listed, the patent may have been later assigned to another entity.

Look also for the **patent title**, which was the title of the patent application when the patent was issued. In this example, you will notice that the patent title was changed at some time after the patent application was published (Figure 7B) and before issuance (Figure 7E).

There are more formalities than we indicated above. For example, issued patents and any published patent applications are further classified similarly as other patent documents in the same **art**. Classifications according to art permit persons sophisticated in patent searching to research an entire art. Plus, the **References Cited** is a list of the prior art references that were considered by the Patent Examiner who examined the application.

7.10 The Claims (C)

As we saw in Figure 7D, the claims are located at the end of the official version of the patent document. They are numbered clauses, which may be split in internal paragraphs. The first of these internal paragraphs starts with a number.

Each patent has one or more claims. Try to find the claims in the patent of Appendix A. Start from the end of your patent document, in column 6. Skimming from the bottom going up, you will find claim 6 that starts in column 6, line 56. Then go immediately above, to find the previous claim. The previous claim is claim 5, which starts in the same column 6, line 42. Then continue going up the claims to find the first—claim 1 starts in column 5, line 52. One line above the text says: "I claim:"—this is the beginning of the claims.

There are two types of claims. An **independent claim** stands alone, in that it does not incorporate any of the other claims. In the patent of Appendix A, claims 1, 4, and 6 are independent claims.

A **dependent claim** is one that references another claim by its number, and therefore incorporates the limitations of that other claim. In Appendix A, claim 2 incorporates the limitations of claim 1, claim 3 incorporates the limitations of claim 1, and claim 5 incorporates the limitations of claim 4.

Just because they are at the end of the patent document, the claims of a patent are not similar to endnotes! Books and paper publications have footnotes and endnotes, which the reader sometimes ignores. Even though they are at the end, the claims of a patent are an important starting point for determining what exactly the patent covers legally. We write a "starting point," because there are further laws about how claims may be construed, and these laws change with time. Accordingly, the claims of a patent may eventually be interpreted to cover more, or less, than what they say literally.

The claims obstruct. Claims of a still-valid patent state what you may not do in the country of the patent without permission from the owner. The hope of receiving claims in a patent is the very business reason that the owner paid money to apply for the patent and teach their invention to others. If you want to understand the overall technology of a patent, you would read the specification, not the claims. You will start looking at the claims when you think of clearing your company's proposed product from earlier issued rival patents. In fact, claims are important to many people, which is why many content providers provide them more prominently than at the end. An example is shown in Figure 7F.

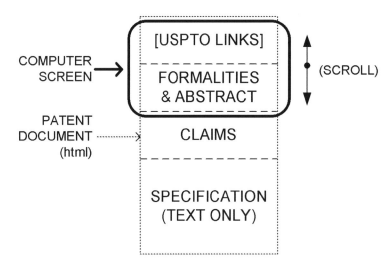

FIG. 7F – VERSION OF HOW PATENT TEXT IS PRESENTED IN THE US PATENT OFFICE WEBSITE

© PATENT INTRODUCTIONS, INC.®
2014 www.patent-introductions.com

Figure 7F is an iconic representation of the order in which parts of a US patent appear on the website of the USPTO itself. The patent text is in html form, and one can scroll through it. In the version of Figure 7F, the claims helpfully appear even before most of the specification, which makes the claims faster to access.

Published patent applications also show the claims that are pending at the time of the publication. The claims may be granted as they are, or as changed later on.

7.11 The Specification (S)

The specification includes all the **drawings** and various text sections. The **Abstract** is a succinct way of describing the invention and appears on the cover page of the patent document—i.e., early in the patent document. As seen in Figure 7F, the Abstract appears early also in the web version of the application.

Figure 7G is a screenshot for a portion of patent content that Figure 7F shows only iconically. The image is for the same patent as in Figure 7E. A few initial formalities are shown, and then the Abstract.

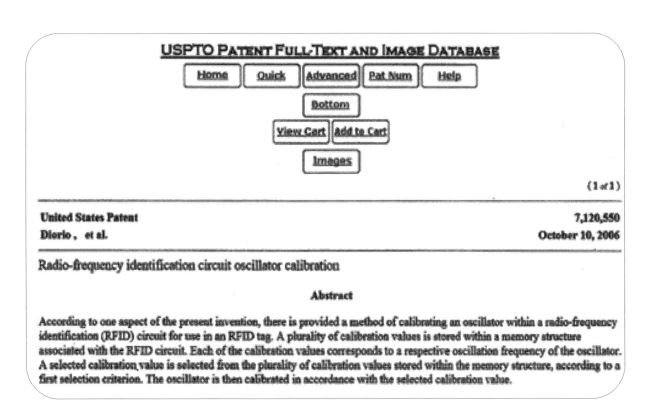

FIG. 7G – SAMPLE BROWSER APPEARANCE OF THE BEGINNING OF A US PATENT IN WEBSITE OF USPTO

The specification instructs, or teaches. The specification is the technical core of the document. As you saw in the issued patent of Appendix A, other sections of the specification include the optional **Background** section, the optional **Summary** section, and the **Brief Description of the Drawings** section to help bridge the text and the drawings. The **Detailed Description** section follows. Even though the content is technical, the legal validity of the patent will also be judged by whether the writing of the specification meets legal rules.

Sometimes you will need to refer to a specific part of the patent text. As described earlier in this chapter, US patents show **column numbers** above each column of the text, plus **line numbers** between the columns. So, you can refer to a portion of the text by quoting the column number and the line number. When the patent document is a published patent application, you can use the page number and paragraph number.

In US patents each of the drawings is designated as "FIG." from the word "figure." Small numbers, which are called **reference numerals**, indicate individual aspects of what is shown in the drawings. The text also includes the reference numerals, to refer to these aspects.

7.12 Patent Families

We first mentioned the concept of a **patent family** in chapter 1. When a single invention is patented in multiple countries, the resulting patents form a polyglot international patent family. Moreover, the legal coverage of the patents in such a family is generally similar. A patent family can be broader, however. For example, a family can include multiple patents within the same country, design patents along with utility patents, and so on.

In some instances a patent application can have follow-up patent applications filed. As seen in the example of Figure 7H, an originally pending patent application becomes informally named a **parent patent application**. If it results in a patent, that patent is informally called a **parent patent**.

While the parent application is pending, another patent application may be filed in the same country, which claims **priority** from the parent and is therefore informally called a **child patent application**. If the child patent application results in a new patent, then that new patent is informally called a **child patent**. The formalities of a child patent application indicate the claims of priority to the parent (without using the term "child" or "parent"!). Note that there is a legal deadline by which a follow-up patent application needs to be filed; after that, the opportunity to file a follow-up patent application is lost.

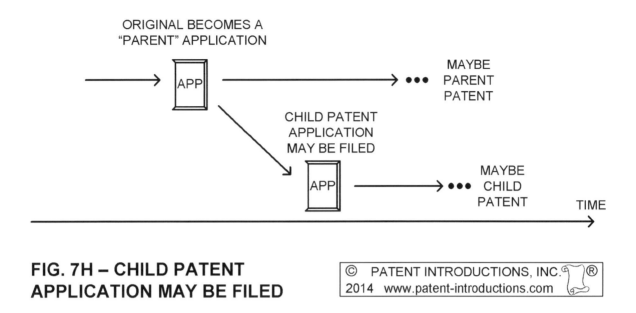

FIG. 7H – CHILD PATENT APPLICATION MAY BE FILED

A child patent application is typically created from largely similar content as its parent. Therefore, the members of a patent family often have similar basic parts, such as drawing sets, specifications, titles, and so on. For example, a parent and a child may have identical specifications and different claims.

In the US there are two kinds of child applications and child patents. The first kind does not require your substantive input and is covered by rules that are beyond the scope of this book. These applications and patents have names like **Divisional** and **Continuation**. Your patent attorney will typically file these without asking you or consulting with you as part of obtaining better coverage.

The second kind of child applications concerns the situation where you or your company is patenting an extension of the invention. For example, you may have reported a follow-up invention that is an extension or refinement of the invention in your pending patent application. A typical example in the United States is called a **Continuation-in-Part** application or patent.

7.13 Information That Is Not Included in a Patent

An issued patent is a reference document. While it includes certain information, it does *not* include a lot of other information that it does not need to (even though you might find it useful or interesting). We mention some such excluded information in this section.

A granted patent is proof that someone applied for a patent and met the minimum requirements of patentability. A patent lists one or more inventors. These are the individuals who were properly reported as inventors at the time of filing a patent application. If a true inventor were not reported, however, the patent will not show it because the Patent Office will not have known otherwise, at the time the patent application was filed.

If a patent lists multiple inventors, it does not show who contributed which aspects. While typically some of the inventors contribute more than others, no requirement mandates that the inventors be listed in the same order as the amount or significance of their respective contributions.

Although a patent mentions the inventor's name, that is only for identification. It does not show the inventor's age. A patent does not mention *when* the inventor invented the invention or how easily. A patent officially makes no comment about whether anyone should consider any of its inventors to be a **person of ordinary skill in the art**. That makes sense, since there is no requirement that someone actually have ordinary skill in an art to be granted a valid patent for inventing in that art.

A patent does not necessarily show whether or not its owner actually built a product, because it does not need to. Indeed, *for your invention to be patentable*, it does not matter whether you tried the idea, built a prototype, or even designed a product that is ready for sale. Your company's IRF will have likely asked about these things, but only to help the Patent Committee decide whether or not it is advantageous to patent the IRF. If your company first waited to see whether a patent would be issued before creating the product, the patent document will not become changed afterwards to indicate that the product was created later.

A granted US patent implies that the explanations in the document are complete for a person having ordinary skill in the art. If, upon reading it, you have follow-up questions about the invention, the patent does not provide a way of answering them; it does not list the inventor's contact information, such as a telephone number or email address. If you are the inventor you should never explain your patent to anyone outside your company, except with permission from your patent attorney—or else your company's patent rights may become compromised. Similarly, you should never contact an inventor about his or her patent without receiving authorization in advance from your patent attorney, lest you raise the other inventor's suspicions that your company might infringe his or her patent. The only exception could be if the patent belongs to your company, and the inventor also presently works for your company.

The claims of a patent document write what others may not do freely in the country that issued the patent. A patent is not obligated to write what one may do instead of what is shown in the claims, so that they benefit from the described invention *while avoiding infringing the patent*. Patent laws for interpreting the legal reach of the claims may have changed since the patent issued, but the patent document will likely not change as a result.

A patent will typically not contain an indication as to whether it is more important than other patents in its field. This will be determined from a context far larger than the patent itself, for example by analyses, reviews that examine alternatives, and so on.

A patent document does not say whether the patent has expired or not. In fact, a patent may legally expire before its nominal full term, or after that if its term is extended. When a patent expires, the appearance of the document does not change. Research will be required to determine whether the patent has expired.

A patent document does not necessarily reflect events that may have happened after the patent was issued. For example, a patent document will not show that it has been litigated in a court. If the patent becomes revised, a different, updated document or certificate may be printed.

One of the events that may have happened after a patent was issued was that its ownership may have changed. While the patent document may show the owner (**Assignee**) as of the time it was issued, it will typically not show if the owner later sold or licensed the patent to someone else. Other records may show that.

> **Chapter Summary**
>
> In this chapter, we looked closely at patent documents. For the US, we saw that there are utility patents based on text and design patents based on drawings. The basic parts of a utility patent are the formalities, the specification that instructs, and the claims that obstruct; these parts may appear in different order in different contexts. An exercise was to read a patent to gain familiarity. In subsequent patent searches you will (a) decide on your purpose for reading the patent, (b) determine which patent parts you need to read for that purpose, and (c) read only those parts. A child patent application has many similar parts as its parent patent application. Some of the information that is used to generate a patent is not included in the final patent document.

Notes:

8
FINDING PAST DOCUMENTS ("PRIOR ART SEARCHING")

8.1 About "Prior Art" Searching

A **prior art search** is an effort to find documents and activities that were published and available before a reference time. A prior art search is often the beginning strategy PSD2 of Figure 3B and can benefit also other patent strategies.

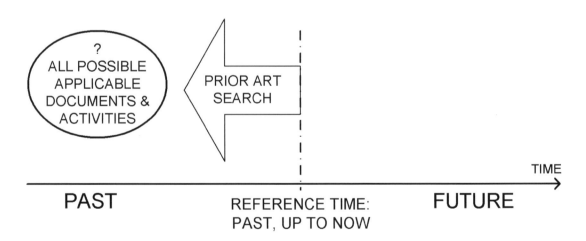

FIG. 8A – THE PROSPECT OF A GENERAL "PRIOR ART" SEARCH

© PATENT INTRODUCTIONS, INC.®
2014 www.patent-introductions.com

Figure 8A depicts graphically the prospect of a prior art search. There is a time axis that includes a "REFERENCE TIME", which ranges from any time in the past until "NOW". A prior art search is only for items dated before the REFERENCE TIME.

Strictly speaking, the prior art search is for documents and activities prior to the reference time. Activities could include prior disclosures, prior products and offers for sale, and so on.

A prior art search can be for all possible documents that are applicable for a specific purpose. These documents are also called "references." The references are also called "prior" because they have a date prior to the reference time. Accordingly, the result of a prior art search is a group of **prior art references**.[28]

Practically speaking, there are two types of prior art references: **patent documents**, plus other documents that are often called **Non-Patent Literature** (**NPL**). Patent documents include issued patents and published patent applications of any country. NPL may include textbooks, journal publications, past product manuals, and so on.

8.2 Reasons for Searching the Prior Art

Searching the prior art can have different purposes based on what you are seeking. In some instances, you seek to understand a field. Those who worked earlier in this field may have reported useful findings. Accordingly, you may perform a **patent landscape search** for a field, which will give you a **patent landscape**. There are different types of patent landscapes. Figure 3D was an example of a patent landscape that was specific to a contemplated product.

In some instances you seek an answer to a question. First understand your question well, and therefore determine what information is relevant for answering it. The question will determine the reference time of Figure 8A. Some examples follow:

As we first saw in chapter 5, a frequent type of question is: *"Does my proposed design clear all others' patents?"* Again, you can answer that, in part, with a **patent clearance search**, which is also known as a **Freedom To Operate** (**FTO**) search (strategy PSD2 of Figure 3B). For this kind of search, your reference time in Figure 8A would be NOW.

Another frequent type of question is: *"Could this threatening patent that I know about be forcibly revised, or even invalidated, so that my contemplated product can avoid it?"* You may develop this question after you have a product in mind, and find a threatening patent from your patent clearance search. You can answer this new question by performing a **patent invalidation search** (strategy PSD6 of Figure 3B) and taking its results to your patent attorney. For this kind

---

[28] There is also a distinction about whether a prior art reference, depending on its content and its source, is applicable for legal purposes, but that is beyond the scope of this book.

of search your reference time in Figure 8A would be earlier than NOW—it would be determined from the dates of the threatening patent that you are hoping can be revised. The question can be also for a pending patent application, as we will see later in this chapter.

One more frequent type of question is: *"Is my invention new enough to be patentable?"* We first saw that question in chapter 5, and you can answer it in part with a **novelty search**, which is also known as a **patentability search**. This search would be to mitigate patent business risk PBR-3 of Figure 2D, while intending to execute according to patent business opportunity PBO-1. For this kind of search, your reference time in Figure 8A would be NOW.

There can be other types of questions. If you are considering getting a job with a company, you can ask yourself whether they try to patent their inventions, and search for their patents and patent applications. (Or maybe you just want to learn whether your cousin got a patent on anything.)

Whatever the question you want to answer, the ability to search patents will help you time and again.

8.3 Confirm That Your Company Permits You to Search

As we saw in chapter 3, some companies do not permit their technical people to search patents. Your company could be one of them. So, ask before searching the prior art. If you receive company guidelines, follow them.

If your company does not have a policy or guidelines, then you are likely expected to be searching the prior art, discovering any threatening patent documents as early as possible, and dealing with them as effectively as possible. You are likely expected to be doing this so that you mitigate patent business risk of infringing (PBR-1, in Figure 2D) for the product you are creating.

8.4 About "Patent Searching"

Many of the possible reasons for searching the prior art specifically require you to search for issued patents and pending patent applications. A **patent search** is a prior art search that searches only for patent documents, not for any other prior art references. The prospect is depicted graphically in Figure 8B.

Figure 8B looks similar to Figure 8A. For example, the reference time could be NOW or sometime in the past. Plus, there is a clarification that your search will not find patent applications that are still protected by the publication delay, or those filed in the United States that will not publish before they issue.

The other important difference is that in Figure 8B you are not searching for activities or for **Non-Patent Literature** (NPL) before the reference time. Patent searches that ignore NPL are very prevalent for a number of reasons:

First, you can do your patent searching for free on the internet, and often from very few databases. You do not need to pay for a searcher or to subscribe to databases as with NPL in specific fields. Of course, if your company provides paid access to NPL, you can use that too.

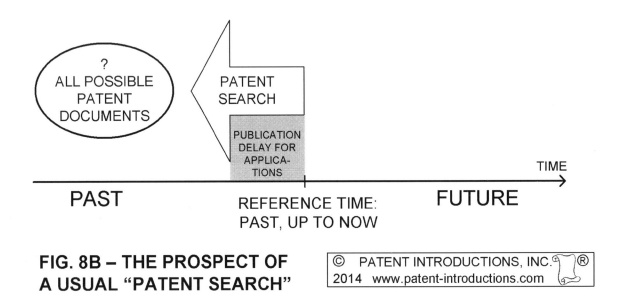

FIG. 8B – THE PROSPECT OF A USUAL "PATENT SEARCH"

Second, even keyword searches often yield enough initial results to provide you an adequate answer for your typical purposes. For example, you may learn that your new idea has been mentioned exactly in a prior patent, which could end decisively your inquiry about the patentability of your idea. Many ideas for a new patent end this way, without ever searching for NPL.

In most other instances patent-only searches cannot be considered complete; NPL should be also searched, especially when the answer is important.

8.5 Update Your Personal Patent Organizer

At this time, we suggest you update your Personal Patent Organizer document, which we initially mentioned at the end of chapter 4. A started sample is in Appendix C.

Find out from an internet search engine where you can search for patents for your country of interest. A link is proposed in Appendix C. As you find ways for searching the prior art, you can update your Personal Patent Organizer.

8.6   Your First Few Patent Searches

Spending some time to search patents as a personal exercise should increase your level of skill. You can search for patents from websites. The websites can be from Patent Offices around the world, plus from many free online patent search services, as long as you understand or can translate their language.

Once you reach the website of a Patent Office, find where it permits you to search for the patent documents that it has issued. In addition, the website will usually teach the proper syntax for queries.

For a first search, create a query. For example, try for patent documents that have both the word "computer" and the word "mouse." Enter your query, and see what happens. If you searched for US patents, did you find the patent of Appendix A? If you get too many results, see how you might narrow your search.

For another search, think of a technical topic that interests you, and then think of appropriate keywords for your topic.[29]

Write your chosen keywords here: _____

Then, search patents according to your keywords. As you find relevant documents, skim a few of them this first time. A patent that you find may reference another patent, which you may want to skim as well. Or you may find results that apply to a different line of thought that you also want to explore.

As you skim the patents you find, notice whether they use specific terms for some elements. Now reformulate your search using the specific terms that they use, and repeat. You may find your new searches focusing better on results that are useful to you.

---

[29]   If no specific technical terms come to mind, see if any of the following are of interest: additive manufacturing, aircraft, allele, antigen, automobile, avatar, balance, battery, bracket, bridge, camera, capacitor, cash, cell, clothing, cloud, communication, credit, database, debit, defibrillator, detector, derivative, door, electron, elevator, filter, fuel, glass, graphene, inhibitor, interface, lattice, lock, medical, microwave, moiety, mouse, music, network, nitrogen, nucleus, package, plant, polymer, printer, protein, receptor, refrigerator, resistor, RFID, scaffold, screen, smartphone, telephone, television, shoe, vehicle, vibration, and watch.

If you find yourself learning, do not become concerned. It is the Patent System, working.

8.7 Your Other Patent Searches

As you may have seen from your first patent search, exploring patents in a topic that you like can be interesting and captivating. You may find yourself distracted by reading your findings instead of staying focused on the search that you are supposed to be doing.

A technique to combat the distraction is to prepare a **search scratchpad document** for your patent search results. In this document, write:
(a) your purpose for searching,
(b) the date, and
(c) the keyword queries that you are trying.

Before starting, review the patent reading prism of Figure 7C. Then decide which *parts* of patent documents you are searching for. Write these also in your scratchpad document. The rest of this chapter provides starting suggestions, depending on what question you want answered.

And then start your search, *preparing to avoid reading what does not matter*. If you find a list of documents of interest, copy and paste the list in your scratchpad document. If you find a promising document, skim it.

Then start from the documents of interest. Do they teach you any new keywords? Use these new keywords to refine your search. Do these documents belong in a patent family? Try to find the parent. Which patents do they reference as their prior art? These findings are valuable, because a Patent Examiner and/or a patent attorney may have thought they were relevant at the time. Often there is text that corresponds to the diagrams. If you find something in a diagram, look for it also in the text.

If you start finding documents that contain your answers, write the answers in your search scratchpad document. Enter in detail the patent number and where exactly the answer is found within the patent document. For example: "Item X found in Patent Number Y, Figure 4, element 422 within element 420, also in the text at column 6, lines 3-10."

Do not throw away or delete your search scratchpad document. It will be useful if you ever want to do an updated search at a later time.

8.8 Searching Patents by Field

When you want to search by a field, patent search engines typically suggest the proper syntax for your query. Figure 8C suggests that searching according to a field is a way of viewing only a "slice" of all patent documents. The slice can be a subset of the formalities, the specification, and the claims. Drawings are not as easily searchable for their concepts as is text.

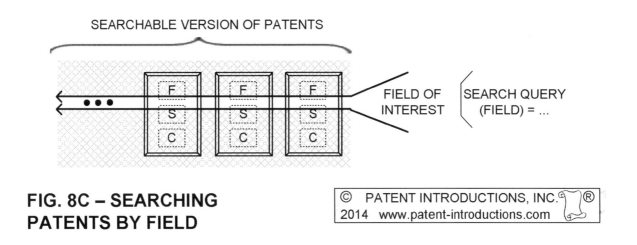

FIG. 8C – SEARCHING PATENTS BY FIELD

Figure 8D shows some fields in the formalities that can be searched for, on the same portion of a patent cover page as in Figure 7E. You can search patents according to the fields that are pointed out in Figure 8D.

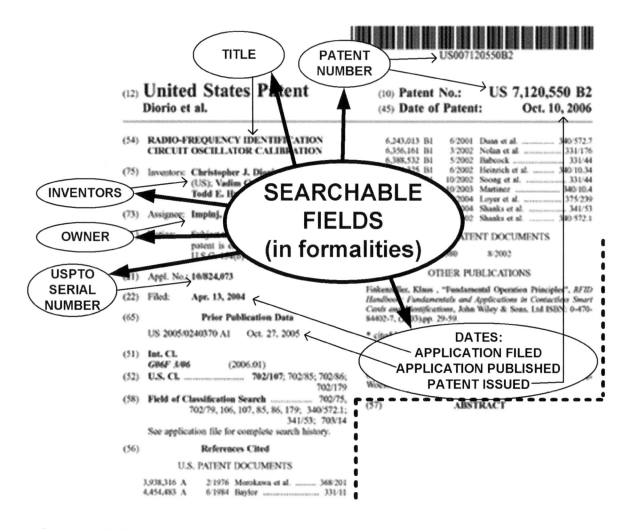

FIG. 8D – SOME OF THE FIELDS THAT CAN BE SEARCHED AMONG THE FORMALITIES

© PATENT INTRODUCTIONS, INC. ®
2014 www.patent-introductions.com

OK, let's try searching for something else. Is there a company that interests you? Do they have patents? Here are some steps to try now:

Write the name of the company that interests you here: _____

Write today's date (the date of search) here: _____

Go to the internet, find a patent search engine, create a query by "assignee name" for this company, and search for its patents and patent applications.

Write the number of patents you found: _____

Write the number of patent applications you found: _____

If you ever happen to read again this part later, think about repeating this search. You can see whether this company has filed more applications, and received more patents since your last search.

8.9 Expected Effectiveness of Patent Searching

Patent searches have limitations.

First, make sure you only need to find patent documents. If it is absolutely critical to find *any* document, then Non-Patent Literature (NPL) should also be searched.

Second, a patent prior art search will not necessarily be fast or straightforward. Even with simple word searches, you need to find the right sets of words and then conduct your searches using the right word combinations. To add to the challenge, sometimes people use different words for the same thing.

Third, no patent prior art search will find every patent document that is findable, unless one searches the records of every Patent Office around the world, in its own language. For many purposes, it is cost-effective enough to search the records of the Patent Office of one's own country or group of countries. For other purposes, one should also search other large databases in prevalent languages.

Fourth, obviously you can only find what can be found. No one can find what is still confidential. In the gray area of Figure 8B are patent applications that have already been filed and are still confidential, and which no search can find today. It is possible that these documents will publish and become issued patents by the time you are planning your activity.

Fifth, the results of your search apply only to today. Even if the search results are "clear" and therefore favorable today, *after as little as one week the patent search results become stale*. This is because the moment NOW and the gray area of Figure 8B continually shift to the right, as time passes. More prior art will become findable over time, and the search will need to be updated. Of course, by then, even more prior art may have been filed by others, and so on.

In some cases you will find exactly the answer you are looking for. For example, it will be a prior art reference, such as a patent, that makes your answer conclusive.

In many other cases where you are seeking clearance of a product or a new idea, however, your answer will never be conclusive. Regardless, you may start developing a level of confidence that what you were looking for is not there. Perhaps a patent or an application that you were looking for does not exist.

You can restate the above as follows: When seeking product clearance in patent searching, there are often no absolutes—only a level of confidence in the reliability of a search. In such cases, the more you search, the higher the reliability of your results and the higher your level of confidence in your results can become.

Figure 8E shows graphically a concept of how the level of confidence can be increased, when seeking clearance. The horizontal axis depicts the resources and effort expended. The vertical axis depicts the resulting level of confidence in the reliability of the patent prior art search.

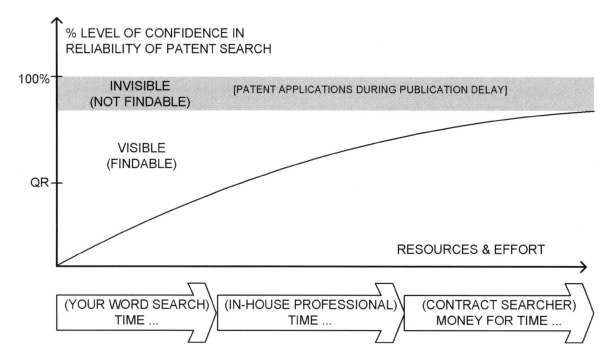

FIG. 8E – THE LEVEL OF CONFIDENCE IN THE RELIABILITY OF A PATENT SEARCH WHEN SEEKING CLEARANCE IMPROVES WITH RESOURCES & EFFORT

© PATENT INTRODUCTIONS, INC.®
2014 www.patent-introductions.com

From the graph of Figure 8E, you can see that a word search alone has some value. Beyond that, the more resources you devote to a search, the higher the level of confidence in the reliability of the answer. Beyond the word search, an in-house patent professional such as a patent attorney or patent agent might advance the effort without spending company money. Moreover, a contracted patent searcher can be engaged, as we will see in the next section.

In Figure 8E note the gray area for invisible patent applications, which stems from the gray area of Figure 8B. The gray area means that your search now cannot find documents that are invisible now. So, for clearance searches, your confidence level might never reach 100%. The confidence level *tends* toward 100% when the IP Alignment of Figure 3E has been achieved and time has passed, because IP Alignment plus time passing make many things visible and risks better understood.

How much confidence is enough? Ordinarily this would be denoted by an intercept, such as QR, but there are no numbers in Figure 8E. Figure 8E is borne out of experience. The required level of confidence should be determined from a number of factors, including how much you can tolerate the down side.

Expect that sometimes you will need to work with some uncertainty. You should take steps to reduce it.

8.10 Engaging Patent Searchers

In Figure 8E, at the far right-hand side of the horizontal axis, is the use of a **contract patent searcher**. You can find one in the internet.

Contract patent searchers ("searchers") can give you services that you often cannot get on your own. For one, they can *search for Non-Patent Literature* that you cannot search as easily because of the cost of subscriptions, etc. Second, when they search for patents, they find better results when they use a **Patent Classification System**, if the art has been classified. Some will add more services regarding, for example, how they process and present their results.

Searchers are acutely aware of the limitations depicted by the graph of Figure 8E. So, at the end of their engagement agreement you may see disclaimers that no search is ever perfect and so on. Moreover, they may list search services and costs that are stratified according to your different *reasons* for searching. Your different reasons require a different amount of work from them to achieve a different level of confidence. For example, you might see a quote for a "patent clearance search" that is higher than a quote for a "patentability search." Of course, all this is fair and reasonable.

Before hiring a searcher, there are some things to keep in mind.

First, before contacting a searcher, *plan in advance* what you will want them to accomplish for you. Some searchers will fairly ask you for a written technical description before they search.

They might help you write one by asking you questions—in which case much of the answer will come from you anyway. So, try to write your question in advance, and make sure it is correct. For example, "I need to clear a product X that includes devices Y and Z together." After you write it, think again whether you want to subcontract the search to a searcher. After forcing yourself to write, you may have developed keywords that enable a keyword search. If you then do the keyword search on your own, your answers may help you refine the question, or discover that you do not need to search anymore.

Second, it is fair to pay a searcher to do *just* a patent search by keywords for you. Think again whether you want to invest 4 hours of your own time or hire someone to do *more* than just a patent search by keywords. Sometimes it pays for you to first do a preliminary search in order to get a sense of how many documents are findable. After that, you can fine-tune the scope of the search you want done.

Third, if you want search results with *a higher level of confidence than from your own keyword search*, ask prospective searchers about their methods or approaches to searching, to see if they are different from the way you search. Searchers should be able to list the NPL databases they use. Ask if they search according to a Patent Classification System. If they say yes, then their report should list what classification(s) they believe your description falls in, the description of what a classification covers, and so on. Searching by the patent classification system often avoids the problem that different people use different words for the same thing.

Fourth, discuss your technical description with the prospective searcher. If your description is vague, you may become inundated by many search results you did not need. Answer your searcher's questions. If you already have a sample patent document that gets close, perhaps give its number to the searcher.

Fifth, before starting, discuss with the searcher *the format of the search results*. In other words, whether the engagement includes that they give you:
(a) "everything" they find in their search,
(b) "everything," but with the relevant results prioritized over the irrelevant results, or
(c) only what seems to them relevant to your description.

In other words, determine whether or not the searcher is expected to think about what they find, apply it to your needs, and make a decision about how to prioritize their reporting. Be aware that option (b) has more value for you than option (a), and requires more effort and risk from the searcher. Option (c) requires even more risk from the searcher.

8.11 Patent Watch Programs

Sometimes companies have institutionalized general periodic patent search programs. A typical program is a **patent watch program**, which could properly be called a "newly appearing patent document watch program." A patent watch program involves periodic searches, for example weekly or monthly, for all patent documents appearing newly in your company's fields of interest. These searches are typically automated according to classifications and keywords, and the results can be emailed to you.

A patent watch program can have many uses. For example, if a list of patents is being maintained per competitor, the program could provide updates to the list. For another example, those receiving the newly published patent applications can determine quickly if one is threatening to a prospective product, and whether an effort should be made to challenge it.

A patent watch program is necessarily general about your field. It will usually find patent applications of interest as soon as they become published and patents as soon as they issue. However, it should not give you a false sense of security that you know all there is to know in a field. Sometimes you must search to answer your questions.

The value of a patent watch program is that, over the long term, you learn the art as it publishes. Of course, every year you might want to reevaluate and update the keywords used, as the fields of interest evolve.

8.12 Patent Searching to Clear a Prospective Product

Sometimes you want to clear a prospective product from patent threats. For example, as seen in Figure 8F, you have an idea for a new feature, shown by the light bulb. You want to implement this feature in your company's future product. You want to make sure, as much as possible, that there is no past patent document that will threaten your product in the future. In other words, you need to mitigate the future patent business risk of infringing (PBR-1), which we saw in Figure 2D.

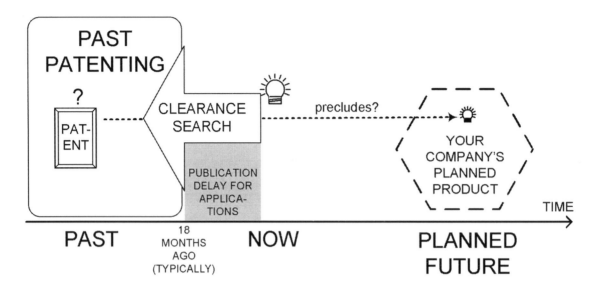

FIG. 8F – CLEARANCE SEARCH TO MITIGATE RISK THAT PAST PATENTING PRECLUDES THE NEWLY CONSIDERED PRODUCT

© PATENT INTRODUCTIONS, INC. ®
2014   www.patent-introductions.com

You will note that Figure 8F starts with the situation of Figure 5C. In addition, Figure 8F shows that you perform a search, called a **patent clearance search** or **Freedom To Operate (FTO) search** (strategy PSD2 of Figure 3B). The reference time for this search is NOW.

Your patent clearance search needs to find patent documents first in the countries where the product will be made or sold, and perhaps also where resold by your company. Such patent documents may have been issued as patents or still be pending patent applications.

Although a clearance search can mitigate the risk of infringing, it cannot eliminate the risk completely. As we saw earlier in this chapter, a patent search that you do today will become stale next week, because more such patent applications could have been published in the interim. Of course, typically one more week does not make much difference, but project managers can make the mistake of relying on positive results of old searches without updating them.

The search results will include patents and patent applications. Among those, you can identify any potentially threatening patents and potentially threatening patent applications. Those will be only patents of others, not those of your own company. Your analysis will become more refined as you start looking at the claims and the specification of each of these documents. The claims of patents are largely fixed,[30] while the claims of patent applications can still be

---

[30] The claims of an issued patent are fixed most of the time. These claims can be changed if the issued patent becomes revised, whether forcibly or not. At least in the United States, the revision can be that the claims are broadened in some instances.

changed. Reading the claims will give you a good starting idea, but the claims must be legally interpreted. Sometimes the claims cover legally more than they say, and sometimes less. The rules for interpreting claims are elaborate, and judgments must be made according to these rules. Patent attorneys are qualified to make these judgments.

If you find a threatening patent document, do not stop there. Search to see if it is part of a patent family, and find any other members of the family.

So when you find threatening patent documents, prepare to take them to your patent attorney. Before you do, gather your proposed design and think whether the next three sections can help.

8.13 Dealing with Potentially Threatening Patents without Disputing Them

Sometimes it is possible to deal with a potentially threatening patent without having to *dispute* it, in other words, where your patent attorney can invoke the legal theory that the patent does not apply to your prospective design. There are a number of ways this can happen, and in this section we explore some ways you can help your patent attorney invoke this theory.

A potentially threatening patent could have expired. We saw some initial considerations in chapter 6 when discussing time T11 of Figure 6A. Sometimes the term of a patent becomes extended beyond the **nominal full term**. Your patent attorney can confirm for you that a patent has, indeed, expired.

Refer again to Figure 3B, strategy PSD5. In some instances, you may be able to legally **design around** the patent claims. Designing around claims is also called **working around** the patent claims, and the result is known as a **workaround**. A **legal workaround** is a design that legally avoids the patent claims.

Your patent attorney may give you some guidelines as to how you might design around the claims. Then you can generate and propose alternative designs as workarounds. When your patent attorney agrees that your proposed design is a legal workaround, in some instances he or she may further advise you to procure a written **legal non-infringement opinion** for it. In other instances, your attorney may think that such an opinion is not merited, for legal strategy reasons beyond the scope of this book.

Keep in mind that *not every patent can be designed around*. Not every patent can be designed around with useful results. You will know that your proposed design is not a legal workaround if a patent attorney who is disinterested in the outcome of your effort privately refuses to give you a written non-infringement opinion for it. In these cases, the legal theory that the patent does not apply cannot be invoked.

8.14 Dealing with Potentially Threatening Patents by Disputing Them

Sometimes it is possible to deal with a potentially threatening patent by *disputing* it, in other words, where your patent attorney can invoke the legal theory that the patent is somehow wrong or has claims that it should not have. Indeed, a potentially threatening patent, or just some of its claims, could be later found to be legally not valid for many reasons, but usually you cannot tell from just reading it. There are a number of ways in which a patent can be disputed, and in this section we explore some ways you can help your patent attorney invoke this theory.[31]

As explained earlier, a patent might be issued with mistakenly broader claims than it should have. The most frequent reason is that there is prior art that the Patent Office did not find or consider before issuing the potentially threatening patent.

Accordingly, you can help by searching *in the hope* of finding such prior art (strategy PSD6 of Figure 3B). So, consider doing a prior art search against the potentially threatening patent, which is called an **invalidation search**. Referring to Figure 8B, ask a patent attorney about what is the proper "reference time" with respect to the threatening patent, that is, how old the prior art references should be.

If you are familiar with the field, you are probably a very good person to define the invalidation search and perhaps even start it. Start searching to find some results, and familiarize yourself with the appropriate terms. After that, you may want to hire a contract patent searcher for the invalidation search. If you do, ask the searcher to map the results they find into the elements of the claims you are trying to invalidate.

If you are lucky, your search will reveal earlier patents or documents that mention the same aspect.

The results of your invalidation search are critical for disputing a patent. Your patent attorney should review and evaluate them. Then he or she might make some decisions as to how to proceed about the threatening patent.

In some instances, based on your results, your patent attorney can procure a written **legal invalidity opinion** about the potentially threatening patent by using the prior art that you or a searcher has found. The invalidity opinion will be based on your search results. Then, in some of these instances, your patent attorney might tell you that it is acceptable to ignore the patent.

In other instances, using the search results, your patent attorney can initiate a **revision proceeding** against the potentially threatening patent. There are a number of possible revision

---

[31] Most legal theories are beyond the scope of this book. For example, patent claims can also fail for legal technicalities in how they are written, etc.

proceedings which, in various countries, have names like **reexamination**, **post grant review**, **inter partes review**, **revocation**, and so on. Each has conditions for when it is available, legal deadlines by which it is permitted to be initiated, and advantages and disadvantages.

When completed, the revision proceeding may result in the Patent Office revising the patent to have broader, the same, or narrower claims, or no claims at all. In the latter case, the patent is said to have been **invalidated**.

Some types of revision proceedings can take a long time—several months or even a few years. Before one is completed, the threatening patent is still presumed valid. This is why, when you find potentially threatening patents, you should address them earlier rather than later.

There is no guarantee that your invalidation search will yield usable results. In other words, it is possible that you will *not* manage to dispute the threatening patent. In these cases, the legal theory that the patent is somehow wrong, or has claims that it should not have, cannot be invoked. Even with usable results, there is no guarantee that a revision proceeding will eventually succeed.

8.15 Challenging Potentially Threatening Patent Applications

It is possible that your patent clearance search has found a potentially threatening patent *application*. This may happen if you have been asked to copy a recent new product by a rival, and your search has found the rival's freshly published pending patent application.

The potentially threatening patent application will have claims that have not yet been in a granted patent. In addition, the same document might be filed again as a new patent application, with additional claims.

It may be possible to *challenge the threatening patent application* (strategy PSD7 of Figure 3B). First, do an invalidation search against the application as described in the previous section. If you have found applicable results, take them to your patent attorney. He or she may be able to submit them against the pending patent application with a proper analysis. This submission is called a **third-party prior art submission**. When the patent application is examined, the Patent Examiner will also consider the third-party prior art submission. If your search results are applicable, the Patent Examiner will likely reject one or more of the broadest claims of the threatening patent application. It is possible that the applicant might never manage to patent these claims.

Do not make a third-party prior art submission by yourself! Sometimes there are good strategic reasons *not* to make one. Sometimes there are good strategic reasons for what comments to include in one.

Often there is a **legal deadline** by which a third-party prior art submission must be filed. To prevent problems caused by missed deadlines, a company may have a **patent watch program** and a process for treating its results, as described earlier in this chapter.

8.16 Searching Patent Specifications for Novelty—Patentability

Another reason for prior art searching is to determine whether your design may be patentable itself. For example, you may have an idea for a future design or product that is not in your company's product pipeline, but might be useful someday. Perhaps you will want your company to patent that design or product now for when that day comes. Accordingly, you can do a prior art search that is called a **novelty search**, or **patentability search**.

The prospect of a novelty search is shown in Figure 8G, which builds on Figure 5D. The reference time will be NOW, as we saw earlier in this chapter.

Accordingly, you do a novelty search to find a past document, such as a rival patent, which would serve as prior art that would prevent your idea from becoming patented. You would search to find such a rival past patent—more exactly, you would search to gain confidence that *it does not exist*. If you cannot find anything, then maybe you can also get your idea patented by your company. Your novelty search is not guaranteed to find everything, but it helps.

A novelty search feels the same but should not be confused with a clearance search. Their scenarios are different, their purposes are to mitigate different patent business risks, their scopes are different, and they justify different amounts of resources.

You would do a novelty search when your invention is not a feature that is concretely planned for incorporating in a product, but instead you want to explore ideas of what is possible to invent, develop, and patent in the future. Your purpose for a novelty search would be to ameliorate patent business risk PBR-3 (see Figure 2D) of investing in patenting and not succeeding. As we see in Figure 8G, you could be searching for more documents than patents, even though it is easier to start with patents. Because risk PBR-3 affects only the much smaller investment in patenting, it is often acceptable to use fewer resources in searching.

Instead, you would do a clearance search when there is a specific feature that you concretely plan to incorporate in an upcoming prospective product. Your purpose for a clearance search would be to ameliorate patent business risk PBR-1 (see Figure 2D) of infringing. As we saw in Figure 8F, you would be searching only for threatening patent documents, and then searching to discover how to counter them. Because risk PBR-1 usually affects a larger imminently planned investment in development, more resources are merited in searching.

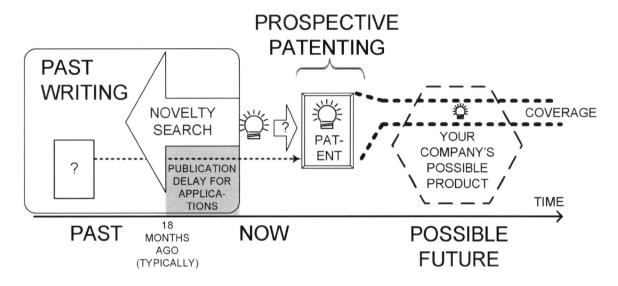

FIG. 8G – NOVELTY SEARCH FOR HIGHER CONFIDENCE THAT YOUR INVENTION CAN ALSO BECOME A PATENT THAT WILL PROTECT THE EXCLUSIVITY OF THE POSSIBLE FUTURE PRODUCT

Regardless of their differences, a clearance search and a novelty search have common elements. First, *a typical novelty search can serve as the beginning of a clearance search.* Whatever it finds should be studied to see if it is a potentially threatening patent or patent application. Plus, it may serve as a guide for defining the more rigorous clearance search.

Second, *a clearance search can serve as the beginning of a novelty search.* If the feature is clear from the clearance search, it may also be patentable. More specifically, if you have done the patent clearance search and found nothing, then you need to consider Non-Patent Literature for your novelty search, plus the fact that a clearance search might not have gone as far back in time as a novelty search needs to go.

Chapter Summary

In this chapter, we learned about prior art searching and got a sense for different types of patent searching. The usual reasons for searching are for the main concern of clearing a proposed design and the patentability of a new idea. We learned that some documents are hard to find and some pending patent applications cannot be found at all. The effectiveness of searching increases with increasing investment, such as with using contract searchers. When threatening patents are found for a proposed design, you might be able to develop a workaround, or search further to develop grounds to dispute a threatening issued patent, or to challenge a threatening pending patent application.

Notes:

PART FOUR

YOU, PATENTING FOR YOUR COMPANY

CHAPTER 9. REPORTING YOUR INVENTIONS FOR PATENTING

CHAPTER 10. A PATENT APPLICATION WILL BE PREPARED FROM YOUR IRF

CHAPTER 11. THE NEXT TWO DECADES

9
REPORTING YOUR INVENTIONS FOR PATENTING

9.1 The Prospect of Your Patenting

Your company wants you to report your inventions for patenting. Your reporting will initiate procedures that may result in a patent for your company.

Figure 9A shows the prospect of your patenting. Along a horizontal TIME axis, the time is NOW. Patenting that you do now is prospective—its rewards will be in the future.

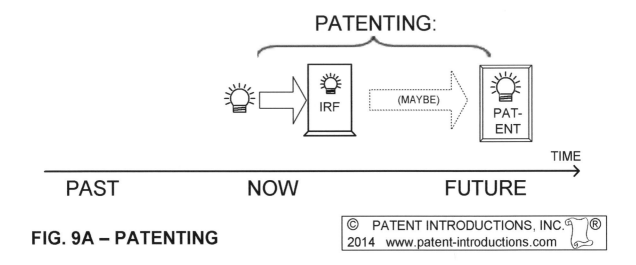

FIG. 9A – PATENTING

Patenting will be *collaborative* between you and your company. You are asked to contribute your idea by writing about it in the company's **Invention Reporting Form** (**IRF**). Sometimes you will be asked to search for prior art against your idea—at least the easily searchable patent prior art. Your company will provide the infrastructure to evaluate your IRF. If your IRF is approved for patenting, your company will also provide the resources for the patenting, and you will be asked to review a patent application that is drafted for your IRF. Finally, your company will try to turn the patent application into a patent.

9.2 Start Managing Your Ideas

As you work, you may notice that you start having ideas. Beyond those for solving your assigned problems, these ideas can be for extensions of your company's products, for alternatives to your company's products, and so on. Your ideas are inventions. Some of your inventions may even be patentable.

You may need to think more on each of your inventions. If you do not write your ideas, you might forget them. As a wise person once said, your mind was made to have ideas, but not to hold them.

So, *learn to capture your ideas as you are having them* by writing them. The more you capture them, the more your mind will be liberated, allowing more and even better ideas to come forth. If your company asks you to use a physical Engineering Notebook, use one. Other companies rely on computer records only.

Also, learn *to store your captured ideas in a findable way*. In your computer records, create a subfolder for your inventions that is separate from your other work. Label the subfolder and file names descriptively.

Occasionally review your stored ideas anew. As time passes, you will think better about your ideas. You will find that some of them will look promising, while others have been done before, either in a product or in a patent. Then you will want to start organizing them according to your insights, and where they will apply in your work.

Importantly, start distinguishing what is a new idea of yours from what is your company's **ambient information**. Ambient information is common knowledge and experience of your coworkers, the kind of which they talk about at the cafeteria during lunchtime. This knowledge and experience may be about your industry in general, or specific products, or products being developed. Large portions of ambient knowledge are often not patented.

Sometimes you are going to recognize that one of your ideas is a complete invention that you could report for patenting. When that happens, report it.

9.3 Streamline Your Process for Reporting Inventions

Your company likely has a business process for your reporting inventions for patenting. The process typically involves filling in and submitting an **Invention Reporting Form** (IRF).[32]

Make the process easy for you to follow. Start your own **Personal Patent Organizer** document, as we suggested at the end of chapter 4 and in chapter 8. See Appendix C for a sample. Perhaps you can keep your Personal Patent Organizer in your subfolder for inventions.

Find and enter in your Personal Patent Organizer the URL that leads to your company's IRF within your company's intranet. If your company gave you this book, that URL might already be written in the Patent Department Contact Information at the beginning of this book.

Read your company's IRF document once, to get a sense for what it asks. If you do not yet work in a company, a sample IRF has been created for you in Appendix B of this book. Take the time to read its questions; doing so will benefit you because many IRFs ask similar questions.

After you read the questions of the IRF, identify the questions that will have the same answers in all of your IRFs. These questions include, for example, your name and contact information. If you use the starting sample IRF of Appendix B, question C provides one block for the data of each inventor. Answer this block once for yourself carefully, and then keep a copy handy in your Personal Patent Organizer document so you can copy and paste it every time.

9.4 Two Types of Inventions to Report for Patenting

There are two basic types of inventions to consider reporting. Different considerations apply to each.

The first type is inventions that you are required to report. When developing a product, focused companies patent its new features (strategies PSD4 and PSI1 of Figure 3B) to mitigate respective patent business risks PBR-1 and PBR-2 of Figure 2D.

The business processes of New Product Development often define milestones that have names such as "Phase 1", "Phase 2", etc. In focused companies, patent clearance and patenting are integrated with clearing these milestones. Clearing one of these milestones typically requires all new aspects in the product to be reported for patenting by their inventors, so that the patenting can start on them. For innovative companies, a single new product may have multiple inventions.

---

[32] The IRF is sometimes called an Invention Disclosure Form (IDF).

The second type is inventions for which reporting is optional. These can be for possibly new products.

Often you will not know whether to invest the few hours to report these. It may help to seek early feedback, even if informally. Good people to ask can be those who will make the decision of whether to patent a new IRF or not. In many companies, the decision is made by a **Patent Committee**. Any informal feedback they give you will not be binding because a single person typically does not speak for the whole committee. Still, such feedback can help.

For example, encouraging feedback can be that the Patent Committee tends to approve this kind of invention for patenting. Or it can be that a coworker of yours is working on something that is related, and your invention could expand it. Maybe you two could work together, and your expanded invention has a correspondingly better chance of being approved for patenting than either of your inventions alone.

Moreover, discouraging feedback can be that the Patent Committee tends not to approve these kinds of inventions for patenting. Or, it could be that the invention seems familiar—be sure to do a patent search as described in chapter 8. Of course, you can report your invention anyway—because discouraging feedback is not the same as preventing you from reporting your invention.

9.5 Improve Your Invention's Chances of Being Patented

You can do things that will help your invention's chances of being chosen for patenting.

First, *report inventions that will be definitely included in a planned product.* Ensure that your IRF shows the name of the planned product. These inventions tend to take precedence in Patent Committees because they tend to protect a company's much larger investment in the planned New Product Development.

Second, *see if you can find your Patent Committee's selection criteria.* Patent Committees typically use both general selection criteria and special considerations for deciding which IRFs to choose for patenting. Progressive Patent Committees actually are open about some of their general selection criteria, but always with the caveat that these are not determinative. Sometimes, Patent Committees announce that they are especially interested in inventions in a topic of interest. Even if the criteria are not posted, you may ask a member of your Patent Committee what type of IRF tends to be approved for patenting. As you learn such selection criteria, use them! Try to see which of your ideas meet them, and prioritize reporting them over the others. Learn what your company considers valuable to patent, and apply it to generate new ideas.

Third, when you start focusing on an idea, if permitted, *do a patentability search*, even a quick one. If your invention is clear, you can include your keywords in the IRF and the few closest prior art references that you found. Create a table to show the differences between your invention and the prior art references you found. Differences can be in terms of:
(a) what your invention does versus what they do,
(b) how your invention works versus how they work, and
(c) whether your invention has an unexpected different application or advantage over them.

A Patent Committee will be more confident in choosing to patent such an IRF. Of course, your search may reveal that your invention has been written about before, in which case you should not submit it and save everyone time.

Fourth, *seek the right colleagues* in your company to collaborate with you on your idea. The right colleague is someone whose daily emphasis is not the same as yours, but complements yours advantageously. If you need more knowledge on a specific topic, approach an expert. If your daily focus is on a technical topic, approach a systems person, and so on. Remain open to new ideas—your colleagues may suggest additions for your IRF that your company may find valuable, even if they are not valuable to the function that you are contributing. *Adding the right colleagues will usually enlarge the scope of your IRF, which will make it more compelling for the Patent Committee to approve for patenting.* If your colleagues contribute, then they have a chance of becoming named additional inventors or **coinventors**. However, there are legal rules as to who can become a coinventor, which your patent attorney will apply later on.

9.6 You Are Responsible for the Invention Reporting Form (IRF)

You are the starting point of patent protection. Patent protection starts with you or one of your coinventors writing the IRF and submitting it. Figure 9B shows the relevant time in the time line of Figure 6A.

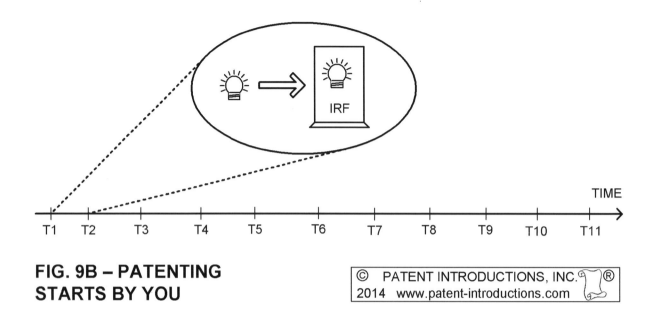

FIG. 9B – PATENTING STARTS BY YOU

© PATENT INTRODUCTIONS, INC. ®
2014 www.patent-introductions.com

The submitted IRF brings your invention to the point in which it can be patented by your company. Conversely, if you do not write or submit the IRF, your invention will not become patented, since your Patent Department has no other way of knowing what you are thinking or inventing.

Writing an IRF should take you less than 8 hours—often less than 4 or even 2 uninterrupted hours. Still, it may be hard to make the time to write an IRF. One problem is the trap of systematically prioritizing other tasks over writing the IRF. When this happens, you can remind yourself of the long-term benefit to your career and to your company of your invention becoming patented.

If you are still not finding the time to write the IRF, consider asking for help. Perhaps your company has created the position of a Junior Technical Officer (JTO) *for this kind of work*. Perhaps a JTO can start the IRF after you describe it verbally, which will make it easier for you to review afterward. However, even if a JTO writes what you say, you will still own the document. The JTO does not start by knowing what you know, and you must proofread the JTO's work. Look for any gaps in what is written. Of course, a JTO working for the company may add his or her own related ideas to the IRF. In this case, the JTO becomes presumptively a coinventor and owns the IRF together with you. If the additional ideas are included in the patent application, the JTO will be listed as a coinventor.

A person such as a JTO may prove very useful where original innovation is to proceed very fast. Such a person can collect the ideas mentioned in planning activities, group them according to topic, and then create the right set of IRFs for the team to read and submit.

9.7 An IRF Is a Separate and Different Deliverable

An Invention Reporting Form (IRF) is a separate deliverable from other deliverables that you may generate. For example, an idea written in your Engineering Notebook or going into a product does not count as being reported for patenting.

Additionally, an IRF is a different deliverable. You cannot submit one of your other deliverables in lieu of the IRF. Here are some examples:

An IRF is not similar to a market planning document. The desire to build a new and improved product is great, and that is what creates progress and fresh revenue streams for the company. An IRF, however, asks further questions, such as *how* to implement your ideas. These further questions must also be answered.

An IRF is *not similar to an internal design report*. The design report is a description of how to make something specific. It does not focus on the invention by isolating what is new from what is known, nor does it discuss any advantages of implementing it.

An IRF is generally *not similar to a scientific paper for publication*. The purpose of the IRF is ultimately to obtain a patent, and patents are very different from such papers. Figure 9C is a table that shows some of the differences.

ASPECT	INVENTION FOR PATENTING	SCIENCE PAPER FOR PUBLICATION
Originator:	An inventor (no education required)	A scientist or engineer
Criteria for approval:	To be allowed as a patent, invention must be "novel"* and "non-obvious"* to "a person skilled in the art"* [*quotation marks because these terms have specific legal meanings]	To be accepted for publication, content of paper must pass peer review
Is usefulness a criterion?	Usefulness is a requirement: invention must have "utility" for patent to be granted.	Usefulness is often NOT a requirement: in fact, paper can be "pure science" and still be approved for publication
Final document informs the world of ...	... what they may NOT do or offer, in the same country, unless they get permission, if available, often by paying	... what the authors did or propose
Business result of final document	Opportunity to have a form of legal monopoly for product; pricing power; reputation	Reputation
Cost (2014)	Often US$10,000 to start	about US$100 (mostly for printing costs)

FIG. 9C – DIFFERENCES BETWEEN INVENTIONS FOR PATENTING AND SCIENCE PAPERS FOR PUBLICATION

© PATENT INTRODUCTIONS, INC.®
2014 www.patent-introductions.com

One of the most significant differences between an IRF and a scientific paper is the aspect in the third row of Figure 9C, which is whether usefulness is required. Some scientists may characterize their work as "pure science," which means "science depending on deductions from demonstrated truths, such as mathematics or logic, studied *without regard to practical applications*"[33] (emphasis added). By definition, then, what is *only* pure science is not patentable, because usefulness *is* required for patenting. When writing an IRF, never write that your invention is "pure science." If you truly believe it is, please take the additional time to find useful applications for your science and report them in the IRF. If you cannot think of such useful applications, start considering additional contributors who might, as mentioned above.

---

[33] Definition from http://www.google.com/, by querying "what does pure science mean" accessed on 2014-12-31.

9.8   Writing the IRF

Writing IRFs becomes easier with practice.

Report each invention separately. If two inventions seem to you that they are related, ask your Patent Department in advance whether they should be reported in the same document, or in two separate documents that cross-reference each other.

The IRF has two kinds of questions, **administrative** and **substantive**. (In this regard, an IRF is like an application for admission to a university as a student.)

The **administrative questions** of the IRF ask for data about who the inventors are, what their contact information is, when the invention was made, whether the invention is intended for a planned product, and so on. The answers are needed for the patenting, and you are the best person to determine the answers.

Pay attention to the exact version of your name. Sometimes people include their middle names or only their middle initials. Some people use nicknames in quotation marks. It may help with your personal brand to decide on a single version of your name, and use it consistently when you report inventions for patenting.

The **substantive questions** of the IRF ask about your invention. Answer the questions. Write from the general to the specific. Give examples, particulars, and details. Read again your answers, to make sure that what you wrote is clear.

The IRF is for others. You are the only person on earth who does not need the IRF to understand your invention, because you know it already. However, your audience does not necessarily know your project, and they should be able to understand what you invented. Have you ever read poorly written instructions for assembling a piece of equipment? Sometimes such instructions are written poorly because those who wrote them already know how to assemble the equipment, and therefore assume you know what their terms mean, or skip steps. Your IRF should be better than that.

Some unsophisticated IRFs do not ask the key substantive question: "What is the difference or improvement of your invention over the prior art you know about?" Sometimes this question is phrased as: "What is the claim of your invention?"

Even if your IRF does not ask the key substantive question, try to answer it anyway—it will save everyone a lot of time later. In your writing, point out what is new versus what is not. What is new could be a new device or arrangement or method of doing something. The patent application will be attempted only for what is new.

Beyond that, *do not answer what is not being asked*. If you do, you will be wasting your time to write and others' time to read. For instance, if the IRF asks for "your earliest date of invention," *write that date only*, for example, "January 7, 2014." That question did not ask that you *prove* your date of the invention by providing copies of your Engineering Notebook, so do not prove it. If more detail is needed, the IRF will ask for it.

9.9 Generating Words

The writing in your IRF should be descriptive, direct, objective, and plain. It should not skip steps. Patents are no place for humor, innuendo, or anything other than what you exactly mean.

It is beneficial to *generate the right words* for what you mean. Using the wrong words is one of the technical reasons that patents can fail afterward, and that can often be traced back to the inventor having used the wrong words in reporting the invention.

The meaning of your technical terms should be well accepted. If a term is not yet well accepted, you should give a definition. Also, if there are similar terms for related concepts, perhaps you can explain those too, in order to prevent confusion. Your referee for the meaning of a word should be an appropriate dictionary for the field, not your personal preference.

Once you decide on a specific word or label for a concept, you should use it consistently throughout the IRF to keep your document unambiguous and clear. Technical writing is different from creative writing, and therefore many of the guidelines you may have learned in high school for creative writing—such as varying your prose by using synonyms—do not apply and, in fact, should be avoided in this context.

Remember that your IRF must be understandable to others outside your working team, confidentially of course. Accordingly, there are **traps**, in that there are types of words you must be careful about. These are words that you use casually and daily within your company, but you should always consider whether a person outside your company would know what they mean.

A first type of trap is to use a **project name** instead of an objective description. When you are working on an upgraded version of your product, internally the project name could be "Star." Of course, as a note to your Patent Committee, you can indicate that this IRF is being implemented in "the front end of Project Star"—your Patent Committee will know what that is and likely approve it. But later inside your IRF, you would need to say what the project "Star" is about, at least with a block diagram.

Second, avoid using **marketing terms** or **product names**, which are sometimes used as trademarks. Marketing Departments are fiendishly good at creating names for products that sound better than the products actually are, or suggest that the products have more or better attributes than the products actually do. Disaster looms when you use these terms as ordinary descriptions because an IRF is expected to be objective about the attributes of its invention, and the wrong description can hurt patentability.

Moreover, there may be an instance where you will have identified an entirely new device or method or concept or composition of matter. For example, you may have invented a device that does something that has never been done before. In such an instance, you can give it a name by *coining a new word*.[34] Of course, there are rules. First, the new word that you choose should not mislead about, or mean something already different than, the device or concept that you identified. Second, do not use a new word without defining it. So, your IRF should include a separate paragraph with the words: "I am coining a new term, namely: '...', and it means: ... ." Explain what device or concept your new word stands for. Third, your patent attorney might not agree to include the new term in the eventual patent application for strategic patenting reasons, if some circumstances apply. Finally, when creating a new word, professionalism and good taste are always good ideas.

9.10 Generating Drawings

Your IRF should include drawings for your reader. The drawings can include diagrams and tables, just like those in engineering textbooks.

Drawings complement text, but the comprehension economics of drawings and text are different. When engineers or scientists read, they usually comprehend faster from drawings than from text. Drawings even help overcome comprehension problems when the reader is not a native speaker of the text's language. For some people, the mind thinks more comprehensively in pictures than in words. Indeed, words force some readers to conjure pictures, which is a mental process that taxes them much less than looking at a well-thought out drawing. Unfortunately, much writing is produced because less effort is required *from the writer* to write words than to create a drawing.

You want your IRF to sell itself to the Patent Committee. They will usually discuss it while looking at a drawing that you may have added. So, for your IRFs, share your mental picture with your reader more directly. Can you describe your invention with drawings? Is there one that clearly describes what happens? If so, include it. It will make everything go so much better downstream. The draft patent application will likely have fewer errors and in turn will require fewer corrections from you.

Think of what drawings to add. For example, generate a drawing to answer some of these questions: "Where does the invention fit?"; "What are the main components?"; "What are variations?" and so on. *Create these drawings*. Continue even though some answers are merely block diagrams that are trivial to you. Label the drawings "FIG. 1", "FIG. 2", etc.—then you can describe them more easily in your text.

---

[34] In the field of patents, the act of coining a new word is also known as "being your own lexicographer."

Insert your drawings into the IRF. If you have captured something on a computer screen, the image can be a screenshot, which you can copy into the text of the IRF. If you have a prototype, take pictures of it from different angles and copy them into the text. If you can, set the camera to stamp each photograph with a date for better record keeping.

In the last few years, it has become very easy to add drawings into a word processing program. You could make drawings neatly by hand on a sheet of paper, take a picture with a smartphone or a tablet, and copy the picture into the IRF. Your drawings need not look perfect or as good as patent drawings—just clear.

9.11 Reporting Prior Art

At least in the United States, *inventors are obligated to report the relevant prior art that they know of*. Your Patent Department will indicate how they want you to report prior art. In many instances, there is a special section in the IRF that asks you about the prior art that you know of.

Your obligation to *report* the prior art that you know of does not mean that you have an obligation to *search* for prior art. In fact, as mentioned earlier, your company may have a policy of no prior art searching, and in that case you should comply with the policy.

If your company permits you to search for prior art, then think of whether it would be helpful to do so. Many inventors find that a 20-minute patent search orients them well in a field, and increases their confidence about the patentability of their invention.

The obligation to report prior art is focused primarily on the patentability of what you think is the new part of your invention. This means reporting any documents that would tend to prove that your invention is *not* new! Plus, if there is an article that provides general background in the field of your invention, you could report it. Also, ask your patent attorney whether you are proposing to report too many prior art documents that merely repeat the background, without teaching anything more relevant to the invention.

Whether you search or not, *strongly consider reporting your own relevant prior work*. This includes public documents related to your invention that have your name on them. Examples are issued patents, published patent applications, published papers, etc. If you do not report these, then in the future it might be very hard for you to explain why you did *not* know about them!

9.12 Coordinating with Coinventors

As we mentioned above, you may have asked people to contribute who may become coinventors. Or you may have been asked to contribute to someone else's IRF.

An IRF is a single document, regardless of the number of contributors. If there are others working with you, it is smart to divide the work among yourselves.

One person can start on the IRF, and another can review. When you pass copies of documents to each other, ensure you follow a format that indicates which version is the latest. One format is to use filenames with an increasing version number, like "v1 IRF", then "v2 IRF", etc., or use version control tools where available.

When ready, accept all the changes in the IRF and submit it.

9.13 Submitting Your IRF for Patenting

Your company will also have instructions for how the completed IRF is to be submitted. Larger companies have online systems for uploading invention submissions and even accepting related files. Related files could be for drawings, but also try to extract an image and copy it into the IRF, as not everyone might have the proper software to read drawings files.

Of course, keep a copy of the submitted IRF for your records. Even if your company does not approve your IRF for patenting right now, they may change their mind in the future. In that case, congratulations for your foresight!

Update your Personal Patent Organizer with your IRF submission. As a result of the submission, your IRF will usually receive an **Idea Submission Number** or an **Attorney Docket Number**—add this number to your records and your copies. You will need this internal tracking number should you ever ask about the status of your IRF.

Your submission will typically go to your Patent Department. After that, start thinking about your next IRF.

Finally, keep in mind that *your submission for patenting does not operate as a suggestion for product development*. Ordinarily your Patent Department will not take your idea and try to suggest to others in the company that they implement it. If you want your invention to become a product as well, you will need to find the right channel for doing so.

9.14 Your Company Will Decide Whether to Patent Your IRF or Not

Companies typically have a process for choosing which IRFs to patent. The process often includes a meeting by a Patent Committee. Figure 9D shows an example.

In Figure 9D, five IRFs are submitted to the Patent Department. Upon receiving them the Patent Department may do a preliminary prior art patentability search. This search is intended to find any easily findable prior art that would preclude patent applications for these IRFs from becoming patented. In other words, the search is intended to mitigate patent business risk PBR-3 of Figure 2D on behalf of your company, before investing in acquiring patent rights.

Afterward, the IRFs are forwarded to the Patent Committee, which generally meets periodically. Since patents are multidisciplinary, the Patent Committee typically includes members of the business side, the legal side, and the engineering side, often in equal representation.

For each IRF in its agenda, the Patent Committee decides whether or not to apply for a patent and, if not, whether to publish defensively. If a complex technical question arises, then the inventor may be called in for an explanation. The decision of whether or not to patent, however, will depend more on the business aspects of the answer.

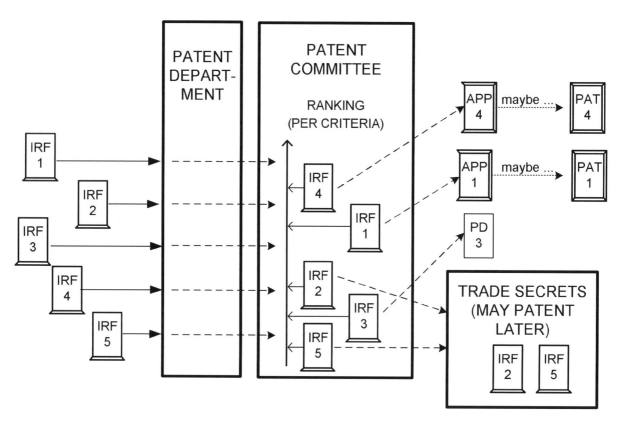

FIG. 9D – SAMPLE DECISIONS OF PATENT COMMITTEE

Patent Committees use criteria for making the patenting decisions. The criteria are often intended to determine whether *the company would benefit from patenting* a particular IRF. In reality, when budgets are tight, even desirable IRFs can go unpatented.

Some Patent Committees aggregate some of their criteria in a number ranking. Submitted IRFs receive numerical scores for these aggregate criteria, and then the IRFs are ranked according to their numerical scores. Then the Patent Committee typically chooses to patent the IRFs with the top rankings.

In the example of Figure 9D, the five IRFs are ranked in the order of IRF4, IRF1, IRF2, IRF3, and IRF5, only according to the criteria used for the numerical score. The top two, namely, IRF4 and IRF1, are selected for patenting. IRF3 is published as a defensive publication due to criteria that were not used for the numerical score. The remaining two, namely, IRF2 and IRF5, are kept as trade secrets, at least in the United States. Perhaps they will be patented later—for example, if your company changes direction.

The Patent Committee is one place where new strategic directions of your company may be implemented. For example, if a company wants to enter a new direction, one of the criteria of the Patent Committee can be that IRFs in that direction face a lower threshold for approval.

Of course you will like hearing that the Patent Committee chose your IRF for patenting. If they don't, you may want to consider the following:

- The decision of whether or not to patent an IRF is not made casually. For every decision to patent, the company will be devoting resources.

- Do you want feedback? It could be that there would not be enough useful expected patent protection to be had. In other words, there was not enough business advantage in precluding the rivals, if what you proposed in your IRF became a company patent. After all, patents are used mostly for business purposes.

- Would another part of the business, with perhaps its own patent budget, be interested in your IRF? If so, find out how to take your IRF to them.

Finally, if it is later decided to incorporate your invention in a product, go back and submit your IRF again, referencing your previous submission. Its ranking may have improved.

Chapter Summary

In this chapter, we saw how you can start managing your ideas and then report them for patenting. There are two types of ideas, those you must report because they will be implemented in a product and those that you may report. Reporting your ideas includes filling in the Invention Reporting Form (IRF) and submitting it. Filling in the IRF involves generating words and drawings. A single IRF may have multiple contributors, with whom you might share some of the tasks. The Patent Committee will decide whether or not to patent your IRF.

Notes:

10

A PATENT APPLICATION WILL BE PREPARED FROM YOUR IRF

10.1 Preparing to Patent

Your Invention Reporting Form (IRF) has been approved for patenting. Now a patent application will be written for your invention, as seen in Figure 10A. Writing a patent application is often called "drafting." The drafting will use your approved IRF as the starting point.

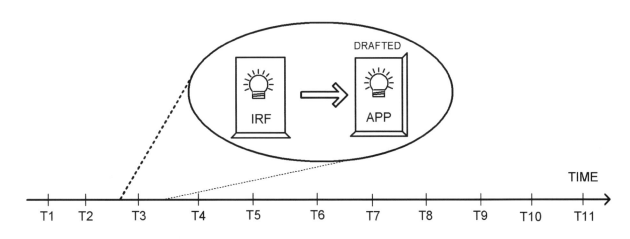

FIG. 10A – A PATENT APPLICATION WILL BE DRAFTED FROM YOUR IRF

Your Patent Department will engage a **patent attorney** or a **patent agent** who is to draft the patent application, with your help. This person might work in your Patent Department or be hired on contract from an outside law firm.[35]

10.2 Initial Inventor Interview

In some instances, an inventor interview will be held. The patent attorney or agent will speak with you and likely also with any other coinventors about your IRF. Sometimes a member of the Patent Department may also attend the interview.

The interview can start by reviewing the IRF together and then answering questions. If your patent attorney is not an employee of your company, do not assume that he or she knows about the project that you have been working on for a long time. The patent attorney talks to many inventors about many different projects.

During the interview, the patent attorney may also ask you for other ways that your invention may be implemented. If you know of any, or can think of any, be sure to mention them at least in broad lines.

In other instances, no interview will be held. Your IRF may be clear enough, or your patent attorney may know the subject well.

10.3 Receiving a Drafted Patent Application for Review

After some time the patent attorney will prepare and send you a drafted **patent application**. The drafted patent application is a document that typically has text and drawings.

As in Figure 10B, *you are expected to review the drafted patent application.* After you review it, you are expected to reply, possibly by sending an email. If you reply that you approve the drafted patent application, then it will be filed with the Patent Office as it is. Otherwise, you should reply with your specific changes and corrections. Then the draft will be corrected and sent to you again, and the process will be repeated until you approve the patent application.

Do not write that you approve the drafted patent application as soon as you receive it, because it could have errors that should be corrected first. (Worse, the draft may include embedded questions for you in bold typeface and, if you approve it without addressing them, it may seem like you did not even glance at it!)

---

[35] The patent attorney does not work for you personally—the attorney works for your company, as do you.

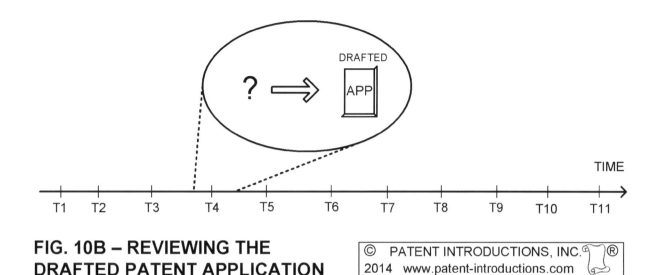

FIG. 10B – REVIEWING THE DRAFTED PATENT APPLICATION

© PATENT INTRODUCTIONS, INC. ®
2014 www.patent-introductions.com

If there are multiple **inventors**, each should review the drafted patent application. Each should give approval or corrections. One person on the team of inventors can be appointed the "captain" for this patent application. (Other words for "captain" are leader, coordinator, quarterback, etc.) Very often the captain is the first person mentioned in the group of inventors. Everyone is to review and send feedback to the captain. To save paper, sometimes one of the inventors prints the draft patent application, reviews it to generate his or her comments, and then gives the printed draft to another inventor. The captain then creates a single set of corrections on behalf of the group, and sends these corrections to the patent attorney.

Sometimes, along with the drafted patent application, *you are given a deadline for your review*, with the understanding that you will read it before the deadline and you do not need to reply if you approve it. If you need more time than the deadline, then you should say so before the deadline passes. (Keep in mind that sometimes the deadlines are absolute, from patent considerations that we described earlier.) In these cases then, if the deadline passes and you have not replied, your approval is presumed.

In your review, you should look for errors. Any error that you do not correct will likely not be fixed at all, and will be propagated into the eventually filed patent application and possibly also into a child patent.

Sometimes, along with the drafted patent application, the patent attorney will send you also the **inventor legal forms** to sign. Sign them only after your review is complete.

It is quite possible that, after you read your drafted patent application, you will have no comments or corrections. In that case, there is no feedback to give, and you should communicate to the patent attorney that you approve the drafted application for filing. Then you will be ready to proceed with signing the inventor legal forms.

10.4 Preparing a Document for Your Feedback

If you do give feedback, *it should be specific to the drafted patent application*. Feedback is specific when it points to the exact portion of the document and writes what should be written. Feedback might also explain why a change is requested, and is a good place to ask a general question.

So, *create a new document* by copying the drafted patent application, and adding your initials to the file name of the copied file. For example, if the file is has the name <P0123_Pat_App>, and your name is John Smith, create a copy for your feedback with the file name <P0123_Pat_App_JS>.

Enter your comments, questions, and corrections in your new document at the appropriate places, with the changes ("deltas") showing. Plus, answer any questions that may be embedded in the text. For example, the drafter may have written the text: <**INVENTOR, HERE I HAVE A QUESTION—how does (element A) receive data from (element B)?**>. The question is often in bold typeface to attract your attention. In other instances the patent attorney will have included such questions in a separate email.

10.5 Perspectives for Reviewing the Drafted Patent Application

It is useful to adopt some mental perspectives when you review a drafted patent application. As we said before, patents are multidisciplinary, and therefore patent writing sometimes seems strange.

A patent application is legal writing, not ordinary writing. Different words in different places have different effects in how the legal system will interpret the application, similarly with how different words in software source code eventually affect how a computer operates, when that source code is interpreted. In patent applications some words repeat, and there are good reasons for that. Just because something seems strange, it is not necessarily wrong. If you are not certain, you should check with the drafting patent attorney. If you find the answer difficult to accept, ask your Patent Department.

Given that the patent application is legal writing, there will be a number of differences from ordinary writing. You may notice the use of the word "embodiment" or "version". Your invention can have different embodiments or versions, because an invention is first an idea.

The drafted patent application that you are reviewing *is a proposed document*. The patent attorney sent it to you with an implied question: "Is this right?" Equivalently, the question to you is: "Do you have any comments or corrections?" or "Do you approve?" The document could include substantive errors, which you should find in your review and correct.

10.6 Criteria for Reviewing the Drafted Patent Application

You should review your drafted patent application in terms of various criteria. The following criteria must be true for every US patent application, and you can use them as a starting checklist.

CR1)   In the specification, spelling errors have been found and fixed: ___

CR2)   In the specification, a section titled: "Brief Description of the Drawings" mentions all the provided drawings (e.g., FIG. 1, FIG. 2, etc.): ___

CR3)   All the reference numerals mentioned in the specification also appear in the drawings: ___

CR4)   All the reference numerals shown in the drawings also appear in the specification: ___

CR5)   ...

Your patent attorney or Patent Department may supply additional criteria. In any event, aspects that do not seem correct should be part of your feedback.

10.7 The Updated Drafted Patent Application

The patent drafter will receive your feedback and will send you an updated drafted patent application. The status will be the same as before: if you approve it, then the updated patent application will be filed as is. Otherwise, you should send your comments.

You should review the updated drafted patent application. In some instances, you only need to review the changes made by the patent attorney from the earlier draft.

In some instances the patent attorney might have disagreed with a change you proposed earlier. The patent attorney does not start by knowing your invention better than you do, but typically knows patenting techniques much better than you do. When the patent attorney disagrees with a comment you made, he or she should also be able to explain why. Of course, the explanation could be legal and, if you are not satisfied, you should involve someone from your Patent Department.

Many patent applications are resolved in this second iteration. The iterations are complete when the end result is text and drawings that everyone agrees upon are ready to file.

10.8   Who Will Be Named as the Inventor(s)?

The patent application will name one or more people as the inventors. Some drafted patent applications include a cover page that lists the proposed inventors. In those instances, any omissions or disagreements can be identified faster.

The final time to resolve who should be listed as an inventor occurs when the drafted patent application is finalized for filing. If there is a dispute, the Patent Department or the patent attorney will take into account the story of each contributor, apply the legal rules, and decide accordingly who should be listed.

Disagreements can be resolved by paying attention to some general rules. First, *one can be listed as an inventor even if* that person is not an engineer, scientist, or other technical person. Keep in mind that knowingly omitting an inventor is wrong, illegal, and can invalidate a resulting patent.

Second, *one should not be listed as an inventor if* that person's *only* attribute is that he or she:
(a)   ranks higher in the company than one of the inventors,
(b)   provided the funding that generated the idea or the patenting,
(c)   wrote the IRF on behalf of the original inventor without adding anything,
(d)   has done other work in this area, or
(e)   knows, works with, or is a friend with one or more of the other inventors.

Third, someone who independently thought of the same idea, and even wrote it in their Engineering Notebook *might* not be listed as an inventor if he or she:
(a)   did not work with the inventors who submitted the IRF, or from their IRF, or
(b)   did not report the invention for patenting in his or her own IRF.

There are other criteria for more refined factual differences. Your patent attorney can resolve them.

10.9   The Inventor Legal Forms for Signing

Every inventor must sign one or more **inventor legal forms**. When signed, these forms are sent to the Patent Office as parts the patent application.

After the application is ready for filing, *do not delay signing your inventor legal forms*. Delaying past a certain point costs your company extra money and work.

Your patent attorney or Patent Department will decide which set of forms will apply in your case. Forms may be combined so that you need to sign fewer times. Sometimes you may have to sign additional forms for your company to file also in foreign countries.

One of these forms for the United States is called the **Oath or Declaration**. With this form, you are declaring that you are indeed an inventor or a coinventor in the invention of the patent application that is being filed.

Another such form is the **Assignment** form. With this form you transfer your patent rights for the invention to your company. As we saw in chapter 4, this is likely part of your Employment Agreement.

One more form can be a **Power of Attorney** document. With this form, as a named inventor, you are permitting the patent attorney to prosecute the patent application with the Patent Office in an effort to make it become a patent.

Before you sign the forms, check your name, address, and also the name of your company. Harried people can make mistakes. If anything appears incorrectly, ask what to do.

10.10 The Patent Application Will Be Filed

After you sign and return the inventor legal forms, the drafted and approved patent application will be filed with the Patent Office. Figure 10C shows the timing of the filing.

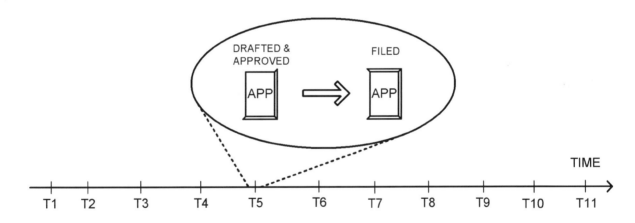

FIG. 10C – YOUR DRAFTED & APPROVED PATENT APPLICATION BECOMES FILED WITH THE PATENT OFFICE

© PATENT INTRODUCTIONS, INC.®
2014 www.patent-introductions.com

Now you have mostly finished what you had to do for this case. Going forward, others will work on it. Officially, you may not hear anything for months or even a few years.

10.11 Update Your Personal Patent Organizer

You may want to *update your Personal Patent Organizer regarding the filing*. The more data you capture, the easier it will be to find this patent application in the future.

For your records, get the **exact title** of the patent application as filed. This will likely be the title as in the last drafted patent application that was sent to you. Exact titles make for very well-targeted patent searches. Of course, the title may be changed during prosecution or in a child patent application.

Try to identify the **Attorney Docket Number** for this patent application. These are numbers that Patent Departments and patent law firms use to keep track of patent applications. There may be more than one number, one from each organization that handles your patent application. You may see these numbers in the header of an email that forwards the inventor legal forms to you or in the footer of a patent application or of the documents you signed. The docket numbers will serve until you have the tracking number of the Patent Office itself, as we will see later.

10.12 Update Your Calendar for the Expected Publication Date

You can anticipate the expected publication of your patent application, and create a reminder to search for it at that time. This will help with your Personal Patent Organizer later on, in case your company does not have a patent watch program.

After the application is finalized and you have signed the forms, you can ask your patent attorney *approximately which month the patent application will be published*—will it be the usual 18 months from filing plus maybe a week?[36] You will be trying to understand when the publication delay will start and end for this application. If there has been a provisional patent application, the publication delay may have started from the filing date of the provisional. The publication delay may be much shorter for child patent applications. The publication delay may be altogether different for US applications— in fact the application might not be published at all while pending.

Then, put a reminder in your calendar for the expected date of publication. The reminder can be for you to *search for your published patent application* on the internet.

---

[36] Remember, typically filing happens shortly after you sign the forms.

10.13 Update Your Calendar for the 19-Month Clearance Milestone

Consider whether this patent application is for a product that your company is developing. If so, you can anticipate the **19-Month Clearance Milestone** that we will describe in the next chapter.

Find the day that is 19 months from when you signed the inventor legal forms. Let's call it the **19-month date**. After the 19-month date, many of the patent applications filed by rivals before your patent application will have necessarily been published, and therefore will have become findable by a search.

Then put a reminder in your calendar for the 19-month date. The reminder can be for you to *do an updated patent clearance search for what your patent application covers*.

The 19-month date could be about the same as the date of the other reminder, which we mentioned in the previous section for searching for the publication. This is fine, but the tasks are different.

10.14 Update Any Relevant Internal Presentations

The patent application is now confidential within your company. Some benefits start now.

Look at the drawings of the patent application. Think of where in your other work you can reuse them. Can you add them in any presentations? If you do, you can also indicate that they are from a pending patent application.

If the patent application is about a product you are developing, inform the project manager that a patent application has been filed and what the title is. When the project manager gives a status presentation about the product, he or she will want to report that your patent application has been filed. This status presentation will become the source for the eventual **Product Patent Report**.

In fact, filing the patent application itself is one of the milestones for product clearance—we can call it the **Filing Clearance Milestone**. The big news is that time range TRA of Figure 3G has ended and time range TRB has started. Accordingly, *the invisible type of patent business risk of infringing (PBR-1) has finally stopped being renewed*; the Cut-Off Time of Figure 3H has been reached, and the Cut-Off Effect for any rival patent application filed afterward will have started.

If New Product Development is already proceeding on the product, perhaps at this time there might not be another Business Analysis Review, such as the one of Figure 3A. However, if the project had not started, then its Business Analysis Review could be that of Figure 10D.

Updated Note N1 indicates that, for the feature of this patent application, strategies PSD4 and PSI1 of Figure 3B have been implemented.

BUSINESS ANALYSIS REVIEW – COMPUTATION OF NPV
NEW PROJECT: [NAME]

DEVELOPMENT COST	$...	
RAMP-UP COST	$...	
MARKETING & SUPPORT COST	$... / year	
UNIT PRODUCTION COST	$... / unit	
PRODUCTION VOLUME	... units / year	
SALES VOLUME	... units / year	*N1, *N2
UNIT PRICE	$... / unit	*N2
SALES REVENUE	$...	*N1, *N2
PROJECT NPV	**$...**	*N1, *N2

*N1 PBR-1) PATENT BUSINESS RISK
    OF INFRINGING A PATENT: * VISIBLE TYPE: There is some; we have continued searching and clearing the patents we find.

    * INVISIBLE TYPE: For feature in the patent application we just filed: there is some risk up to (filing date). Beyond that date, this type of risk is no longer being renewed, even if we postpone entering the market. Patent searches & clearance will continue.

*N2 PBR-2) PATENT BUSINESS RISK
    OF BEING FOLLOWED: We may have been the first to apply for patent; if we succeed in patenting, rivals may be deterred.

FIG. 10D – PROJECT'S BUSINESS ANALYSIS REVIEW (FILING CLEARANCE MILESTONE: SEARCHED, THEN FILED PATENT APPLICATION)

© PATENT INTRODUCTIONS, INC. ®
2014 www.patent-introductions.com

As Figure 10D indicates, searches should be repeated periodically, because they become stale as time passes. At this time 18 months have not yet passed since your patent application was filed, and searches still reveal patent applications filed before yours, as they publish. These need to be cleared. If they are patent applications, they need to be monitored.

10.15 Maybe You Will Receive a Small Patent-Filing Bonus

After the patent application is filed, your company may give you a small patent-filing bonus as an additional reward for inventing and filing a patent application for your company. This is different from a possible patent-issuance bonus that we will discuss in the next chapter. Keep in mind that sometimes companies have good reasons for not paying such bonuses.

The patent-filing bonus may arrive in a few weeks or a few months. Do not be surprised if a large company needs 6 months to pay it due its large bureaucracy.

Note that sometimes mistakes do happen. If you hear or receive nothing for a few months after filing, it is acceptable to ask discreetly whether your company has a bonus program, and if so, what the status of your bonus is. When you do ask, identify which application you mean by at least the **Attorney Docket Number**. (Patent Departments deal with a blizzard of such information, and it is often hard for them to identify which particular application you are asking about without its docket number.)

> **Chapter Summary**
>
> In this chapter, we saw how your approved IRF will become a filed patent application. A patent attorney will read it, likely interview you, and draft a patent application for your review and approval. After you send your comments, the patent application can be updated. Then you will sign the inventor legal forms, and the patent application will be filed with the Patent Office. You can update your Personal Patent Organizer, calendar, and your presentations.

Notes:

11

THE NEXT TWO DECADES

11.1 Your Patent Application Is Filed and Pending

Now your regular non-provisional patent application has just been filed and has **Patent Pending** status. Figure 11A shows where you are in the process, using the time line of Figure 6A. Your patent application is under its publication delay time, so a patent search cannot find it yet.

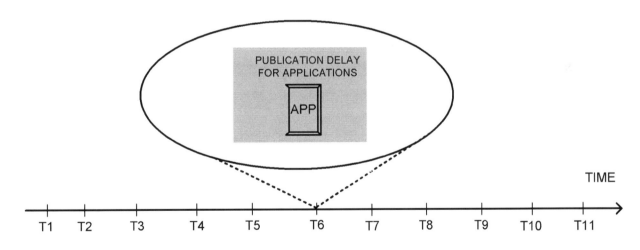

FIG. 11A – YOUR PATENT APPLICATION HAS JUST BECOME FILED

© PATENT INTRODUCTIONS, INC. ®
2014 www.patent-introductions.com

The process is now out of your hands. In fact, you may often not be told what is happening. The rest of this chapter can help you observe the process and benefit from the progress of your patent application, especially in the context when you are developing a new product, and your filed patent application covers a feature of it.

11.2 Your Patent Application Becomes Published While Pending

One day, your pending patent application will likely be published by the Patent Office, as seen in Figure 11B. For the time that this happens, hopefully, you will have put a reminder in your calendar to search for your patent application, as we suggested in the previous chapter. Recall that your application might *not* be published if it had been filed in the United States and your company had requested it not be published.

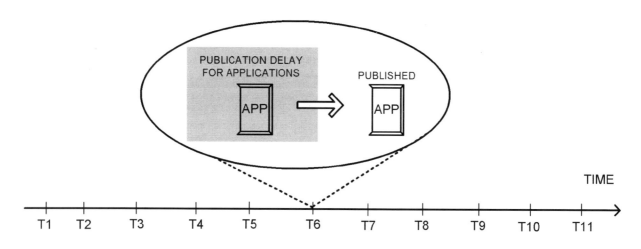

FIG. 11B – YOUR FILED PATENT APPLICATION BECOMES PUBLISHED WHILE PENDING

© PATENT INTRODUCTIONS, INC. ®
2014 www.patent-introductions.com

Since your application has been published, it is now findable by a patent search. So search for it. Use the data in your Personal Patent Organizer. Search for the invention title and your name as inventor. Or, if you know any listed coinventors, search for their names along with yours—this tends to restrict the search results.

Your search should find your newly published patent application. If 20 months have passed from when you signed the forms and you cannot find it, it is acceptable to ask your Patent Department or patent attorney about it. In that case, you should ask by referring to the **Attorney Docket Number**.

When you do find your newly published patent application, recall that it is still an **application**, which means: **not (yet) a patent**. What you see is only a snapshot of how your patent application is now pending in the Patent Office. You may notice that some of the claims are listed as canceled; when this is done, it is intentional and often not final. For example, in some instances the same document might be filed again later as a child patent application that includes the claims that are now canceled.

Once your search finds your patent application, there is more that you can do.

First, *update your Personal Patent Organizer* with data that you can identify from your now published patent application. This data includes the **document number**, the **publication date**, the **Application Serial Number**, and the **filing date**. With these, you can track your document more easily in the future.

Second, *try to find an image file of the official document that the Patent Office created*. An example of an image file is a pdf file. Although Patent Offices typically do not offer pdf files, other free web services do. Store the image file with your other invention records.

11.3 The 19-Month Clearance Milestone for Managing the Risk of Infringing

If your patent application is for an invention that your company is developing into a product, then another milestone for managing your risk of infringing comes on the **19-month date**, i.e. 19 months after your non-provisional patent application has been filed. We can call this the **19-Month Clearance Milestone**. Hopefully you will have put a reminder for this date in your calendar, as we suggested in the previous chapter.

From what you will see below, the 19-Month Clearance Milestone does not occur exactly 19 months after any specific date; strictly speaking, it occurs 18 months plus maybe two weeks from the exact date that your non-provisional patent application was actually filed. Typically, however, when you proofread your patent application for filing, you will not know exactly when it will be filed, but you can fairly guess that it will be a few days after you sign the inventor legal forms. So, given this uncertainty, choosing this date to be 19 months from when you sign the inventor legal forms is usually a convenient way to decide on the time of your 19-Month Clearance Milestone.

Let's review what will have happened by this milestone. Your patent application will likely have been published. More importantly, many of the possibly earlier-filed threatening rival patent applications *will have also been published by then*, because their publication delay will have ended. These are the patent applications that were filed within time range TRA of Figure 3G, and they were your rivals' substantially last chance to patent what is in your patent application before you, and thus **cut off** your patent application. After that, any patent applications they may have filed will likely eventually be cut off by your filed patent application.

The **19-month date** is therefore a very good time to do an updated patent clearance search, and this is what makes it a milestone. Of course, if your company has a vigorous **patent watch program** in place, you might not need to do an updated patent search, because you will have been learning of such rival patent applications as they publish.

In the worst case, you will find a patent application that was filed before yours for the same or a similar invention. The invisible type of the patent business risk of infringing (PBR-1 of Figure 2D) will have become mostly visible. Plus, you may be precluded from receiving a patent.

On the other hand, if your updated search on the 19-month date is favorable, you will have a higher chance for two good outcomes. First, the chance of the invisible type of patent business risk of infringing (PBR-1) will have become less, as to the feature of your patent application. Second, your patent application will have a correspondingly better chance of actually becoming a patent, which can further protect the product in the future.

Even if your updated search on the 19 month date is favorable, your confidence level should not become absolute, for at least two reasons. First, you will need a high confidence in how your searches are done. So, your updated patent search should be with terms that are finding at least your newly published patent application. Second, even on the 19-month date, your search will not be able to find patent applications that will not be published on their 18th month, such as in Figure 6B. You can decide accordingly how your project is impacted, and what your level of confidence should be.

Again, if New Product Development is already proceeding with the product, perhaps at this time there might not be another Business Analysis Review of the type that we saw in Figure 3A. However, if the project has not started yet, then its Business Analysis Review could be that of Figure 11C, with regard to this patent application.

PATENT READY®

BUSINESS ANALYSIS REVIEW – COMPUTATION OF NPV
NEW PROJECT: [NAME]

DEVELOPMENT COST	$...	
RAMP-UP COST	$...	
MARKETING & SUPPORT COST	$... / year	
UNIT PRODUCTION COST	$... / unit	
PRODUCTION VOLUME	... units / year	
SALES VOLUME	... units / year	*N1, *N2
UNIT PRICE	$... / unit	*N2
SALES REVENUE	$...	*N1, *N2
PROJECT NPV	**$...**	*N1, *N2

*N1 PBR-1) PATENT BUSINESS RISK OF INFRINGING A PATENT:

* VISIBLE TYPE: There is some; we have spent some resources in patent searches, and we have cleared what we found today. By now we have also found and cleared most of what was filed before our own patent application, and published while pending.

* INVISIBLE TYPE: For feature in the patent application we have filed: this type of risk has stopped being renewed. Patent searches to continue only for any few late-publishing patent applications and issuing patents.

*N2 PBR-2) PATENT BUSINESS RISK OF BEING FOLLOWED:

We may have been first to apply for patent; if we succeed in patenting, rivals may be deterred.

FIG. 11C – PROJECT'S BUSINESS ANALYSIS REVIEW (19-MONTH CLEARANCE MILESTONE: AFTER FILING, THEN SEARCHED & CLEARED AGAIN)

© PATENT INTRODUCTIONS, INC.®
2014 www.patent-introductions.com

Since 19 months have passed from when you filed your patent application, Figure 11C reflects that most of the patent applications filed before yours have also been published and are findable. Statistically these are the majority of those that could **cut off** your application, *and are no longer invisible.*

In Figure 11C it is assumed that you have been clearing what you have been finding. The Business Analysis Review shows an increased comfort level about the risk of the feature in your patent application infringing another patent. Now the risk is reduced to mostly looking for the statistically fewer patent applications being published for the first time more than 18 months after being filed, and patents issuing without having been published as applications.

11.4 Third-Party Prior Art May Be Submitted against Your Patent Application

Now that your patent application is a public document, your company's rivals can also find it if they happen to search. Or, if they have a patent watch program in place, they are likely to see it shortly after it becomes published.

Upon finding your patent application, a rival may want to challenge it. The rival may determine that they have prior art references that are applicable against the patentability of your invention. So, they might report these references to the Patent Office via a **third-party prior art submission** against your patent application, as we saw in chapter 8.

11.5 Reporting Follow-Up Inventions

Now there is not much for you to do. Consider reporting any follow-up inventions. For example, if the application relates to a product you are developing, are there subsequent related improvements? Has the design shifted from what you originally reported for patenting?

When you write the next **Invention Reporting Form** (IRF) for a follow-up invention, do mention your earlier and now pending patent application by its Attorney Docket Number. Perhaps your new IRF will become a **child patent application**. Of course, if a few drawings in your earlier patent application apply in your follow-up invention, use them!

11.6 The Patent Office Examines Your Pending Application

Once your patent application is filed, the Patent Office will put it in a queue, which is substantially of the type "first in, first out," although there can be exceptions. In some rare instances, your patent application will be substantially accelerated within the queue.

At some time, your patent application will be examined. In terms of Figure 11D, the application is at time T7.

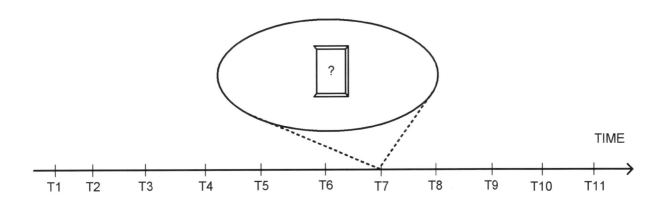

FIG. 11D – YOUR FILED & PENDING PATENT APPLICATION IS EXAMINED BY PATENT OFFICE

The Patent Office will examine your application to determine whether all the requirements for patenting are met. If the Patent Office determines that they are, then it will allow your patent application to become a patent. Otherwise, it will write to your patent attorney a document called an **Office Action**.

In chapter 5, we saw that the requirements for a patent application are both formal and substantive. The substantive requirements of a patent application include that the claims of your patent application be legally patentable over the applicable prior art. We show this in Figure 11E, whose left side is similar to that of Figures 5E and 8G, except that the Patent Office is not subjected to the publication delay. In other words, they can see all the pending applications, even the ones that are not published yet. The applicable prior art may also properly include products that were introduced to market before the filing date of your patent application, but often the Patent Office does not have a way of knowing about them.

The Patent Office will make a legal determination of whether the applicable prior art prevents the claims from being patentable. The determination is based on legal concepts that are beyond the scope of this book. Then the Patent Office will send your patent attorney the Office Action.

Your patent attorney will respond to the Office Action to try to fix any problems that can be fixed. If the prior art references are close to your claimed invention, your patent attorney may need to reduce the scope of the claims in the pending application. If no claim is allowed, there will be no patent.

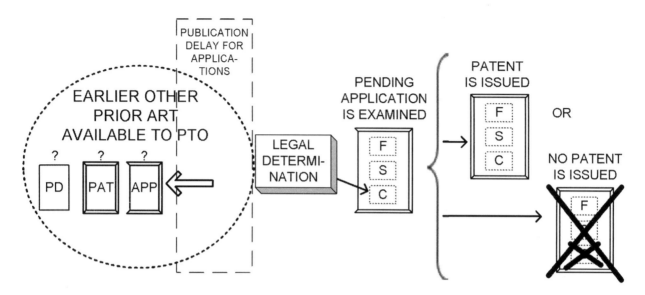

FIG. 11E – PATENT OFFICE EXAMINES CLAIMS OF YOUR PENDING PATENT APPLICATION AGAINST PRIOR ART

© PATENT INTRODUCTIONS, INC. ®
2014 www.patent-introductions.com

As we can see in Figure 11E, even though the investment was made to create and file a patent application, the patent application can fail at the point when the Patent Office examines it. In this case, the investment of patenting can generate inadequate returns (patent business risk PBR-3 of Figure 2D). It was this risk that you were trying to reduce, when you did a patentability prior art search before submitting the IRF that became this patent application. After all, if you were not going to get a patent in the end, you and your company might as well not have invested the effort to apply.

Ultimately, if at least one claim is allowed, then the patent application can be issued as a patent. This will happen if your company chooses to pay the additional required fees to the Patent Office. The rest of the time line assumes that your patent application will be allowed to issue into a patent.

11.7   Helping with Responding to the Office Action

The substantive requirements for patentability include proving legally that the claims are patentable over the prior art references. Very often patent attorneys read the references themselves and respond without involving you, because they understand the invention anyway. Moreover, and this may seem strange, at this time it does not matter much anymore what your invention is, as much as what the filed patent application *says* that your invention is. Of course you ensured that the patent application said correctly what your invention is when you proofread it before signing the inventor legal forms, and before the patent application was filed. If now you find an error that you did not find then, ask your patent attorney if there is anything that can be done at this time.

Your patent attorney may ask you to help with responding to the Office Action in two particular circumstances. First, you may be given a prior art reference that the Patent Office sent, and be asked to explain it.

Second, in some legal systems and in some circumstances, your patent attorney may ask you about the facts of your invention, such as which day you invented what. Based on these facts, your patent attorney may then be able to draft an affidavit for you to sign. Of course, you would sign the affidavit only if it is true.

Your patent attorney will do the rest.

11.8 The Examination Clearance Milestone for Managing the Risk of Infringing

The time of examination (T7 in Figure 11D) can be another milestone for managing your risk of infringing—it can be called the **Examination Clearance Milestone**. The Patent Office will have sent your patent attorney the Office Action. The Office Action can list prior art references, including those that were used against the patentability of your invention, plus others possibly applicable in the art.

Your patent attorney will typically address the Office Action and the prior art from the perspective of *patentability*. However, it is possible that your patent attorney has not been asked to perform any clearance of your product.

Read the Office Action to see which prior art references are mentioned, *above and beyond those used against the patentability of your invention*. Ensure that your product will clear them as well. If uncertain, discuss the results with your Patent Department. Even if there is a risk of infringing (PBR-1 of Figure 2D), at least it has become better known.

The clearance that you do at this stage is a milestone because these prior art references came from an independent Patent Examiner at the Patent Office, who could also look for any other patent applications for the same feature that had not become public yet. The Patent Examiner might have even delayed the examination of your application until such other patent application would first become public.

Of course, *the prior art references in the list from the Patent Office cannot be trusted as a complete product clearance search*—and it was not intended to be one. Rather, it was intended as a list for a search against the patentability of your patent application. As such, the Patent

Office's list is not complete for a clearance search. Indeed, the task of the Patent Office during examination is to try to give a few sound **rejections** as to the patentability of all the claims in your application; once it has, the task is done and the Patent Examiner may have fairly stopped searching for additional prior art references to give more rejections—but which you would still need to clear if you find.

Again, if the project is already proceeding, perhaps at this time there might not be another Business Analysis Review. If, however, the project had not started before, then its Business Analysis Review for this feature could be similar to that of Figure 11C, if the prior art references in the Office Action are cleared.

Note that the Examination Clearance Milestone may be reached more than once, for the same patent application. For example, your patent attorney may be able to overcome the rejections of the first Office Action that were based on some prior art references that the Patent Examiner found. In this case, however, the Patent Examiner is permitted to search again, find additional prior art references, and form additional rejections in an additional Office Action, etc. In such a case, you would have to clear the additional prior art references, and so on.

11.9   Your Patent Application Becomes Issued as a Patent

One day your pending patent application may be issued by the Patent Office as a patent. Figure 11F shows this as a diagram.

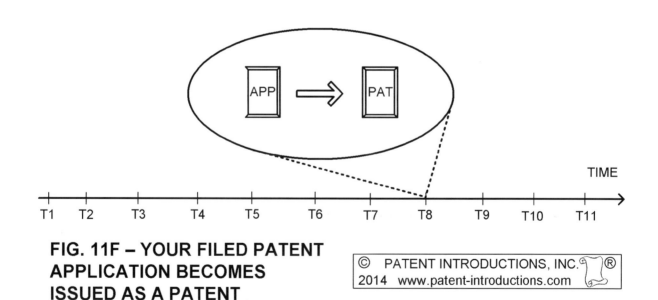

FIG. 11F – YOUR FILED PATENT APPLICATION BECOMES ISSUED AS A PATENT

Congratulations! Now you have become a named inventor in an issued patent.

Your patent is now findable by searching the website of the Patent Office, if you knew to search for it. In reality, you will learn about your patent in different ways. For example, your company might inform you in some way—you might receive a patent-issuance bonus. Recall that, just like with patent-filing bonuses, sometimes companies have good reasons to not pay patent-issuance bonuses.

Now you can search for your patent. Use the data in your Personal Patent Organizer and especially the Patent Office's unique serial number.

Once you find your patent, there is more that you can do. First, *update your Personal Patent Organizer* with the patent data, which is different from the patent application data. Identify from your patent the **patent number** and the **patent date**. Also try to find an image file of the official patent document, as you did with your published patent application document.

11.10   A Patent Protects the Product Better

Given the new patent, your Patent Department may want to update your company's **patent marking**. If the patent is for a product that you are familiar with, your Patent Department may ask you particulars, to determine whether the issued patent claims cover the product.

If New Product Development is proceeding, you may want to notify the appropriate project manager that the patent has issued. He or she will appreciate knowing this for the next status report.

In the context of New Product Development, the issuance of your patent is another milestone, which can be called the **Patent Issuance Milestone**. Issuance means that that Examination Milestones have been completed, and the existence of an earlier-filed application for the same feature has become even less likely.

Again, if New Product Development is already proceeding, perhaps at this time there might not be another Business Analysis Review. If, however, the project had not started before, then its Business Analysis Review for that patent could be that of Figure 11G, where it is assumed that all prior art references from any Office Actions have been cleared.

BUSINESS ANALYSIS REVIEW – COMPUTATION OF NPV
NEW PROJECT: [NAME]

DEVELOPMENT COST	$...	
RAMP-UP COST	$...	
MARKETING & SUPPORT COST	$... / year	
UNIT PRODUCTION COST	$... / unit	
PRODUCTION VOLUME	... units / year	
SALES VOLUME	... units / year	*N1, *N2
UNIT PRICE	$... / unit	*N2
SALES REVENUE	$...	*N1, *N2
PROJECT NPV	**$...**	*N1, *N2

*N1 PBR-1) PATENT BUSINESS RISK
    OF INFRINGING A PATENT: * VISIBLE TYPE: For our patented feature, this type of risk has been understood better since our patent application was examined.

    * INVISIBLE TYPE: For our patented feature, this type of risk is no longer being renewed, and became a lot less likely since our patent application was examined.

*N2 PBR-2) PATENT BUSINESS RISK
    OF BEING FOLLOWED: We have a patent on the feature; rivals may be deterred.

FIG. 11G – PROJECT'S BUSINESS ANALYSIS REVIEW (PATENT ISSUANCE MILESTONE)

© PATENT INTRODUCTIONS, INC. ®
2014 www.patent-introductions.com

Moreover, because of the issuance, the product differentiation from rival products can become more durable. Accordingly, the unit price might be higher, and the higher price might be sustainable for a far longer time. As we saw in chapter 3, this can become a situation of IP Alignment. Rivals may be deterred from copying a feature that the patent protects, or may spend more resources trying to avoid it.

11.11   Revision of Granted Patents

A patent is never final. Even after being granted, a patent can be revised by the Patent Office that issued it, or by a court. A revision is possible because, as we saw earlier, the Patent

Office may have missed some prior art, and therefore sometimes a patent is granted when it should not have been. See Figure 11H.

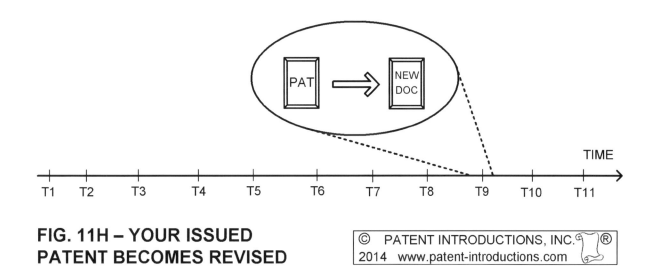

FIG. 11H – YOUR ISSUED PATENT BECOMES REVISED

As we saw in chapter 8, there are different kinds of **patent revision proceedings**. A patent revision proceeding, such as a reissue proceeding, can be initiated by your company. Typically, however, a patent revision proceeding against your patent will be forced by another party. The reason will be that this other party finds your patent threatening and wants to limit it or invalidate it completely.

During a patent revision proceeding, the Patent Office typically examines the patent again. It uses prior art references, some of which might not have been available for consideration before the patent was issued. Your patent attorney might not contact you, for the same reasons that he or she did not contact you for responding to an Office Action.

After the revision proceeding, the Patent Office will typically issue a new document, or a certificate about the revised patent. The new document will indicate that this patent has been through the revision proceeding. The revised patent's claims could be broader, the same, or narrower than in the issued patent, or the new document may have no claims at all. In the last case, the patent is no longer valid—it has become **invalidated**.

11.12   Is Your Patent Infringed?

It is possible that your patent will be infringed by another company. It is not your job to monitor for that, unless you are told otherwise by someone with authority in your company. Rather, you should focus on your daily duties.

Regardless, when you have no other duties ("free time"), it will be helpful to your company if you *research* whether your patent is infringed. *There are restrictions on such research, however.* For example, you are not authorized to spend company funds for this research unless you receive permission in advance. You may not contact anyone outside your company or do anything that could let people outside your company know or suspect that you are researching the possibility. It would not be good if they suspected this, because these other people might start thinking reciprocal thoughts about their patents and your company's products. However eager you may be, you should not do anything illegal, either.[37] You may research only information that is public, such as websites, data sheets, rival products that you have access to, and so on.

Of course, recall that determining infringement means matching the claims of your company's patent to the rival product according to legal reasoning. This determination is something that you can start but you cannot complete with finality because it calls for a legal opinion, as described earlier. In the end you will not be certain, but perhaps you will have a strong idea about whether infringement is actually taking place.

If, after researching, you suspect that your patent is indeed infringed, you should notify the person responsible for patents in your company. Your notification could be an email as follows:

"Dear [person responsible for patents]:

I have discovered that our company's patent [number] is probably infringed by [product name] that is offered by [other company name]. Here is a link to a [photograph/data sheet/product announcement] of the [product name].

Best regards

[Your name]"

Beyond notifying that person, however, you should not publicize your finding within your company, lest the wrong rumor starts. In addition, *you should never contact about this matter anyone working for the rival company*. If you do, they may take steps to disadvantage you in a future patent litigation. Instead, ask your patent attorney what to do and how to do it.

A challenge with such research is an asymmetry of information between you and the recipient, such as your Patent Department. Your company will likely benefit from your notification, but the Patent Department will have good legal reasons to keep such information secret. So they may reply, "Thank you for your email," without ever telling you whether you are right or wrong, and that will be the end of their discussion with you. Do not be frustrated if they say nothing more to you, or if nothing seems to happen as a result of your notification.

---

[37] For example, pretending or "pretexting" to be someone you are not is illegal in many contexts, and you and your company may face adverse legal consequences if you do. Worse, your company may not be interested in defending you, and you will need to pay for your legal defense and deal with the consequences.

Most companies do not sue for patent infringement casually, because suing is a complicated, expensive, distracting, and often risky undertaking, and many variables must be considered first. In fact, you may never see any action. It could be that, thanks to your notification, your company will grant a license to the infringing other company for money, and that the license will not be publicized as is often the case.

11.13 Patent Litigation

As mentioned in chapter 2, patent litigation can start when two parties have a dispute that they cannot resolve by negotiation, mediation, or arbitration. Again, exploring or pursuing the dispute with another party is a business decision that will be made by others in your company.

Figure 11I shows a patent dispute that also involves a product. Nominally the dispute starts with the patentee asserting in a court that its patent is infringed by the rival's products. The accused side may raise various legal defenses—for example, allege that the patent is not infringed, perhaps because the product is a legal **workaround**; or that the patent is not valid, because there is applicable prior art that was not considered during the examination; or that the patent is not enforceable, perhaps because some rules were not followed in procuring the patent. Of course, you recognize from much of this book how your prior actions could have helped your company here.

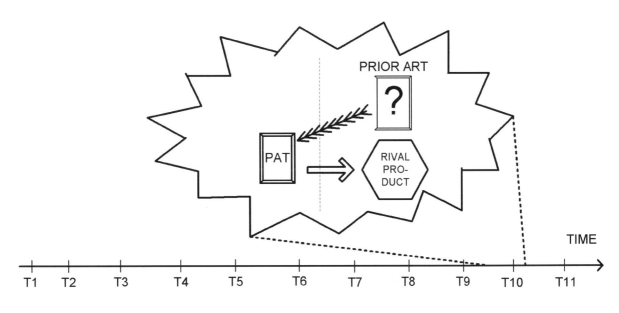

FIG. 11I – PATENT LITIGATION

In the United States, patent litigation includes a phase called **discovery**. Then there can be a trial, unless the parties settle before that. The process can last a few years. In other countries, the process can be faster or slower.

During the discovery phase, an attorney from the other side will have the opportunity to look at your company's documents. If you are the inventor, the documents would be records about the patent and its invention. If your company is the defendant, then the documents would be records as to whether you knew about the patent, whether you tried to respect it by designing around it, etc. The attorney will also ask you questions, and you must reply truthfully.

Discovery often happens long after patenting and product introduction. With the passage of time, memories fade. They can fade faster if you have changed employers by then. However, your written records persist. You do not want these documents to embarrass you, which is why you should be careful in what you write in the first place.

Your patent attorney will help you prepare as to what to expect. If you testify at trial, it also helps if you have the right mental attitude. Most people do not recognize that jurors, as a set, can be rather smart; your **humility** and **earnestness** will not antagonize them needlessly.

And always tell the truth.

11.14 Your Patent Expires

One day, without any notification to you, your patent will expire. In Figure 11J, that day is at time T11. That day is nominally about 20 years from when the original patent application was filed at time T5, but different factors can make that day come earlier or even later than 20 years.

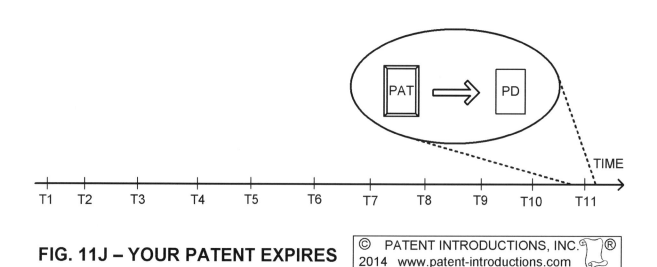

FIG. 11J – YOUR PATENT EXPIRES

When the patent expires, the document will not look any different to someone who finds it by searching. It remains as a publicly available document that teaches your invention. If a rival company starts using your invention after its patent has expired, the rival cannot be accused of infringing the patent.

> **Chapter Summary**
>
> In this chapter, we saw an accelerated time line of what happens after your patent application is filed until the end of the patent's life. The process is mainly out of your hands as your patent application becomes published, perhaps challenged by third parties, examined by the Patent Office, and hopefully issued as a patent. We also saw how, at various milestones, you can update your Patent Organizer and any Business Analysis Reviews.

Notes:

ABOUT PATENT INTRODUCTIONS, INC.

Patent Introductions, Inc. is a company whose mission is to publish materials that educate generally about patents without being particular enough to offer legal advice. Its website is at www.patent-introductions.com.

The contents of this book and any related websites are not legal advice. Purchasing, reading, or otherwise interacting with this book and any related websites does not form an attorney-client relationship with Patent Introductions, Inc., or with the author. Anyone wanting legal advice should contact a patent attorney.

ABOUT THE AUTHOR

Mr. Gregory T. Kavounas has been pursuing the generation of patent value for more than twenty years. While working in law firms, he procured patents in numerous technologies for his clients. Moreover, he has published articles on how patents could be written more effectively.

Mr. Kavounas has further worked as an in-house patent attorney, managing all aspects of the patent function in companies ranging from Fortune 500 to start-up. While doing so, he studied the dynamics at all levels of how inventions happen and how patent value is generated. Additionally, he has published on how Senior Management could manage these dynamics, for pursuing different patent strategies.

Mr. Kavounas holds a Bachelor of Science degree in Electrical Engineering from California Institute of Technology, a Master of Science degree in Electrical Engineering (Electrophysics-Optics) from University of Southern California, an Engineer degree in Electrical Engineering (Electrophysics-Optics) from University of Southern California, a Juris Doctorate from Loyola Law School (Los Angeles), and an Executive MBA from Seattle University. Before becoming a patent attorney, he worked as an engineer in the Defense Industry. Mr. Kavounas is a Senior Member of the Institute of Electrical and Electronics Engineers (IEEE).

ACKNOWLEDGMENTS

I am grateful to my parents, Apostolos and Vassiliki, for bringing me into this life and raising me. My father further taught me to do not only what was asked of me, but also to ponder its purpose, determine what else needs doing for that purpose, and do that too. I have also been helped by teachers and mentors in life, patent law, and patent practice.

I am grateful to my inventors. A repeating reward of being a patent attorney is being exposed to their new ideas. It was their questions, concerns, and sometimes misunderstandings that helped me realize that, regarding patents, they do not always fully understand what happens around them or why. The law, and especially patent law, can seem strange to those who have not learned it in depth, and it is not always clear how to work within it successfully. Hence, this book was created.

I want to thank Karin Bartels, Kirk Haselton, Lawrence Lycke, Richard C. Nova, Ian C. Nova, Ron Paulsen, and George Tolomiczenko for giving me valuable feedback and ideas that I used to enrich the text. I further want to thank Stephen Lynch for help with the manuscript.

Greg Kavounas

DEDICATION

This book is dedicated to my wife, Angeliki, and my son, Panayiotis, whose sustained personal support and encouragement made it possible.

GLOSSARY

19-Month Clearance Milestone
In the context of clearing a prospective new product from the invisible type of the patent business risk of infringing (PBR-1), a milestone of increased confidence that is reached in the event that the search of the 19-month date is clear, from knowing that many of any possible rival patent applications filed before it will have been published and thus become findable by then.

19-month date
A date that can be calendared, chosen to occur conveniently 19 months after an inventor signs the inventor legal forms for a patent application to be filed, the calendared date to include a reminder to search against the filed patent application.

Abstract
A section of the specification of a patent document.

African Regional Intellectual Property Organization (ARIPO)
An organization formed according to an international patent agreement.

ambient information
Ambient information is knowledge and experience readily shared by one's coworkers about one's industry, products, projects, etc.

art
A field of an invention or a patent application.

assign
A legal activity of transferring patent rights.

assignee
An entity to which a patent has been assigned; the assignee at the time a patent is issued is found in the formalities of the associated patent document.

Assignment form
An inventor legal form.

Attorney Docket Number
A number assigned internally within a company to keep track of filed patent applications.

authorized private exceptions (to confidentiality)
Disclosures about your company that are authorized to be made under a Non-Disclosure Agreement (NDA).

authorized public exceptions (to confidentiality)
Disclosures about your company that are authorized to be made to the public.

Background
An optional section of the specification of a patent document.

barrier to entry
An obstacle that makes it difficult for an entity to enter a market.

Brief Description of the Drawings
A section of the specification of a patent document.

Business Analysis Review
A review for making a business decision of creating a new product.

Certificate of Correction
An addendum to a patent document, intended to correct errors.

challenge (a patent application)
(verb) The act of where, while a patent application is pending, a rival takes action to diminish its prospects of becoming issued as a patent.

child patent
A patent that results from a child patent application.

child patent application
A patent application filed in the same country as, and claiming priority from, another filed ("parent") patent application, both in the same patent family.

claims
A part of a patent document that determines the legal coverage of a patent.

coinventors
A group of two or more persons who have cooperated in generating an idea that could be patented.

column numbers
Numbers along the top of a US patent document intended to identify columns of text.

commoditized
A state where a product or service lacks differentiation from rival products or services.

compensatory damages
In a court verdict finding patent infringement, a portion of the assessed money damages that the infringer has to pay and is attributable to the fact that the patent was infringed.

competitive convergence
A notion about the extent of competition by different entities in similar products and in patenting.

Continuation
A type of a child patent application.

Continuation-in-Part
A type of a child patent application.

contract patent searcher
A professional who can be hired to perform prior art searches.

cover page
The first page of a patent document.

cut off
(verb) What happens according to the Cut-Off Effect when the earlier disclosure prevents a later-filed patent application from becoming issued as a patent.

Cut-Off Effect
The phenomenon that a patent application is prevented from becoming a patent if, before it is filed, its disclosure has already been made in another way, such as by an earlier-filed patent application.

Cut-Off Time
The time that the earlier disclosure is made, which cuts off all patent applications filed afterward.

defensive patent strategy
A patent strategy intended to mitigate a product's patent business risk of infringing (PBR-1).

defensive publication
A publication disclosing an idea made in a forum appropriate for preventing others to patent the idea.

Department of Commerce
A branch of the US Government.

dependent claim
A claim in a patent document that references at least one other claim.

design around
(phrasal verb) An act of designing a product with the further constraint of trying to avoid the legal coverage of a patent.

design patent
A type of patent, at least in the US, intended to protect shapes and the appearance of things.

Detailed Description
A section of the specification of a patent document.

differentiation
A state of a product or service being distinguishable from rival products or services, so it can be more attractive in the market place and/or command a higher price.

discovery
A phase during litigation in the US, where the opposite party has the right to look at a company's documents and ask questions of employees.

Divisional
A type of a child patent application.

document number
A unique number for a patent application publication document, found in the formalities of the associated patent document.

drawings
A part of the specification of a patent document.

duty of confidentiality
An employee's frequent obligation towards his or her employer.

duty of loyalty (legal)
An employee's obligation towards his or her employer.

Employment Agreement
A legal agreement about the employment of an employee by a company.

Eurasian Patent Organization
An organization formed according to an international patent agreement.

European Patent Convention (EPC)
A set of international patent agreements.

Examination Clearance Milestone
In the context of clearing a prospective new product from the invisible type of the patent business risk of infringing (PBR-1), a milestone of increased confidence that is reached in the event that the Patent Office's examination is clear, from knowing that many of any possible rival patent applications filed before it that a Patent Examiner would consider relevant would have been published by then and used in an Office Action against the filed patent application.

false marking
Patent Marking that suggests that a product or process is protected by an issued patent or a pending application at a time when it is not.

Filing Clearance Milestone
In the context of clearing a prospective new product from the invisible type of the patent business risk of infringing (PBR-1), a milestone of increased confidence that is reached from knowing that any subsequently filed rival patent application should be cut off.

filing date
A date that a patent application was filed that resulted in a patent, found in the formalities of the associated patent document.

follower
A company that executes the business strategy of following.

following
A business strategy of competing against a leader with a product that is similar, even identical to that of the leader.

formalities
A part of a patent document that includes administrative data about the patent.

Freedom To Operate (FTO)
A state of having mitigated a product's patent business risk of infringing (PBR-1).

Freedom To Operate (FTO) search
A patent clearance search.

future patenting
Patenting that has not been started yet.

Gulf Cooperation Council
An organization formed according to an international patent agreement.

idea submission number
A number assigned internally within a company to keep track of submitted IRFs; sometimes it is the same as the Attorney Docket Number.

independent claim
A claim in a patent document that does not reference any other of the claims.

Innovation Landscape
In a country, a web of people, education, culture, economic circumstances, institutions, and laws that relate to innovation.

innovator patent strategy
A patent strategy intended to mitigate a product's patent business risk of being followed (PBR-2).

Intellectual Property
A regime of laws that protect products of the mind such as inventions.

inter partes review
A type of a revision proceeding in the US.

Interactive patent strategies
A patent strategy pursued by an entity that requires another entity to cooperate.

international patent agreement
An agreement between countries to cooperate about patents, and/or to recognize a patent application filed in one country as an acceptable priority patent application in another.

invalidated (for an issued patent)
The result of a revision proceeding to a patent, when the legal coverage of the patent is completely eliminated.

invent
The activity of identifying a problem and a solution for it.

Invention Reporting Form (IRF)
A company form that must be used by a company inventor to report his or her invention, so as to enable the patenting process to start.

inventor
A person who has an idea that could be patented.

inventor legal form(s)
A legal form that an inventor must sign for a patent application to become filed with the Patent Office.

invisible type PBR-1 risk
A type of the patent business risk of infringing (PBR-1), which arises from patent applications that have not yet been published, and therefore cannot be found by a patent search.

IP
A frequent abbreviation for "Intellectual Property."

IP Alignment
The state where the legal coverage of an entity's patent protects the entity's product or feature.

legal deadline
A deadline by which an act must take place, or else it can no longer be done.

legal invalidity opinion
An opinion by a patent attorney, usually in writing, detailing why a claim of a patent should not be found valid.

legal non-infringement opinion
An opinion by a patent attorney, usually in writing, detailing why a proposed design avoids the legal coverage of a patent.

legal workaround
A workaround that legally avoids the patent it designed around.

license fee
A rent payable to the owner of a patent in exchange for permission to use the patent.

line numbers
Numbers in a US patent document intended to identify lines of text.

loss of IP
Loss of Intellectual Property rights, or loss of opportunity to obtain Intellectual Property rights.

market plane
A visualization device intended to show market transactions.

market share
A fraction of a relevant market that is captured by a product, over a given time.

money damages
In a court verdict finding patent infringement was committed, an amount of money that the infringer must pay to the owner of the patent for past infringement.

negative know-how
An accumulation of information about techniques that do *not* work well, or do not work at all, for building a product.

Net Present Value (NPV)
A statistic for determining an expected return if a contemplated new product is created.

nominal full term
The nominal time duration of when a patent is valid, prior to adjustments.

Non-Disclosure Agreement (NDA)
An agreement between two parties to exchange information and to keep confidential the information they learned this way.

Nordic Patent Institute
An organization formed according to an international patent agreement.

not obvious to a person having ordinary skill in an art
A legal requirement for an invention to be patentable.

novelty
A legal requirement for an invention to be patentable.

novelty search
A patentability search.

Oath or Declaration
An inventor legal form.

Office Action
A document that a Patent Office prepares and sends to the patent applicant that details why it is not allowing a patent application to become a patent.

Organisation Africaine de la Propriété Intellectuelle (OAPI)
An organization formed according to an international patent agreement.

parent patent
A patent that results from a parent patent application.

parent patent application
A patent application for which a child patent application has been filed.

past patenting
Patenting that has already been started.

patent
As a noun, a bundle of temporary legal rights; as a verb, the act of obtaining a patent.

patent agent
An individual qualified to represent a patent applicant.

patent applicant
An entity applying for a patent.

patent application
A document by which a patent applicant applies for a patent.

patent attorney
An individual qualified to represent a patent applicant, and who is also an attorney.

patent battles
Operations by entities that involve patents and can be adverse to other entities.

patent business opportunity to reserve future exclusive patent rights (PBO-1)
A business opportunity created for entities by a country's Patent System.

patent business risks and opportunities
Business risks imposed on, and business opportunities created for, entities by a country's Patent System.

patent business risk of infringing (PBR-1)
A business risk imposed on entities by a country's Patent System.

patent business risk that inadequate or no returns will be generated (PBR-3)
A business risk imposed on entities by a country's Patent System.

patent business risk that a new product will be followed or copied (PBR-2)
A business risk imposed on entities by a country's Patent System.

patent certificate
An original document that is given by the Patent Office to the owner of a newly issuing patent.

Patent Classification System
A system used by a Patent Office for classifying various arts.

patent clearance search
A patent search intended to mitigate a product's patent business risk of infringing (PBR-1) another's patent.

Patent Committee
An internal company committee that chooses which of the reported inventions to patent.

Patent Cooperation Treaty (PCT)
An international patent agreement.

patent date
A date that a patent was issued, found in the formalities of the associated patent document.

Patent Department
A department within a company that deals with patents.

patent dispute
A dispute between entities that involves a patent and possibly also a product.

patent document
A document published by the Patent Office about an issued patent, copies of which are freely available to the public.

patent family
A group of patents and patent applications generated for the same invention or for related inventions, sometimes from the same patent application.

patent infringement
At least the act of making, using, selling, or offering to sell an invention that is legally covered by a patent, without permission from the owner of the patent.

patent invalidation search
A prior art search intended to establish that a particular patent should have been granted with less broad a legal coverage, or not at all.

patent landscape
A visualization device intended to show the coverage of multiple patents.

patent landscape search
A patent search intended to reveal a patent landscape.

patent litigation
A patent battle fought in a court between at least an owner of a patent and a producer or importer of a product.

patent marking
An act of indicating on a company product the numbers of company patents that cover the product.

patent number
A unique number for a patent, found in the formalities of the associated patent document.

Patent Pending
A status of a product, if it is covered by a pending patent application.

patent plane
A visualization device intended to show patent operations.

patent race
A scenario where two rivals file patent applications for substantially the same invention; the scenario is called a race because the first one to file usually wins.

patent reading prism
A visualization device intended to help the reader mentally separate a patent into its basic parts.

patent-related facts
Facts significant for determining patent rights.

patent search
A search for prior art references that are patents, and which are legally applicable for a specific purpose.

patent strategies
Strategies pursued by entities to mitigate their patent business risks and capitalize on their patent business opportunities.

Patent System
A system of laws and institutions within a country's Innovation Landscape.

patent title
A title of a patent, found in the formalities of the associated patent document.

patent watch program
A program where typically automated patent searches are performed periodically in specified fields of interest.

patentability search
A search for prior art references intended to establish that a particular invention has not been disclosed before.

PCT application
A patent application filed according to the Patent Cooperation Treaty.

person having ordinary skill in an art
A hypothetical person postulated by law at least in the US, whose level of skill is used as a standard in making legal determinations.

Personal Patent Organizer
A private document intended to help organize one's patent information.

post grant review
A type of a revision proceeding in the US.

Power of Attorney
One of the inventor legal forms.

prior art references
Reference documents having a date prior to a specific date and including a certain disclosure.

prior art search
A search for prior art references, which are legally applicable for a specific purpose.

priority
A notion that a later-filed patent application can be officially treated as if it had been filed earlier, on the same day as another earlier-filed patent application, if the later-filed patent application is for the same invention as the earlier-filed patent application.

priority patent application
A patent application from which another patent application claims priority.

Product Patent Report
An internal, usually attorney-confidential company report that lists which company patents cover a company's product.

provisional patent application
A type of a tentative patent application that does not become a patent.

publication date
A date that a patent application was published, found in the formalities of the associated patent document.

publication delay
A time duration from when a non-provisional patent application is filed until it is published while pending.

published patent application document
A document published by the Patent Office about the published patent application, copies of which are freely available to the public.

punitive damages
In a court verdict finding patent infringement, a portion of the assessed money damages that the infringer has to pay and is attributable to the fact that the patent infringement was willful.

reexamination
A type of a patent revision proceeding in the US.

reference numerals
Numbers on drawings of a US patent document intended to indicate individual aspects of what is shown in the drawings.

References Cited
A listing, found in the formalities of a patent document, of prior art references that were considered in evaluating whether to allow the underlying patent application to become issued as this patent.

reissue
A type of a patent revision proceeding in the US.

rejection (for a patent application)
In an Office Action, a reason given as to why a pending patent application is not being allowed to become a patent.

revised (for an issued patent)
The result of a revision proceeding to the legal coverage of a patent.

revision proceeding
A proceeding intended to have a patent's legal coverage revised.

revocation
A type of a revision proceeding under the European Patent Convention (EPC).

search scratchpad document
A private document intended to help organize one's prior art search.

serial number
A tracking number assigned by the Patent Office to the patent application that was filed for a patent, found in the formalities of the associated patent document.

Solo patent strategy
A patent strategy pursued by an entity that does not require any other entity to cooperate.

specification
A part of a utility patent document that teaches the invention of the patent.

stealth mode
A way in which a company develops a new product secretly, with no specific announcements made during development.

Summary
An optional section of the specification of a patent document.

Technical Standard
An agreed upon specification for products offered by different entities, even rivals, in the expectation that the products will be technically compatible with each other.

third-party prior art submission
A usual method for challenging a pending patent application.

trade secret
Information that an entity tries to keep secret, and benefits from keeping it secret.

US Patent and Trademark Office (USPTO)
The US federal agency for granting US patents and registering trademarks.

utility
A legal requirement for an invention to be patentable.

utility patent
A type of patent in the US and in many other countries, intended to protect machines, processes, articles of manufacture, compositions of matter, and their improvements.

Venture Capitalists (VCs)
Entities that provide capital to start-up companies or small companies.

visible type PBR-1 risk
A type of the patent business risk of infringing (PBR-1), which arises from patents and patent applications that are findable by a patent search.

work around
(verb) See design around.

work product
The useful output of an employee's work.

workaround
A design resulting from working around.

World Intellectual Property Organization (WIPO)
An organization formed according to the Patent Cooperation Treaty.

APPENDIX A

IMAGE OF PATENT DOCUMENT OF SAMPLE US PATENT NO. 4,369,439

United States Patent [19]

Broos

[11] 4,369,439
[45] Jan. 18, 1983

[54] CURSOR POSITION CONTROLLER FOR A DISPLAY DEVICE

[75] Inventor: Michael S. Broos, Kittery, Me.

[73] Assignee: Massachusetts Institute of Technology, Cambridge, Mass.

[21] Appl. No.: 225,123

[22] Filed: Jan. 14, 1981

[51] Int. Cl.³ G09G 1/00
[52] U.S. Cl. 340/710; 340/706
[58] Field of Search 340/710, 706, 709, 711

[56] References Cited

U.S. PATENT DOCUMENTS

3,541,521	11/1970	Koster	364/521
3,541,541	11/1970	Engelbart	340/710
3,625,083	12/1971	Bose	74/471 XY
3,643,148	2/1972	Brown et al.	318/628
3,668,685	6/1972	Horvath	340/710
3,835,464	9/1974	Rider	340/710
3,872,460	3/1975	Fredrickson et al.	340/711
3,883,861	5/1975	Heartz	340/705
3,892,963	7/1975	Hawley et al.	340/710
3,967,266	6/1976	Roy	340/709
3,987,685	10/1976	Opocensky	74/471 R
4,085,443	4/1978	Dubois et al.	364/900
4,101,879	7/1978	Kawaji et al.	340/709
4,118,695	10/1978	Ogawa et al.	340/709

Primary Examiner—Marshall M. Curtis
Attorney, Agent, or Firm—Arthur A. Smith, Jr.

[57] ABSTRACT

A position indicator or cursor is moved over a visual display in response to signals generated by corresponding movement of a keyboard relative to a fixed point on the surface supporting the keyboard.

6 Claims, 3 Drawing Figures

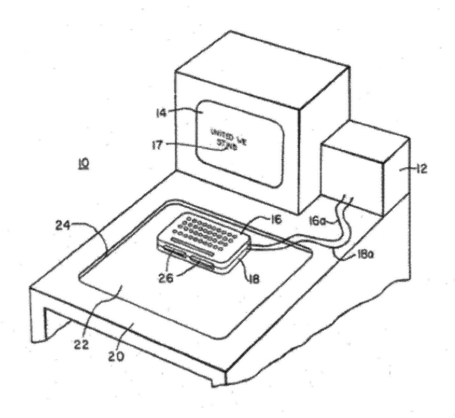

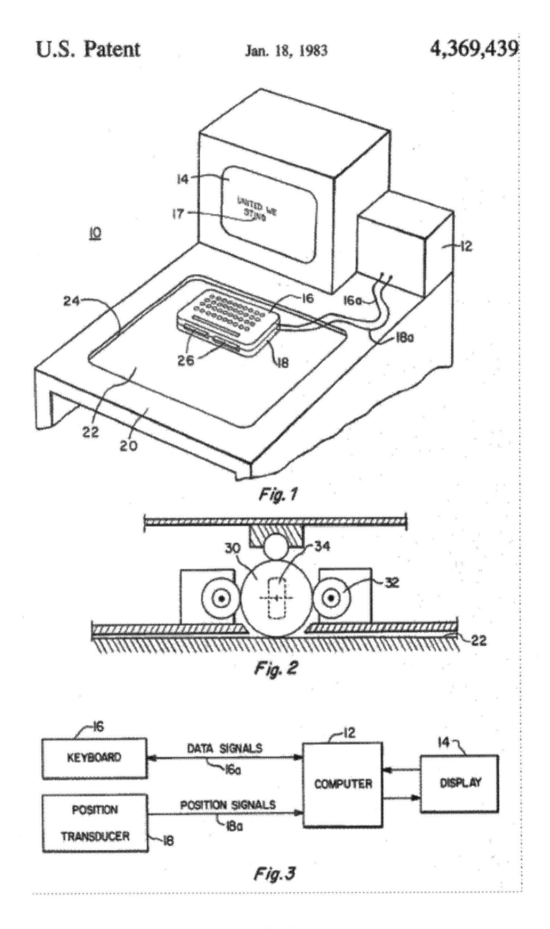

CURSOR POSITION CONTROLLER FOR A DISPLAY DEVICE

BACKGROUND OF THE INVENTION

In many general-purpose computer systems and in most commercial "word-processing" or document creation systems, the editing of textual data is performed by a human operator, using a typewriter-style keyboard to enter editing commands and data, and viewing the edited text on a CRT display. The computer maintains a "current position" in the text being edited, which most editing commands imply as an argument. For example, if the operator presses the "rubout" key, it is interpreted by the computer as a command to remove the character to the left of the current position from the text being edited and from the display of that text being viewed by the operator. The computer normally indicates the current editing position by displaying a distinctive marker, called the cursor, on the CRT along with the text being edited.

The operator controls the position of the cursor in a variety of ways. In the majority of such systems, a particular keystroke or combination of keystrokes is interpreted by the computer as a command to move the cursor to the right, left, up, or down in increments of a single character or, in some systems, an entire word, line or paragraph. In many systems, special keys are devoted to these functions and are usually located in a special keypad separate from and often adjacent to the typewriter keypad.

A smaller number of editing systems use a position-indicating device whose position is sensed by the computer and used to control the cursor position in the display and text being edited. Examples of such devices are: light pens, tablet pens, joysticks, thumb wheels, and "mice" (devices which sit on a table top and are moved about by hand). Devices of this type are disclosed in U.S. Pat. No. 3,541,521 to Koster, U.S. Pat. No. 3,541,541 to Engelbart and U.S. Pat. No. 3,835,464 to Rider.

All of the aforementioned prior art position-indicating devices enable an operator to "point" at a position on the display where the cursor is to be located. However, the typical editing sequence is; (1) manually adjust a control to position the cursor at the place to be edited; and (2) enter one or more keystrokes to modify the text. This sequence is then repeated for the next editing operation. If the operator needs to stop typing to pick up a light pen, or grasp a "mouse" or like device or to use a special keypad to adjust the cursor position, and then to return to the typewriter keyboard for the editing operation, he or she uses a lot of time getting his or her hands repositioned over the "home" typing keys. Often, one of the operator's hands is incorrectly positioned, upon return to the keyboard. For example, the operator's hand may have drifted one key to the right or left of the correct position, and many typing errors result. Touch typists especially find this type of interaction annoying, which is probably why such systems have found little acceptance outside of the computer research field.

Accordingly, it is an object of the present invention to provide a system for facilitating the generation of two-dimensional coordinate data for input to an electronic digital computer to control the position of a visible marker, or "cursor", displayed on the face of a cathode ray tube or other dynamic display device under control of the computer.

It is another object of the present invention to provide such a system which may be operated in conjunction with a typewriter-style keyboard in a manner which does not require the operator to remove a hand from the keyboard.

These and other objects and features of the present invention will be understood from the description to follow, taken in conjunction with the accompanying drawings.

SUMMARY OF THE INVENTION

The present invention provides a system that includes a data entry keyboard mounted on a carriage which is freely movable on a support surface within a bounded horizontal plane. The carriage is mechanically constrained to movement within the bounded horizontal plane by a suitable barrier provided on the support surface. A sensor for detecting motion of the keyboard carriage relative to a fixed point within the bounded horizontal plane is mounted either on the keyboard carriage or is fixed within the support surface. The motion detected by the sensing element is translated into position signals representative of the coordinates (e.g. X and Y) of the keyboard's position within the bounded horizontal plane. These position signals are applied to a computer, which in turn generates a cursor at a corresponding position on a visual display. The cursor's position is automatically changed responsive to detected changes in the position of the keyboard carriage.

In the preferred embodiment two brakes independently operable by hand, are provided on the keyboard carriage. One brake, when applied, restricts the keyboard carriage to movement along an X axis within the bounded plane, while the other brake restricts the keyboard carriage to movement along a Y axis within the bounded plane.

In operation, in a data entry mode, a user may enter text data to the system using the keyboard or by alternate conventional means (e.g. magnetic disc, paper tape, OCR, or the like. In a text editing mode, the operator may re-position the keyboard and carriage by selectively operating the brakes and applying forces to the carriage in a manner positioning the cursor to the location of a desired text change. The operator may then enter the appropriate editing command as required by the text editing system.

The main difference between the apparatus of the present invention and those devices currently used for cursor control is that the present system uses the keyboard (coupled to the carriage) as a position indicating device. Accordingly, the main advantages of the present invention over the current devices and methods used for control of a cursor are: (1) the operator may selectively control the cursor position without removing his or her hands from the keyboard; and (2) the naturalness attributed to the "pointing" capabilities of a position indicating device is retained. The combination of these two qualities is the real advantage of the invention and is expected to make it possible to perform text editing tasks in a way which is much more natural and efficient than with conventional systems.

The present invention is useful in computer applications involving the editing of text displayed on a CRT or other display device, such as order-entry systems, word processing or document creation systems and pre-press text preparation systems for the publishing industry. The invention may also be utilized in the editing of non-textual data on display devices, such as graphs, line drawings, or telemetry data.

BRIEF DESCRIPTION OF THE DRAWINGS

FIG. 1 is a pictorial illustration of a cursor positioning system in accordance with the invention;

FIG. 2 is a partial elevational view, in cross-section, showing a motion sensor mounted within a keyboard carriage in accordance with the invention; and

FIG. 3 is a simplified block diagram of the system of the invention.

DESCRIPTION OF THE PREFERRED EMBODIMENTS

FIG. 1 illustrates a cursor positioning system 10 for an information processing system constructed in accordance with the present invention. The system 10 includes a programmed digital computer 12 and associated cathode ray tube (CRT) display 14, and a data entry keyboard 16 mounted on a carriage 18.

The keyboard 16 is a conventional data entry keyboard having a plurality of selectively operable, pressure sensitive switches which provides data signals on an output line 16a representative of this state of the switches. Line 16a is coupled to the computer 12, as described below. In the present embodiment, the computer 12 and CRT display 14 generally have the form of a conventional word processing system such as the Model 8000 distributed by CPT Corporation of Minneapolis, Minn. In FIG. 1, the image on display 14 shows text with a cursor 17 identifying a text character for which an editing operation is desired.

Unlike conventional systems which generate cursor position signals in response to signals generated by the operation of switches on the keyboard, the present embodiment generates cursor position signals directly from the position transducers associated with carriage 18.

The carriage 18 is positioned on a table 20 and is movable in the horizontal plane of the table surface 22 bounded by walls 24. In the present embodiment, the carriage 18 includes selectively locking casters (not shown) positioned at each of the corners of the lower surface of the carriage, to permit selective free motion of the carriage on the surface 22. In the embodiment of FIG. 1, the bounded support surface 22 is shown as a depression in the top surface of table 20. Of course, the movement of carriage 18 about the support surface 22 may be mechanically constrained in an alternative manner, for example, by walls protruding from the surface of the table 20.

In the present embodiment, a pair of control bars 26 extend from the carriage 18 for controlling the operation of electromechanical brakes (not shown) which selectively lock and unlock the casters. In the present embodiment, the control bars 26 are positioned in a manner similar to the space bar of a conventional typewriter keyboard. With this configuration, the operator's palms may rest lightly on the upper surfaces of the bars 26 and 27 (which thus form palm pads). The palm pads provided by control bars 26 and 27 have a two axis concave upper surface so that when the operator's palms are resting thereon, a transverse motion of either of the operator's palm transmits a force in either the X or Y or both directions (depending upon the direction of the force of the operator's palms) to the carriage assembly 18. In the present embodiment, with little or no operator applied downward force on either of bars 26, the casters remain locked and the position of carriage 18 is fixed on surface 22. However, in response to a downward force on either of bars 26 and 27, a force sensor in bars 26 and 27 generates a signal which releases the caster brakes so that the carriage may be freely moved about surface 22 in response to horizontal forces applied by the operator to the palm pad of either bars 26 and 27. In other embodiments, the carriage 18 may alternatively be constrained to movement on either an X or Y or both axes by selective operation of electromechanical brakes associated with respective ones of bars 26 and 27.

The carriage 18 further includes a position transducer 28 which cooperatively interacts with the top surface 22 of table 20 and provides position signals on signal lines 18a indicative of changes in position of the carriage 18 from an initial starting point within the walls 24. Thus in the present embodiment, the transducer signals are incremental, representing changes in position from a calibrated reference position. In other embodiments, those signals may be in absolute form.

By way of example, this transducer assembly 28 may have the form shown in FIG. 2 which shows a sectional view of such an assembly having a spherical member 30 positioned within the carriage 18 which protrudes below the lower surface 31 of carriage 18 in a manner so that it is in constant frictional contact with the support surface 22. The spherical member 30 is adapted to rotate as the carriage 18 is moved about the surface 22. A pair of conventional rotary encoders 32 and 34 with friction driven input wheels are coupled to the spherical member 30 at 90° separated points on the surface of member 30 in a plane parallel to the surface 22 and passing through the center of the spherical member 30. With this configuration, as the carriage 18 is moved about the surface 22, the rotation of spherical member 30 is detected by the position transducers 32 and 34, which in turn provide X and Y position change signals on signal lines 18a, which in turn are applied to the computer 12 (which generates digital signals representative of the X and Y coordinates changes of the position of the carriage 18). In alternate forms of the invention, the position transducers may have other forms, such as optical detectors which detect motion of the carriage relative to a set of bars (or grid lines) on surface 22.

In alternative embodiments, the spherical member 30 may be positioned within the table 22 and protrude from that surface to be in frictional contact with the lower surface 31 of the carriage 18. In a similar manner, the transducer 28 provides signals representative of the changes in carriage position in response to motion of the carriage 18 with respect to the surface 22. In this latter form, the dimensions of the bottom of the carriage 18 and those of the support surface 22 ensure that the spherical member 30 mounted beneath the support surface 22 is always covered by the bottom of the carriage 18 during its movement about the support surface 22.

FIG. 3 illustrates the system processing of the digital carriage position signals generated by position transducers 32 and 34. These signals are transferred from the transducers of carriage 18 (or in an alternative embodiment from the transducers of the table 20) to the computer 12 by signal line 18a and an interface internal to the computer 12.

In the present embodiment, the computer 12 and a CRT display 14 generally have the form of a conventional word processing system, such as the Model 8000 distributed by CPT Corporation of Minneapolis, Minn. However, unlike that conventional system which generates cursor position signals in response to signals generated by the operation of switches on the keyboard, the present embodiment generates cursor position signals directly from the position transducers provided on lines 18a. As a result, the operator may manually position the keyboard 16 by way of its carriage 18 to a point within the bounds of walls 24. In keeping with this motion, the cursor is positioned correspondingly throughout the field of view of the CRT display 14. The operator may then perform word processing operations in the normal manner for the word processing system.

In practical configurations, the present invention requires relatively little motion of the keyboard while in order to provide full travel of the cursor across the screen of display 14 (it is desirable to keep this motion within a few inches or less). At the same time, the ratio of the distance moved by the keyboard 16 and the corresponding distance the cursor moves should be kept as large as possible. In order to effect accurate positioning of the cursor even when relatively small movements of the keyboard produce proportionately large movements of the cursor, the computer 12 may be readily configured to restrain cursor position on the screen of display 14 to be in the nearest one of a plurality of discrete elemental areas within the image, such as the areas occupied by characters within that image.

The invention may be embodied in other specific forms without departing from the spirit or essential characteristics thereof. For example, the system of the present invention may alternatively be configured in a manner where the keyboard does not move, but rather the palm pads from the control bars 26 and 27 would include a plurality of force sensors adapted to detect horizontal orthogonal forces applied by an operator. The sensors would operate so that forces applied by the operator's palm would be detected and would sense the magnitude and direction of those horizontal forces and translate those detected forces into motion of the cursor in the display 14. The present embodiments are therefore to be considered in all respects as illustrative and not restrictive, the scope of the invention being indicated by the appended claims rather than by the foregoing description, and all changes which come within the meaning and range of equivalency of the claims are therefore intended to be embraced therein.

I claim:

1. A system for controlling the display of data for a visual data display controlled by a computer, wherein said system comprises:
   an operator controlled keyboard for selectively generating said display data alteration signals;
   a support surface for said keyboard;
   means for supporting said keyboard on said support surface whereby said keyboard is movable by said generator;
   constraining means for limiting the movement of said keyboard on said support surface whereby each elemental area in the allowed region of movement of said keyboard corresponds to an elemental area of said display,
   means for generating said position signals representative of the position of said keyboard relative to a fixed reference point on said support surface, and
   means for altering the data displayed at the points in said display defined by said position signals, said position signals being indicative of the positions on said display of portions of said data to be altered, and in accordance with display data alteration signals indicating the nature of the change to be made at the indicated position.

2. The system of claim 1 wherein said means for generating said position signals is attached to said keyboard for movement therewith and includes rotatable contact means for frictionally contacting said support surface and transducer means for translating the rotational motion of said contact means into coordinate position signals corresponding to said position signals.

3. The system of claim 1 wherein said means for generating said position signals includes rotable contact means mounted in said support surface for frictional contact with said keyboard, and includes transducer means for translating the rotational motion of said contact means into coordinate position signals corresponding to said position signals.

4. An information processing system comprising:
   A. display means for displaying a data field representative of stored data,
   B. keyboard and associated carriage means adapted for translational movement under control of an operator in a region corresponding to said data field,
   C. transducer means for generating a position signal representative of the location of said keyboard with respect to a reference point in said region,
   D. means responsive to said position signal for identifying a location in said stored data corresponding to said location of said keyboard in said region,
   wherein said display means is responsive to said identifying means to display a cursor at the point in said displayed data field corresponding to the location of said keyboard.

5. A system according to claim 4
   wherein said carriage means includes a selectively operable brake system, said carriage means being fixed with respect to said reference point when said brake system is operative in response to a lock signal and being freely movable when said brake system is operative in response to an unlock signal, and
   wherein said carriage means further includes at least one palm rest having a force sensor, said force sensor being responsive to a predetermined force selectively applied by an operator's palm to generate said unlock signal, and to generate said lock signal otherwise.

6. An information processing system comprising:
   A. display means for displaying a data field representative of stored data, and for displaying a cursor,
   B. keyboard including a palm rest transducer means for generating a position signal representative of the magnitude and direction of horizontal forces applied to said transducer means by an operator's palm,
   C. means for controlling the position of said cursor in response to said position signal.

* * * * *

APPENDIX B

INVENTION REPORTING FORM (IRF) (STARTING)

PATENT INTRODUCTIONS, INC.

INSTRUCTIONS:
Find your company's standard Invention Reporting Form. Use the following form only if your company does not have one. You can download the latest version of this form from: www.patent-ready.com/downloads.html

IN DOCUMENT HEADER:
LINE 1: COMPANY NAME CONFIDENTIAL
LINE 2: INVENTION REPORTING FORM (IRF) – DOCKET NO.: ...

INVENTION REPORTING FORM (IRF) (STARTING)

A.   TITLE OF THIS INVENTION:

\>

B.   ANY RELATIONSHIP OF THIS WITH OTHER IRFS:

(Check one:) This is:
[ ] a wholly new IRF
[ ] an updated IRF from a prior IRF (with Docket No. # ___)
[ ] a new IRF, having common elements with another IRF (with Docket No. # _____)

This disclosure is specific to a project of the company:
(Check one:) [ ] No   [ ] Yes: (project name) _____

C.   INVENTOR(S):

(copy the following block once for each inventor)

Inventor Data:
Full legal name: _____
Telephone number: _____
Email address (accessible from outside our company:) _____@ [company name/domain].com
Residence (city, state): _____
Country of citizenship: _____
Inventor's Supervisor:
Name: _____
Telephone number: _____

222

D.   **FIRST RECORD OF THIS INVENTION:**

The first notes about this invention were made on (date): _____, in:
(Check one)
[ ] Engineering Notebook # _____, page # _____
[ ] this form
[ ] other: _____

E.   **FIRST PRACTICE OF THIS INVENTION, INTERNAL TO COMPANY:**

The first time anyone in our company internally made a device that embodies the invention OR practiced a method that embodies the invention:
(Check as appropriate)
[ ] happened on (date): _____,
[ ] as an experiment
[ ] for project_____
[ ] other _____
[ ] has not happened yet

F.   **FIRST PUBLIC DISCLOSURE AND/OR SALE OF THIS INVENTION:**

1.   Has the invention been disclosed outside our company in a printed publication?
[ ] No [ ] Yes: (publication and date) _____

2.   Has the invention been disclosed outside our company in another way (e.g., presentation, conference, demonstration, standards committee, market research, conversation, product announcement), *without a Non-Disclosure Agreement*?
[ ] No [ ] Yes: (to whom and when) _____

3.   If #1 and #2 are No, is our company planning a public disclosure?
[ ] No [ ] Yes: (to whom and when) _____
Before disclosing publicly, please ask for clearance by the Patent Department after this form has been filled in completely and submitted; and ask whether a provisional patent application can be filed quickly.

4.   Has a product (that incorporates the invention) been sold, or offered for sale by our company or others?
[ ] No [ ] Yes: (which product and when) _____

5.   If #4 is No, does our company plan today to offer such a product for sale?
[ ] No [ ] Yes: (which product and when) _____

PATENT INTRODUCTIONS, INC.

G. DESCRIPTION OF YOUR INVENTION:

The invention is (briefly):

>

The invention in detail: (Write here. Include drawings. If possible, insert the drawing directly into this document. Also describe in words what the drawings show)

>

Advantages (and additional benefits) of the invention:

>

The problem that the invention solves:

>

What is new about the invention?

>

What are embodiments of your invention?
Devices [ ] no [ ] yes, namely:
Methods [ ] no [ ] yes, namely:
Software [ ] no [ ] yes, namely:

H. PRIOR ART:

Did you search the prior art to see if anyone else has thought of this before? (You are not required to.)
[ ] No
[ ] Yes Where: _____
If you searched online, what keywords did you use?
_____

_____

List all the relevant prior art that you knew of or found: (This includes publications, patents, and everything relevant that you found in the your search. For each item, include how your invention is different from it: What does your invention have or do, that the prior art does not?)

Item 1: _____
But this invention is different because: _____

(repeat for other items)
Item 2: _____
But this invention is different because: _____

APPENDIX C

PERSONAL PATENT ORGANIZER (STARTED)

PATENT INTRODUCTIONS, INC.

INSTRUCTIONS: You can download the latest version of this form from: www.patent-ready.com/downloads.html

PERSONAL PATENT ORGANIZER (STARTED)

My information, as I will enter it into Invention Reporting Forms

```
Inventor Data:
Full legal name: _____
Telephone number: _____
Email address (accessible from outside our company:) _____ @ [company name].com
Residence (city, state): _____
Country of citizenship: _____
Inventor's Supervisor:
Name: _____
Telephone number: _____
```

My organization's patent intranet is at: ...

PATENT SEARCH LINKS:

International patent applications: http://patentscope.wipo.int/search/en/structuredSearch.jsf

US Patents and US Patent Applications: http://patft.uspto.gov/

European Patent Office – Patent Searches: http://www.epo.org/searching.html

(Other)

Can download.pdfs of patent documents from: ...
(search internet for sources of free patent. pdfs)

MY PATENTABLE IDEAS:

My company's Invention Reporting Form (IRF) is at: ...
Instructions for submitting the IRF are at: ...

(copy the following block as needed)

Invention Title: (as in ... submitted IRF ... filed patent application)		
Possible coinventors:		
Invention Report:	Submitted on: ... (date)	Docket #: ...
Patent application:	Filed on: ... (date)	Application Serial #: ...
Patent application:	Published on: ... (date)	Document #: ...
Patent:	Issued on: ... (date)	Patent #: ...

INDEX

Page numbers with an n denote a footnote; *f* refers to a figure.

A

advance patenting, 29, 73
    See also prospective patenting
affidavits, 181
African Regional Intellectual Property Organization (ARIPO), 13, 199
agreements, international, 11–13, 204
alignment with intellectual property (IP), 43–44, *44f*, 129, 205
ambient information, 144, 199
application preparation
    about, 161–62, *161f*
    drafting, 82
    error propagation, 163
    inventor names/interviews, 162, 166–67
    review/feedback, 162–65, *163f*
    signatures, 166
    updating paperwork, 168–171
applications
    Attorney Docket Numbers. *See* Attorney Docket Numbers
    challenges to, 23, 83, 86, 178
    child. *See* child applications
    claims. *See* claims
    Continuation, 115, 201
    Continuation-in-Part, 115, 201
    deadlines. *See* deadlines
    definitions, 205, 207
    design. *See* design patents
    Divisional, 115, 202
    filing. *See* filing applications
    issuance. *See* issuance of patents
    non-provisional, 83, *96f*
    parent. *See* parent patent applications
    pending. *See* pending applications
    priority. *See* priority applications; priority claims
    provisional. *See* provisional applications
    publication of. *See* publication process
    as risk mitigation, 47–49, *47f*
    serial numbers, 111, 175, 183, 212
    threatening. *See* threatening patents
    utility. *See* utility patents
    visible/invisible, 45–47, *46f*, 92, 129, 205
ARIPO (African Regional Intellectual Property Organization), 13, 199
art, definition, 199
assets, patent portfolios as, 28
assignee (ownership), 111, 199
assigning patented inventions, 56, 199
Assignment form, 167, 199
Attorney Docket Numbers
    about, 168
    definition, 200
    as identification, 171
    for tracing applications, 155, 175

B

bankruptcies, patent portfolios as assets in, 28
bonuses
    for employee inventions, 55
    for filing, 171
    for issuance, 183
business analysis reviews
    five-year computations, limitations of, 36
    for product development, 33–36, *34f*, 169–171, *170f*, 176, *177f*, 182–83, *184f*, 200
business processes
    about, 63
    for deadlines, 75
    for reporting inventions, 145

business risks. *See* risks; PBR-1; PBR-2; PBR-3
buying patent rights, 15

C

Certificate of Correction, 108, 200
challenges
    to applications, 23, 83, 86, 178
    definition, 200
    threatening patents. *See* threatening patents
    See also disputes/dispute resolution; prior art searching
child applications
    about, 114–15, *115f*
    claims from parent application, 175
    follow-up inventions as, 178
    rivals' filing of, 46
child patents, definition, 200
China, patent system, 6
citizenship requirements, 8, 9
claims
    about, 107, *108–9f*, 109, 111–13, *112f*
    after revision proceedings, 185
    cancellation of, 174–75
    definition, 200
    dependent, 111, 202
    designing around, 133, 202
    fixed/modifiable, 132–33
    independent, 111, 204
    legal coverage in, 30–31
    Patent Office determinations, 179–181, *180f*
coining words, 153, 153n34
coinventors
    about, 147
    coordinating with, 154–55
    definition, 200
    junior technical officer as, 149
    See also inventors
commoditized products
    about, 20
    definition, 201
    technical standards and, 62
company business, patent impact on
    commercial battles, 20–21, *20f*
    finances, 19–20, *19f*
    opportunities. *See* opportunities, patent business; PBO-1
    patent battles, 22–23
    patent plane, 21–23, *21f*
    risks. *See* risks; PBR-1; PBR-2; PBR-3
company patents
    about
        inventions, 69–75
        patent departments, 67–68, *68f*, 208
        time domains, 76
    employee role in
        about, 143–47, *143f*
        company rules, 57, 121
        Invention Reporting Form (IRF). *See* Invention Reporting Form (IRF)
company presentations, 169–171
compensatory damages. *See* damages
competitive convergence, 31, 201
confidentiality, 57–59, *59f*
Continuation, 115, 201
Continuation-in-Part, 115, 201
contract patent searchers, 129–130, 201
copyrights, 5n2
corrections, certificate of, 108, 200
court interpretations of patents. *See* litigation
covenants, 56
cut off, definition, 201
cut-off effect
    about, 48–49, *49f*
    definition, 201
    provisional applications and, 97
    of rivals, 169
cut-off time
    definition, 201
    example of, 88
    infringement risks and, 47–49, *47f*, *49f*
    product introduction as, 49n16
    reaching, 169

D

damages
    compensatory, 201
    definition, 206, 211
    infringement, 24, 26, 30, 35, 186
    liability for, 6
    punitive, 26, 211
deadlines
    for filing applications
        about, 11, 74

international differences, 74
legal, 11, 74, 75, 92–93, 205
for non-provisional applications, 96
patent-related facts, 75, 209
third-party prior art submissions, 136
defensive patent strategies, 38, 201
defensive publications
definition, 201
as patent alternative, 156, 157
as patent prevention, 23, 88–90, 89f
deliverables
Invention Reporting Form (IRF) as, 149
patent-related, 38
See also milestones
Department of Commerce, 21, 22, 202
dependent claims. See claims
design patents
about, 101–2
definition, 202
provisional applications and, 97
designing around claims. See claims
disclosure, exceptions to
about, 58–60
authorized public/private exceptions, 59, 200
non-disclosure agreements (NDAs), 59, 60, 206
discovery, 61n17, 188, 202
disputes/dispute resolution, 6–7, 15–16, 208
Divisional, 115, 202
drawings
for Invention Reporting Forms, 153–54
for patents. See patent contents
duty of confidentiality, 57, 202
duty of loyalty (legal), 56, 202

E

18-month publication delays, 168
email retention, 61
employment
agreements, 55–56, 167, 202
business processes, 63
company revelations, 58–60
company rules, 57
confidentiality, 57–59, 59f
interviews, 55
litigation risk mitigation, 60–61
non-disclosure agreements (NDAs), 59, 60, 206
résumés, 55
technical standards, 62
See also company patents
entry barriers
definition, 200
negative know-how, 58
patents as, 22
EPC (European Patent Convention), 13, 203
error propagation, 163
ESL readers, drawings and, 153
ethics, 57
Eurasian Patent Organization, 13, 203
European Patent Convention (EPC), 13, 203
European Patent Office, 13
Examination Clearance Milestone, 181–82, 203
exclusivity, 38
expiration
about, 84, 117
international variations in, 15
of patents, 189, 189f
of provisional applications, 95
of threatening patents, 133
use after, 43

F

false marking. See products
fees
as infringement penalties, 24, 26, 187
license, 205
for patenting, 8, 84–85, 180
fields, searching by, 125–27, 125–26f
filing applications
about, 8, 167, 167f
bonuses for, 171
date of, 111, 175, 203
international, 10
patent rights from, 22
planning for, 92
timing of, 92
Filing Clearance Milestone, 169, 203
firewalls, patent searches and, 41
followers, market
advantages for, 14
definition, 203, 207

risks, 25, 27, 27n11, *37f*, 72
following, definition, 203
formalities. *See* patent contents
Freedom To Operate (FTO)
    defensive strategy and, 38, 41
    definition, 203
    searches, 120, 132, 203
future patenting, 76, *76f*, 204

G
Gulf Cooperation Council, 13, 204

I
idea submission number, 155, 204
imitation of rival's products. *See* followers, market
inadequate/no returns on investment. *See* PBR-3
independent claims. *See* claims
infringement
    about, 22
    avoidance costs, 22–23
    damages. *See* damages
    definitions, 205, 207, 208
    inventions and, 71–72, *71f*
    liability for, 6
    monitoring for, 186–87
    patent marking and, 40
    risks
        about, 24–28, *26f*
        mitigation of, *37f*, *42f*, 47–49, *47f*, 121, 181–82
        19-month clearance milestone, 175–76
    sales impact of, 35
    technical standards and, 62
    visible/invisible, 35, 205, 213
    willful, 26
    See also disputes/dispute resolution; prior art searching; PBR-1
Innovation Landscape
    about, 5–7
    definition, 204
    international, 13
    stealth mode in, 85
innovator patent strategies, 38, 204
intellectual property (IP)
    alignment with products, 43–44, *44f*, 129, 205
    definition, 204, 205
    forfeiting rights, 93, *93f*
    loss of, 39
    patents as, 5
inter partes review, 135, 204
interactive patent strategies, 38, 204
International Bureau. *See* World Intellectual Property Organization (WIPO)
international patent agreements, 11–13, 204
international patent families. *See* patent families
International Patent Office. *See* World Intellectual Property Organization (WIPO)
interviews, preparation for, 55
invalidation
    definition, 204
    forcible, 120
    by inventor name omission, 166
    legal opinions, definition, 205
    by rivals, 23
    searches, 120, 134–35, 208
    of threatening patents, 134–35, 185
invalidity opinion, 134
invent, definition, 204
Invention Reporting Form (IRF)
    about, 81
    definition, 204
    as deliverable, 149
    drawings, 153–54
    follow-up inventions, 178
    patent committee feedback for, 146–47
    patenting decision, 155–57, *156f*
    prior art reporting, 154
    on provisional applications, *94–95f*
    sample, *221–25f*
    submitting, 155
    updating, 95
    writing, 147–48, 150–53, *150f*, 164
inventions
    bonuses for. *See* bonuses
    creating, 69–70
    definition, 204
    description of, 73
    fact clarification, 181
    follow-up, 178
    implementing, 70–71, *71f*, 155
    infringement and, 71–72, *71f*

ownership of, 56
patentability of, 72–75, *72f*, *74f*
problem-solution approach, 69
reporting for patenting, 145–46
scientific papers vs., 150, *150f*
separate/co-reporting, 151
inventors
definition, 205
draft review, 163
interviews, 162
legal forms, 116, 163, 166, 205
names listed as, 111, 116
See also coinventors
investment cost estimates, 27n11
invisible risks, definition, 205
See also applications; infringement; risks
IP (intellectual property). *See* intellectual property (IP)
IP Alignment, 205
IRF (Invention Reporting Form). *See* Invention Reporting Form (IRF)
issuance of patents
about, 182–84
nominal full term after, 101
revision after, 185–87

J
job search preparation, 55, 121
junior technical officer (JTO), 149

K
keywords in search refinement, 124

L
language in Invention Reporting Forms, 152
leaders, market, 14
legal deadlines. *See* deadlines
legal duty of loyalty, 56
legal invalidity opinion, 134, 205
legal monopolies, patents as, 28
legal non-infringement opinion, 133, 205
See also infringement
legal privilege exemptions, 61n17
legal rules, 102
legal workaround, 133, 187, 205
"lexicographer" in patent language, 153n34
liability, for patent infringement, 6

licensing
definition, 205
fees. *See* fees
patent rights, 15
technical standards and, 62
Lincoln, Abraham, 1, 25
litigation
about, 23, 187–88, *188f*
cost impact of, 35
court interpretations, 26n9
as defense, 23n6
definition, 209
prospective defendants as initiators, 23n6
revision and, 84
risk mitigation, 60–61
sales impact of, 35
loss of IP, definition, 39, 205
See also intellectual property (IP)

M
market plane
about, 21–22, *21f*
definition, 205
impact from patent plane, 89
market share
definition, 206
five-year computations and, 36
followers' impact on, 35
product success as, 20
marketing terms, 152
milestones
about, 38, 145–46
examination clearance, 181–82, 203
filing clearance, 169
19-month date, 168, 175–78, *177f*, 199
patent issuance, 183
mitigating risks. *See* risks
monetizing patents, 28
money damages. *See* damages; infringement
monopoly, patents as, 28

N
NDA (Non-Disclosure Agreements), 59, 60, 206
negative know-how, 58, 206
Net Present Value (NPV), 33–36, *34f*, 206

19-month clearance milestone, 168, 175–78, 199
19-month date, 169, 199
nominal full term of patents
    definition, 206
    extension of, 133
    from issuance date, 101
    of US utility patents, 84
non-core patents, 28
Non-Disclosure Agreements (NDA), 59, 60, 206
non-obvious requirement, patentability, 73
non-patent literature (NPL)
    about, 120, 127
    cost of, 122, 129
non-provisional applications, 83, *96f*
Nordic Patent Institute, 13, 206
not obvious to a person having ordinary skill in an art, definition, 206
novelty
    definition, 206
    of inventions, 73
    searches, 75, 121, 206
NPL (non-patent literature). *See* non-patent literature (NPL)
NPV (Net Present Value), 33–36, *34f*, 206

O

OAPI (Organisation Africaine de la Propriété Intellectuelle), 13, 206
Oath or Declaration, 167, 206
"obvious" in patent law, 73
Office Action, 179–181, 206
opportunities, patent business
    definition, 207
    of patent rights, 28–29
    of patents, 24–25, *24f*
    See also PBO-1
ordinary skill in an art, definition, 210
Organisation Africaine de la Propriété Intellectuelle (OAPI), 13, 206
ownership (assignee), 111
ownership changes, 117

P

parent patent, 114, 207
parent patent applications, 114, *115f*, 207
past patenting, 76, *76f*, 207
past writings, patentability and, 74
patent anatomy. *See* patent contents
patent attorneys/agents
    about, 8
    definition, 207
    patent drafting, 162
patent business opportunity to reserve future exclusivity (PBO-1), *24f*, 25, 28–29, 50, 207
patent business risk of infringing (PBR-1)
    about, 24, *24f*, 25–27, 31
    business analysis review, 34–35
    clearance searches and, 136
    cut-off effect and, 48, 169
    definition, 207
    examination clearance milestone and, 181
    imitation and, 72
    IP alignment and, 43–44
    mitigation, 29, 121, 131, 145
    patent races and, 89
    product planning and, 41–43
    provisional applications and, 97
    strategies and, 38
    understanding, 49–50
    visible/invisible risks, 45–47, 176
    See also infringement; risks
patent business risk that inadequate or no returns will be generated (PBR-3)
    about, *24f*, 25, 29–30
    definition, 207
    mitigation, 121, 156
    novelty searches and, 136
    Patent Office review and, 180
    See also risks
patent business risk that product will be followed (PBR-2)
    about, *24f*, 25, 27–28
    advance patenting, 73
    business analysis review, 34–35
    definition, 207
    ignoring, 39
    mitigation, 28, 29, 50, 145
    patent races and, 89
    provisional applications, 97
    strategies and, 38
    See also risks
patent certificates, 102–3, 208

patent classification system, 129, 208
patent clearance
   milestones in, 145–46
   searches, 120, 132, 136–37, 176, 203, 208
patent committees, 146–47, 208
patent contents
   about, 107, 108, *108–9f*, 113–14, *113f*
   abstract, 113, 199
   background, 114, 200
   brief description of the drawings, 114, 200
   claims, dependent/independent. *See* claims
   column numbers, 103, 114, 201
   definition, 212
   detailed description, 114, 200
   drawings, 103, 113–14, 200, 202
   exclusions, 115–17
   formalities, 107, 108, *108–10f*, 110–11, 203
   line numbers, 103, 114, 205
   specification, 107, 108, *108–9f*, 113–14, *113f*, 212
   summary, 114, 212
Patent Cooperation Treaty (PCT), 12, *12f*, 208, 210
   See also World Intellectual Property Organization (WIPO)
patent departments, 67–68, *68f*, 208
patent documents
   about, 102–3
   certificates, 102–3, 208
   cover page, 103, 201
   definition, 208
   image files, 175
   as prior art references, 120
   sample, *215–220f*
patent families
   about, 114–15
   Continuation, 201
   Continuation-in-Part applications, 115, 201
   definition, 208
   Divisional, 115, 202
   identifying, 124
   international, 10, 114
   threatening documents in, 133
patent landscape, 42, *42f*, 50, 208
Patent Office
   determinations by, 83, 178–180, *179f*

difficulties of, 83n21
rejection limitations, 182
responses to, 180–81
revisions by, 185
See also US Patent and Trademark Office (USPTO)
patent plane
   about, 21–22, *21f*
   battles in, 22–23, 207
   definition, 209
   impact on market plane, 89
   infringement risks in, 42, *42f*
patent races
   about, 11, 31, 87–89, *88f*
   definition, 209
   provisional applications and, 87n23
   uncertainty of, 91–92, *91f*
patent reading prism, 209
patent rights
   about, 6, 207
   assigning, 56, 111, 167
   defining, 14–15
   reserving, *24f*, 25, 28–29
   waiver of, 89
patent systems
   overview
      components of, 6–7
      dispute resolution, 15–16
      international, 8–14
      navigating within, 16–17
      patent rights. *See* patent rights
      theory of, 5–6
      US patents, 7–8
   company operations within, 67
   definition, 209
patent time lines
   about, *82f*
   defensive publications, 23, 89–91, *90f*
   design patent differences, 101
   filtering options, 86–87, *86f*
   patent races, 87–89, *88f*, 91–92, *91f*
   provisional applications, 93–98, *94–96f*
   public disclosures, 92–93
   for a sample patent, 81–84, *82f*
   for start-up companies, 97–98
   for US patents, 84–86, *85f*
patent watch programs, 131, 176, 210

patentability
    damaging, 153
    determining, 69n18
    of inventions, 72–75, *72f*, *74f*
    prior art searching, 75, 121, 154, 156, 210
    in product development decisions, 28–29
    of technology, 13
    See also prior art searching
patenting
    about, 6
    agreements, 11–13
    international, 8–9, *9f*, 11–13
    milestones in, 145–46
    in multiple countries, 9–11, *10f*, *11f*
    in the US, 7–8
patent-related facts
    company activities and, 75
    definition, 209
    employee actions as, 16, 68–69, 98
    in litigation, 15
patents
    about, xxi–xxiii, 101–2
    applications. *See* applications
    company patents. *See* company patents
    definitions, 207–10
    expiration of. *See* expiration
    infringement. *See* infringement
    invalidation. *See* invalidation
    issuance of. *See* issuance of patents
    Lincoln on, 1
    as multidisciplinary, xxi, 102, 106, 156
    numbers/dates/titles, 110–11, 183, 208, 209
    opportunities. *See* opportunities, patent business
    patent markings. *See* products
    pending applications. *See* pending applications
    revision of. *See* revision of patents
    risks. *See* risks
patents, overview
    appearance of, 102–3
    exclusions, 115–17
    as multidisciplinary, 102
    patent families. *See* patent families
    publishing. *See* publication process
    reading, 106–7
    sections of, 107–14, *108–10f*
    types of, 101–2
PBO-1. *See* patent business opportunity to reserve future exclusivity (PBO-1)
PBR-1. *See* patent business risk of infringing (PBR-1)
PBR-2. *See* patent business risk that product will be followed (PBR-2)
PBR-3. *See* patent business risk that inadequate or no returns will be generated (PBR-3)
PCT (Patent Cooperation Treaty). *See* Patent Cooperation Treaty (PCT)
pending applications
    about, 82, 173–74, *173f*
    after issuance, 185–87
    challenges to, 178
    definition, 209
    examination clearance, 181–82
    follow-up inventions, 178
    19-month clearance milestone, 175–78
    patent issuance, 182–84, *182f*
    Patent Office examination of, 178–180, *179f*
    provisional applications as, 95
    publication of, 8, 9, 104–5, *104–5f*, 174–75, *174f*
    searches for, 38
    third-party prior art submission, 135
Personal Patent Organizer
    about, 63, 145
    attorney docket number, 168
    definition, 210
    patent numbers/dates, 183
    sample, *227–29f*
    updating, 122–23, 155
post grant review, definition, 135, 210
Power of Attorney, 167, 210
pricing power
    after patent issuance, 184
    five-year computations and, 36
    followers and, 35
    patents and, 28
    risk mitigation, *37f*
prior art
    improvements on, 151
    in litigation, 187
    Patent Office determinations, 179–181, *180f*
    references, 120, 181–82, 210

reporting, 154
during revision proceedings, 185
third-party submissions, 135, 178, 212
prior art searching
    overview
        about, 119–121, *119f*
        company restrictions on, 41, 57, 121, 154, 186
        effectiveness of, 127–29
        engaging patent searchers, 129–130
        by field, 125–27, *125–26f*
        how-to, 121–24, *122f*
        novelty/patentability searches, 136–37, *137f*
        patent watch programs, 131
        prospective products, 131–33
        search engines, 125
        threatening patents, 133–36
    definitions, 209, 210
    procedure for, 42–43, *42f*
    of prospective products, 41
    of rival products, 38
priority, definition, 210
priority applications
    definition, 210
    international, 11–12
    from PCT applications, 13
    from provisional applications, 96
    rescinding right to, 84
priority claims
    about, 11–13
    design patents, differences, 97, 101
    pledges not to claim, 84
    from provisional applications, 96, 98, 101
Product Patent Reports, 39, 40, 169, 210
products
    about
        false marking, 40, 203
        patent marking, 39–40, *40f*, 183, 203, 209
        prior art searches, 182
        recalls, 57
        See also prior art searching
    planning strategies
        business analysis, 33–36, *34f*, 169–171, *170f*
        infringement risks, 41–43

        intellectual property alignment, 43–44, *44f*
        patent decisions, 39, 47–49
        patent marking, 39–40
        risk/reward calculations, 33
        risks and opportunities, 36–39, *37f*, 49–50
        searches. *See* prior art searching
    development cycle
        certainty in, 29
        invention implementation, 155
        milestones in, 145–46
        patent issuance, 183
        patentability as factor in, 28–29
        project names, 152
    differentiation after issuance
        after patent issuance, 184
        definition, 202
        erosion of, 25, 35
        in market share, 20, 35
        risk mitigation, *37f*
project names, 152
property rights, patents as, 15
prospective patenting
    about, *72f*, 73, *74f, 137f*
    reasons for, 28
    See also advance patenting
provisional applications
    about, 83, 93–96, *95f*
    definition, 211
    design patent differences, 97, 101
    as enabling non-provisional applications, 96, *96f*
    Invention Reporting Forms (IRF), *94–95F*
    misconceptions about, 96–97
    publication delays, 168
    for start-up companies, 97–98
public disclosure
    imminent, 92–93, *93f*
    international, 75
public domain availability, defensive publications and, 89
publication process
    about, 104–6, *104–5f*
    dates, 111, 175, 211
    delays
        about, 168

benefits of, 12–13
definition, 211
duration of, 8, 83
invisibility and, 45, *46f*
design patents exclusion from, 101
publications
defensive, 23, 89–91, *90f*
disclosure of during employment, 56
pending applications. *See* pending applications
punitive damages. *See* damages

R

races against rivals. *See* patent races
reading patents, 106–7
records, as legal tools, 61
reexamination, 135, 211
reference citations, 111, 211
 See also prior art searching
reference numerals, 106, 114, 211
regional organizations, 13
rejection
definition, 211
Patent Office search limitations, 182
reliability confidence, 128, *128f*
requirements, patentability, 73–74
research and development, patentability as factor in, 28–29
residency requirements, 8, 9
résumés, patent listings in, xxii, 55
retroactive validity, 83
returns on investment, inadequate/none, 25, 29, 207
reverse engineering, 58
revision of patents
about, 84, 86
definitions, 211
forcible, 120
post grant review, 135, 210
proceedings, 134–35, 185
reexamination, 135, 211
as shown on documents, 117
revocation, definition, 211
risk/reward calculations, 6, 14, 33
risks
entry barriers for, 58
of followers, 14

foreseeable, *24f*, 27
by industry, 30–31
mitigation
about, *37f*, 42–43, *42f*
examination clearance, 181–82
patent clearance searches, 136–37, 156
patents as, 47–49, *47f*
threatening patent searches, 72, 121
at 19-month clearance, 176
patent business risks
about, 24–29, *24f*
definition, 207
of followers/imitators. *See* PBR-2
of inadequate/no returns on investment. *See* PBR-3
of infringement. *See* PBR-1
rivals
about, 5
application challenges, 23, 83, 86, 178
invisible applications, 46, 205
at 19-month milestone, 169
patent destruction, 23
products from, 20, *20f*
races with, 11
 See also disputes/dispute resolution; followers, market; patent races

S

sales of patents/patent rights, 15, 28–29
scientific papers, inventions vs., 150, *150f*
search scratchpad document, 124, 212
searches. *See* prior art searching
serial numbers, applications, 111, 175, 183, 212
software
code restrictions, 57
patentability of, 13
solo patent strategies, 38, 212
specification. *See* patent contents
start-up companies, provisional applications for, 97–98
statutes of limitations. *See* deadlines
stealth mode, 85, 212
syntax for queries, 125

T

technical know-how, confidentiality of, 58
technical standards, 62, 212

technical writing, 152
third-party prior art submission, 135, 178, 212
threatening patents
    challenging/disputing, 134–35
    identifying, 72, 121, 132–33
    non-threatening approaches to, 133
    responses to, 38–39
    revision/invalidation of, 120, 185
time domains, 76, *76f*
time periods, 30
"traction" in venture capital appeal, 29
trade secrets
    about, 5n2, 14
    confidentiality of, 57–58
    definition, 212
    vs. inadequate patent, 84–85
    records as, 61
    résumés and, 55
    technical standards and, 62
trademarks, 5n2, 152

U
updating
    calendars, 168–69
    company presentations, 169–171
    Invention Reporting Forms, 95
    patentability decisions, 13
    as shown on documents, 117
    See also Personal Patent Organizer
US Congress, 7, *7f*
US Constitution, 7, *7f*
US Department of Commerce, 21, 22, 202

US Patent and Trademark Office (USPTO)
    about, 7, *7f*
    authority of, 22
    definition, 212
    documents issued, 102–3
    fees, 8, 84–85, 180
US patents
    design patent differences, 101
    implications of, 116
    publication delay differences, 168
    time lines, 84–86, *85f*
utility of inventions, 73, 212
utility patents
    about, 101–2
    definition, 212
    design patents vs., 97

V
validity
    duration of, 30
    retroactive, 83
    See also invalidation
venture capitalists (VCs), 29, 212
visible risks, definition, 212
    See also applications; infringement; risks

W
websites, patent sales/licensing, 29
work products, 56, 212
workarounds, 133, 187, 205, 212
World Intellectual Property Organization (WIPO), 12–13, 212
    See also Patent Cooperation Treaty (PCT)